WORLD WAR II
WAR IN THE SHADOWS

"My main weapons were to be lies and deceptions, and I would have to ask friends to commit treason— that is, what was considered treason and punished as such. I myself had indulged in acts outside the normal social conventions, including murder. After this night of actually witnessing the legalized murder of war, I felt no qualms. It was my baptism by fire."

Dusko Popov, double agent for the British

SECRETS OF THE CENTURY

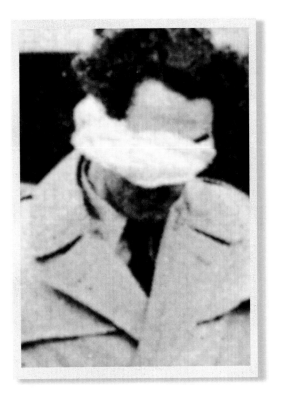

WORLD WAR II
WAR IN THE SHADOWS

BY THE EDITORS OF TIME-LIFE BOOKS, ALEXANDRIA, VIRGINIA

CONSULTANTS

David Kahn holds a doctorate from Oxford University and is a longtime historian and student of cryptology. He is the author of *The Code Breakers*, *Hitler's Spies: German Military Intelligence in World War Two*, and *Seizing the Enigma*. Dr. Kahn is the coeditor of *Cryptologia*, a scholarly quarterly on the study of codes and ciphers.

H. Keith Melton is an internationally recognized expert on espionage artifacts and clandestine devices and is a consultant to U.S. intelligence agencies on historical espionage equipment. He is the author of *CIA Special Weapons and Equipment*, *OSS Special Weapons and Equipment*, and *The Ultimate Spy Book* and the coauthor of *Clandestine Warfare*.

CONTENTS

COVER:
Two German agents face an uncertain future after being arrested in Great Britain during the early stages of World War II. Captured agents who refused to cooperate with authorities sometimes paid with their lives.

PRELUDE: A GATHERING STORM

The world was still at peace in July 1939 when the well-known Australian aviator and businessman F. Sidney Cotton flew to the Frankfurt Air Show in Germany to show off his Lockheed 12-A Electra, the latest thing in executive aircraft. While others shunned the Nazi regime and denounced Adolf Hitler's aggressive moves that threatened war, the big, brash, 45-year-old pilot seemed intent on cultivating close ties with German leaders. Among the officers who stopped by to admire his Lockheed in Frankfurt was General Albert Kesselring of the Luftwaffe, Germany's fast-expanding air force. When Kesselring asked for a ride, Cotton obligingly took him high up over the Rhine and invited him to fly the plane.

As Kesselring took over the controls, he noticed a green light flashing in the cockpit and asked what it meant. The light indicated that fuel was flowing smoothly to the engines, Cotton replied casually. Kesselring seemed reassured, and when they landed back at Frankfurt, he thanked Cotton for a pleasant trip.

For the plane's owner, however, the flight had been anything but a joyride. Sidney Cotton was secretly a British spy, and his Lockheed had three long-range cameras hidden in its belly behind retracting flaps. Cotton had activated the equipment before handing over the controls—and the flashing green light that Kesselring had noticed while flying the plane actually signaled that the cameras were operating automatically and snapping pictures of German military and industrial sites below.

It was a daring mission, and one of many for Cotton, whose reconnaissance flights were not always conducted in the public eye. To avoid notice on other

Officers of the French secret service hide their faces as they leave a German liner empty-handed in 1938. Their elusive quarry—a witness to a suspected German spy ring—was one of many players in the secret espionage struggle before the war.

occasions, his Lockheed 12-A was painted a pale, duck-egg green, making it hard to spot high in the sky.

Like spies throughout history, Cotton and other secret agents for the world's major powers operated in secret, risking serious consequences—at a minimum, immediate arrest—if they were discovered. But they were prepared to take risks. Long before hostilities were declared, Cotton and others had begun waging war in the shadows, fighting for precious scraps of intelligence that might spell the difference between victory and defeat when the shooting started.

Sidney Cotton was a relative newcomer to this shadow war, having enlisted as a British agent in September 1938. But the man who recruited him, Group Captain F. W. Winterbotham of the Royal Air Force, had been spying on Nazi Germany since 1934. Although he was indeed an RAF officer, Winterbotham was also, secretly, an officer with MI-6—the branch of

High-altitude photography pioneer Sidney Cotton (right), shown here in 1920 with a fellow pilot, made daring spy flights for the British agency MI-6 in 1939.

British military intelligence (thus the "MI" acronym) that was responsible for espionage abroad. For years, Winterbotham had posed as a Nazi sympathizer and gained the confidence of Adolf Hitler and some of his top aides, who briefed him on their plans to rebuild the Luftwaffe. Not until 1938 did Nazi leaders begin to suspect Winterbotham of spying—at which point they booted him out of the country and warned him never to return.

Intent on monitoring Hitler's military buildup in spite of his banishment, Winterbotham settled on a scheme to photograph German airfields and other strategic installations from civilian aircraft. The plan required a daring pilot, and Winterbotham had found just the man in Sidney Cotton. Cotton was "extremely keen to go ahead," Winterbotham later recalled. Cotton also had some reason to be in Germany, since he had business ties to a company that was trying to promote the use of color photography there. His daring excursion with Kesselring at the Frankfurt Air Show was just one of several spy flights he made in the months before war broke out in Europe in September 1939, years after the rival powers had begun dueling with each other in secret.

AGENCIES AT ODDS

Each of the major powers that became embroiled in World War II boasted more than one spy service, and those sibling agencies were not always on good terms. In Britain, the major services generally came up with ways of pulling together when it mattered most. MI-6 had occasional spats with MI-5—the agency responsible for counterespionage—but supported MI-5 in its vital task of catching German agents and turning them against their masters. During the war, a similar spirit of teamwork enabled Winterbotham and offi-

cers from competing services to exploit to mutual advantage the precious intelligence known as Ultra, produced when Allied code breakers penetrated the German cipher machine called Enigma and gained access to some of the enemy's top secrets.

Whereas British agencies overcame their differences, rival intelligence services in other nations remained sharply at odds. Under Hitler, for example, the Nazi Party's own security service, known as the Sicherheitsdienst, or SD, emerged as a dangerous rival to Germany's military intelligence service, the Abwehr, which conducted counterintelligence at home and both espionage and sabotage abroad. As early as 1930—eight years before Sidney Cotton started snooping in his Lockheed—the Abwehr had initiated spy flights over Poland by Colonel Theodor Rowehl. The colonel went on to command a secret reconnaissance squadron that photographed much of the Soviet Union, France, and Britain in military aircraft that flew as high as 40,000 feet, making them virtually invisible from the ground.

Meanwhile, the Abwehr was assembling large rosters of agents on foreign soil. By 1938 it had some 250 spies in Britain, surveying airfields, harbors, and other strategic targets. That network was devastated in the opening weeks of the war when British authorities rounded up enemy aliens, forcing German spymasters to hastily recruit new agents and sneak them into Great Britain at great risk of detection. Across the Atlantic, however, scores of German operatives continued unhindered to spy on shipping in ports from New York to as far as Buenos Aires, gathering intelligence that supported Germany's emerging U-boat cam-

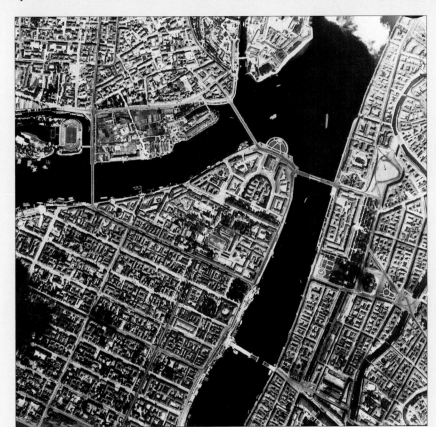

The remarkably detailed photograph of Leningrad at left was taken from a height of 25,000 feet by one of the special aircraft operated for the German Abwehr by Theodor Rowehl.

paign against vessels that were trafficking with Britain.

The rival SD had long looked enviously on these foreign operations and tried to outdo the Abwehr by carrying out special assignments for Hitler abroad. In 1937, for example, the SD went after Joseph Stalin's top generals, whom Hitler wanted to eliminate as part of his long-range goal of crushing the Soviet Union and eradicating Communism. SD agents forged and sold to Soviet officials documents that made it appear some of their top generals were plotting with German commanders against Stalin. Those forgeries helped fuel Stalin's subsequent bloody purge of the Red Army leadership, and the SD took credit for undermining the regime. But there was another layer to the story. In reality, the phony documents simply gave Stalin a cynical excuse to eliminate generals he

already distrusted—and the three million rubles he paid for the forgeries were themselves counterfeit.

The Soviet agents who carried out Stalin's purges belonged to his own state security agency, known as the NKVD (People's Commissariat for Internal Affairs). Much like the Nazi SD, the NKVD hunted down perceived enemies of the Soviet dictator and spied for him at home and abroad. During the 1930s, NKVD agents recruited as spies a group of talented young leftists at Cambridge University, later known as the Cambridge spy ring. Members of the ring went on

Below, members of an SS unit study a plaster cast of a footprint during training at a school run by the notorious Nazi security agency, the SD.

Head of the People's Commissariat for Internal Affairs, or NKVD, in the 1930s, Genrikh Yagoda (left) oversaw Stalin's purges until he himself was arrested and later executed.

officers eliminated by Stalin. Anti-Nazi Germans recruited by the GRU beginning in the mid-1930s, for example, formed the nucleus of a highly effective wartime spy network known as the Red Orchestra, which grew to include cells in a number of European countries and used clandestine radio transmitters to convey Hitler's war plans to Moscow. Other Soviet agents planted in the United States helped track American intentions before, during, and after the war.

Compared with the venomous feuds between rival spy services in the Soviet Union and Germany, relations between the various American security agencies in the years before the United States entered the war were polite but distant. The army, navy, and State Department each had their own intelligence functions, while the FBI conducted counterespionage. In 1942 a new American agency emerged to support the war effort—the OSS (Office of Strategic Services). The OSS was modeled loosely after the recently established British SOE (Special Operations Executive). Both services sponsored sabotage, guerrilla warfare, and other resistance activities in occupied territory; OSS agents also gathered intelligence for U.S. commanders behind enemy lines.

Before the war began, U.S. army code breakers scored a major coup by constructing a device that duplicated the workings of the standard Japanese diplomatic cipher machine, allowing analysts to understand enciphered radio messages

to occupy sensitive positions at MI-5, MI-6, and the foreign office and betrayed to Stalin some of the top secrets of those whom he embraced publicly as Allies.

While serving as Stalin's spy service, the NKVD engaged in a murderous feud with Soviet military intelligence, known as the GRU (Chief Intelligence Directorate of the General Staff). Not long after Stalin purged the leadership of the Red Army, he targeted the GRU for cleansing. NKVD agents gladly rounded up their rivals in military intelligence for execution—although some in the NKVD themselves fell victim to Stalin's terror campaign.

Like the Red Army, the GRU was reconstructed after the purges; it went on to achieve success during World War II by building on the foundations that had been laid by intelligence

Identity cards like this were carried by officers of the NKVD; the badge shown here indicated its wearer was a five-year veteran of the shadowy agency, one of the predecessors of the KGB.

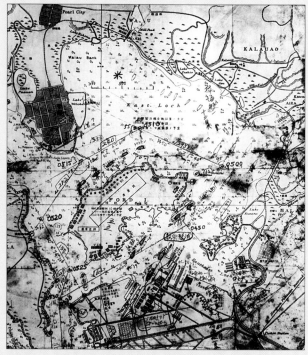

A 1933 Japanese Naval Academy graduate, Yoshikawa Takeo (left) had begun flight training when illness forced his resignation. He joined naval intelligence in 1936 and later became a key agent in Pearl Harbor.

Yoshikawa and others supplied vital data like that handwritten on this U.S. hydrographic chart of Pearl Harbor by Japanese planners.

sent to and from Tokyo. But lack of coordination between agencies hampered other American efforts to learn precisely what the Japanese were planning in the Pacific. In 1940, for example, a former sailor and bit actor in Hollywood named Al Blake informed naval intelligence that he had been approached by a Japanese agent to spy for Tokyo. Employing a typical counterintelligence tactic, the navy then ran Blake as a double agent as a way of penetrating the Japanese espionage network. This promising operation was cut short, however, when the FBI decided on its own to arrest Blake and two of his Japanese handlers. Had Blake been left in place, he might have learned that the Japanese had a special interest in Pearl Harbor— home to the U.S. Pacific Fleet.

A SPY AT PEARL HARBOR

One leading Japanese agent who eluded detection by American authorities was Ensign Yoshikawa Takeo, a naval intelligence officer. Yoshikawa reported for duty in April 1941 as the Japanese vice consul in Honolulu. Beneath the feckless exterior of

a party-going young diplomat, he was to pursue the secret mission of spying on Pearl Harbor and nearby American bases. He already knew when he arrived that Japan would attack the United States, and he assumed that Pearl Harbor would be a target, but his superiors gave him no warning of when that strike might come. As he wrote later, "To entrust knowledge of such a vital decision to an expendable espionage agent would have been foolish."

As a diplomat, the 27-year-old Yoshikawa moved freely about Honolulu. He strolled the hills to observe the fleet coming and going, rented aircraft to survey airfields from above, and disguised himself several times as a barefoot Filipino laborer in an attempt to enter the harbor area, only to be shooed away by sentries. At night, he frequented a Japanese restaurant to take in its commanding view of the brightly illuminated Battleship Row and chat with geishas who innocently offered him bits of information gleaned from American sailors they entertained. He never revealed his mission to them, for he found the local Japanese "essentially loyal to the United States."

Most of his reports were sent by radio to Tokyo and intercepted by the Americans, whose code-breaking feats allowed them to read this diplomatic traffic. But Yoshikawa's messages appeared deceptively similar to those sent by Japanese diplomats at other ports who were asked by Tokyo to supply information about ship movements. American officials tapped the phones at the Honolulu consulate, but Yoshikawa knew the place was bugged and threw his listeners off the scent by making most of his calls to local women he was dating, leaving the impression that the only clandestine activities he had time for were of an amorous nature.

In late November, Yoshikawa got his first inkling that an attack was imminent. A Japanese naval officer disguised as a ship's steward visited the consulate and left behind a ball of crumpled rice paper that contained a list of 97 questions, including one that stood out above the rest: "On what day of the week would the most ships be in Pearl Harbor on normal occasions?" Yoshikawa readily supplied the answer—Sunday.

Nine days later, on Saturday evening, December 6, 1941, Yoshikawa sat at his desk in the consulate, composing what proved to be his final radio message to Tokyo. The Pacific Fleet's three aircraft carriers had put out to sea, he reported, but there were 39 warships in Pearl Harbor, including all nine battleships.

The attack came at dawn the next day. Even as explosions rocked the harbor, FBI agents descended on the Japanese consulate seeking signs of espionage. All they turned up was "a half-finished sketch of Pearl Harbor, forgotten in my waste basket," Yoshikawa recalled, "and this one item of evidence was doubtless disregarded as a result of my diplomatic status."

Released after a period of confinement, Yoshikawa returned to Japan in 1942, along with other expelled diplomats. He never saw battle, but like other secret agents on both sides of the struggle, he prided himself on the vital role he played behind the scenes. "For a moment, at least," he wrote of his mission to Honolulu, "I held history in the palm of my hand."

Events of the War

September 1939
Germans invade Poland; Great Britain and France declare war.

May 1940
Fall of France.

June-September 1940
Battle of Britain—air war of RAF and Luftwaffe above Great Britain ends in German defeat.

February 1941
German Afrika Korps lands to assist Italians in North Africa.

June 1941
Germans invade Soviet Union.

December 1941
Japanese bomb Pearl Harbor; U.S. enters war.

May 1942
U.S. naval victory at Battle of Midway in Pacific.

August 1942
U.S. Marines land at Guadalcanal.

October-November 1942
British victory in North Africa at El Alamein.

November 1942
U.S. landings in North Africa; Germans surrender at Stalingrad, starting defeat on eastern front.

September 1943
Allies invade Italy.

June 1944
D-Day landings at Normandy.

December-January 1945
Battle of the Bulge—last major German counterattack.

June 1945
Germany surrenders.

August 1945
U.S. drops atom bombs on Hiroshima and Nagasaki; Japan surrenders.

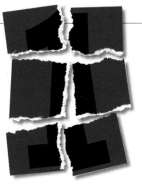

A CLASSIC
DOUBLE CROSS

ermany was at war, but the man striding briskly to work in the city of Hamburg on this September morning in 1939 seemed to have other business in mind. Blond, stout, and neatly attired, he had the preoccupied air of an executive with appointments to keep. Nothing in his appearance or demeanor suggested that his real trade was espionage or that the firm he represented was in fact the Abwehr, Germany's military intelligence service. "When I dressed as a civilian I behaved like one," Major Nikolaus Ritter later recalled, "though of course I am one hundred percent a soldier!"

Reaching his destination on Sophienterrasse in a quiet residential neighborhood, Ritter entered an unassuming three-story gray stone building that housed the headquarters for the Abwehr's covert operations in Britain and America. In his office on the third floor, he often took calls related to the various businesses he kept up as cover for his work as head of the Abwehr's air intelligence unit. On this occasion, however, he was awaiting a message of real consequence, from a Welshman named Arthur Owens, whom he had recruited to spy for Germany. Ritter had made a sizable commitment to this agent, entrusting him with secret codes and the best the Abwehr had to offer in two-way radios, and he wondered if the investment would pay off.

Ritter had first made contact with Owens two years earlier while the Welshman was visiting Germany on business. An electrical engineer with knowledge of the latest developments in Britain's aviation industry, Owens described himself as a Welsh nationalist, opposed to British rule as a matter of principle. Despite his supposed high ideals, however, he did not mind being rewarded for the secrets he betrayed. Ritter escorted the unhappily married Owens to Hamburg's steamy red-light district, provided him with female companionship, and footed the bill for him at beer halls, where the thirsty Welshman learned the only German phrase in his repertoire: "Ein Glas Bier!"

At left, a grinning British soldier escorts two German agents captured in the south of England; one is blindfolded, while the other covers his own eyes. Once caught, such agents were questioned at length by Britain's MI-5 service, then urged to switch their loyalties to the Allied side. Those who refused faced imprisonment or death.

Arthur Owens

Unknown to his German handlers, double agent Arthur Owens (inset) was in residence at Britain's Wandsworth Prison (above) when he transmitted reports soon after the outbreak of war. Each misleading message had been carefully scripted by his British controllers.

In between sprees, Owens—known to the Abwehr by the code name Johnny—was trained in sending coded messages by shortwave radio. Ritter then designated his promising new agent a "deep sleeper," meaning that he would remain inactive until a crisis arose. By early 1939, hostilities seemed inevitable, and it was time for Johnny to wake up; Ritter smuggled a two-way radio to him in London. On September 3, Britain responded to the invasion of Poland by declaring war on Germany, and British authorities began questioning and interning enemy aliens and suspected spies. Ritter waited anxiously at his office for word from Johnny.

If Johnny was still in play, his message would come not directly to Ritter at headquarters, but to a separate communications post in Hamburg, where radio operators listened intently through earphones for signals from foreign agents on designated frequencies. Like most of the messages from spies during the war, these were transmitted in Morse code, but knowledge of Morse was not enough to make sense of the contents, which consisted of cryptic jumbles of letters or numbers that could be interpreted only by those familiar with the Abwehr's codes.

A day or two after the war broke out, Ritter's man in London broke the silence by transmitting a message that was quickly decoded and relayed to headquarters. Johnny opened with a sly greeting—"Ein Glas Bier!"—a reassuring signal to Ritter that his old drinking buddy was back in touch. Then he got down to business. "Must meet you in Holland at once," he signaled. "Bring weather code." One of his duties was to transmit the latest weather reports from London—forecasts of vital interest to the Germans if they launched air raids against Britain—and Johnny needed a special code from Ritter to speed the transmission of those lengthy reports. Happy to oblige, Ritter arranged for a meeting in Rotterdam in late September.

Ritter would have been far less pleased to hear from his long-lost agent had he known where he was broadcasting from. Johnny had made radio contact with Ritter from a prison cell in London, where officers from MI-5—Section 5 of British military intelligence, responsible for counterintelligence—were watching his every move. Arthur Owens was their man now, and they were playing him back against his former German masters.

This maneuver marked the first move in a spectacularly successful operation that brought every last German agent operating in Britain under British control. Known as Double Cross, this scheme, which continued for the duration of the war, not only deprived Hitler and his commanders of vital intelligence but also exposed them to well-orchestrated campaigns of deception that hastened their defeat. Such a remarkable accomplishment did not come easily. To achieve their goal, the planners of Double Cross first had to learn how to deal with agents of shifting loyalties like Arthur Owens, who changed colors as readily as a chameleon.

Before enlisting with Ritter and the Abwehr in 1937, Owens had spied briefly for the British, peddling information he picked up on his German business trips, until he concluded that working for the Abwehr would be more profitable. This work for the Germans did not go unnoticed. British authorities kept an eye on him and hauled him in

Like most other German agents in Britain, Owens relied on an Abwehr-supplied radio similar to the one below. Its three stainless-steel compartments—containing, from left to right, a receiver, a battery, and a transmitter—could be stored in a leather case when not in use.

when the war began. Owens then agreed to broadcast deceptive messages to Ritter scripted by his MI-5 handlers, who gave him the code name Snow.

But could a spy as shifty as Snow be trusted to keep faith with his new masters? Although he was kept under constant surveillance in London after being released from prison, he had more room to maneuver when he met abroad with Ritter in late September and on several subsequent occasions. Even when Ritter later learned that Owens had been working for MI-5, he remained convinced that the agent he called Johnny had offered him intelligence of real value at those meetings early in the war and that Johnny was playing both sides.

The British, for their part, were not so dazzled by Snow that they ceased to be suspicious of him. Doubts about his loyalty resurfaced after a fiasco in the spring of 1940, when Ritter asked Owens to enlist a subagent and smuggle him out of Britain aboard a trawler for training in Germany as a spy and saboteur. Seizing the chance to introduce an agent into the enemy camp, MI-5 supplied Owens with a likely candidate—a reformed con man—and launched the pair across the North Sea. En route, however, Owens began talking like a genuine German agent, so alarming his companion that he locked the Welshman in his cabin and ordered the trawler back to England.

Afterward, a thorough search of Owens revealed that he was carrying stolen documents for an acquaintance, who had hoped to sell the documents to the Germans. But Owens insisted that he had only been acting the role of a German agent aboard the trawler because he thought that the other man really was a Nazi sympathizer. His MI-5 handlers decided to give him the benefit of the doubt.

In the end, the strain of playing two parts, Johnny and Snow, was more than Owens could bear. Early in 1941, after another rendezvous with Ritter abroad, he informed MI-5 that his Abwehr overseer had pressed him hard at that meeting and forced him to admit he was working for the British. Strangely, however, his reported confession resulted in no harm to MI-5 or anyone in its service. The British came to suspect that Owens had concocted the story as a way out of an assignment that had become too much for him.

Whatever the facts of the matter, he was through as a spy. Henceforth, the men who pulled the strings at MI-5 would rely on double agents they deemed more trustworthy. They sent Owens back to prison for the duration of the war and broadcast a few parting words to Germany on his behalf that came uncommonly close to the truth: Johnny had lost his nerve and could no longer carry on.

COUNTERINTELLIGENCE BY COMMITTEE

The man who ran Owens for MI-5—and pioneered the Double Cross system in the process—was Major Thomas Andrew "Tar" Robertson, a shrewd Scotsman who set out to demonstrate that it would be more fruitful to turn an adaptable spy like Owens against the Germans than to imprison or execute him. The results of that trial run were encouraging. Through Owens, MI-5 fed misinformation to the Germans, learned how the Abwehr recruited its spies and communicated with them, and enlisted additional double

Thomas Andrew "Tar" Robertson

John Cecil Masterman

Two of the many clever minds behind the Double Cross system included Major Tar Robertson, who headed the MI-5 section that ran the agents, and committee chairman John Masterman. A historian and avid sportsman who had spent much of World War I in a German prisoner-of-war camp, Masterman viewed his role as that of an amateur among military intelligence professionals.

The Secret Revealed

Like many intelligence feats of World War II, the Double Cross system remained a deeply held secret long after the dust of battle had settled. During the 1950s and 1960s, John Cecil Masterman —eager to counteract bad publicity arising from scandals in the British secret service—tried to reveal the extraordinary story by publishing his own report from 1945. After the government refused to give permission to publish it, he faced years of frustration until a friend suggested releasing it in the United States —a scheme Masterman eagerly dubbed Plan Diablo. Before Diablo could unfold, however, the British government requested several deletions. Once these were made, the book (below) was published in Great Britain and the United States in 1972— more than a quarter century after Double Cross played its last trick, and five years before its author's death at the age of 86.

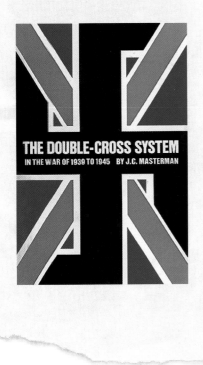

THE DOUBLE-CROSS SYSTEM
IN THE WAR OF 1939 TO 1945 BY J.C. MASTERMAN

agents, many of whom had been instructed by Ritter to contact Owens and ended up in the clutches of MI-5.

Meanwhile, still other German spies sent to Britain were arrested within hours of entering the country, before they could contact anyone. By late 1940 the Abwehr had attempted to sneak some two dozen agents into Britain to gather intelligence for Germany's ongoing air war and for a possible invasion of Britain should that campaign succeed. Whether those spies parachuted down over the countryside by night or came ashore in dinghies under cover of darkness or fog, they were soon spotted by alert British authorities or the highly spy-conscious general public. Indeed, the only spies who remained free and sent reports back to Germany were those working secretly for MI-5.

As Robertson's original notion expanded to include a roster of double agents, MI-5 faced a growing burden. It was not so much a problem of manpower, although just one double agent could require several handlers, including a case officer, a radio technician, and various guards and caretakers. The larger challenge for MI-5 was that the Abwehr might lose faith in a spy who failed to provide credible reports—and that meant feeding the Germans genuine nuggets of intelligence along with the fool's gold. Deciding which truths to reveal to the enemy and which to conceal was a delicate task that required consultation with civil defense authorities and the various intelligence units of the armed forces as well as MI-6—in charge of espionage abroad and responsible for double agents overseas.

In January 1941 an interagency board began holding weekly meetings to supervise the rapidly expanding operation. Formally known as the Twenty Committee—for the Roman numerals XX, or Double Cross—it was often called simply the Double Cross Committee. Chairing the group was John Cecil Masterman, who once described himself as a "junior officer in that section of MI-5 which controlled double agents, a backroom boy whose duties were advisory rather than executive." A relative newcomer to MI-5, the 50-year-old Masterman may have been junior in rank, but he was a master of many trades—a history don at Oxford, an accomplished cricket player, and a mystery writer. His position at Oxford gave him clout in an intelligence circle dominated by old boys from the best schools and prepared him to run a committee brimming with powerful egos from competing departments.

A collaborative effort like the Double Cross Committee was no small feat during World War II, when intelligence agencies operating under the same flag sometimes worked at cross purposes. "In the course of its history a vote was only once taken at the Committee," Masterman noted proudly. All other issues that arose in the course of 226 meetings over four and a half years were resolved by consensus.

Each week, 14 high-powered committee members convened to enjoy tea and buns provided by the congenial Masterman and to debate matters of great consequence. At the first meetings in January 1941, for example, they decided that their double agents should provide the Germans with fairly accurate reports on bomb damage, but they should exaggerate the strength of British defenses to discourage a German invasion.

As time went on, Masterman and company also had to determine the fate of double agents who were declining in value. "Running a team of double agents is very like running a club cricket side," he later explained. "Older players lose their form and are gradually replaced by newcomers." Those who lost form were referred to what Masterman called the "execution sub-committee," which either reprieved the agents in question for further duty or "executed" them; despite the grim term, this usually meant retiring them from service or imprisoning them.

According to Masterman, MI-5 favored keeping captured German agents alive even if they were ill suited for use as double agents, but some had to be put to death to satisfy the British public and present a plausible rate of failures to the German spymasters. Such was the fate of a spy named Joseph Jakobs, who landed by parachute in rural England on January 31, 1941, breaking his ankle in the process. Local authorities were on high alert for suspicious strangers, and Jakobs was promptly arrested amid much publicity. Masterman summed up his case with clinical detachment: "His arrival was widely advertised, his character was truculent, he could not be used, and he was eventually executed in August."

Members of the Double Cross Committee could not afford to be tender hearted if they hoped to win the dangerous game they were playing. By mid-1941, they had more than a dozen double agents operating against the Germans. (Over the course of the war, Masterman reckoned, MI-5 enlisted more than 100 double agents, of whom he rated nearly 40 as significant players.) But the committee was not yet ready to claim absolute control over the Abwehr's spy network in Britain. German agents were still infiltrating the country, and it remained possible that one or two might slip through the net and expose the Double Cross before it ripened to perfection.

Meanwhile, the operation's planners looked ahead to their ultimate goal, which was not simply to mislead the Germans about British defenses but to deceive them on a grand scale when the Allies were ready to take the offensive and reclaim occupied territory. In that momentous end game, the potential payoffs for Double Cross would

With humor and flair, posters like the one above warned British residents to be wary of spies everywhere. Such public campaigns helped ensure that newly arriving German agents would be noticed—and arrested—right away.

be enormous—and the risks if the Germans saw through the scheme would be correspondingly great.

Not surprisingly, the Double Cross system was among the war's most closely guarded secrets. When peace came in 1945, Masterman prepared an official report on the operation. But not until 1972, when the author was past 80, was he able to publish his book, *The Double-Cross System (page 19).*

The operation that the book divulged—and that other participants fleshed out through their own accounts—involved far more than committee meetings or strategy sessions. This covert campaign was planned at headquarters but waged and won in the field, by dedicated case officers and by the double agents they controlled, some of whom ventured abroad at great risk. For the case officers, the first battle was to win over those slippery Johnnies, Joes, or Janes—for several double agents recruited by MI-5 were women—and mold them into trustworthy traitors, prepared to deceive their former masters without a twinge of regret.

A GIFT FROM HEAVEN

No double agent who went to bat for Britain during the war had longer innings than a man whom the British code-named Tate. He fell into MI-5's hands like a gift from heaven after parachuting into Britain in the fall of 1940—before the formal creation of the Double Cross Committee—and remained in play against the Germans until the end of the war. Tate was not easily induced to switch sides, however, and his case demonstrated that patience could be just as effective as pressure in achieving a successful conversion.

Tate was a short, slender young man named Wulf Schmidt, recruited by Ritter for the Abwehr at the age of 26. Like many sent to spy in Britain, he came not from Germany but from one of the neutral or occupied countries—in this case, Denmark. A German agent who spoke anything less than flawless English would naturally attract suspicion, whereas a Dane like Schmidt might pass for a harmless Scandinavian refugee.

On the evening of September 19, 1940, Schmidt sat huddled in a German warplane, darkened with black paint, as the craft slipped into

Training for a mission to Scotland, three Abwehr agents paddle away from a seaplane off the coast of occupied Norway. German spies also tried to reach the British Isles by U-boat and by parachute drops.

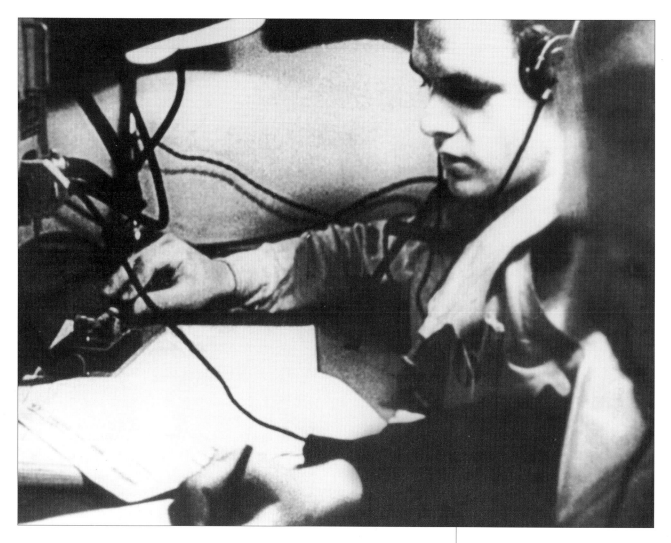

With a watchful British handler at his side, Double Cross agent Wulf Schmidt—code-named Tate—transmits one of hundreds of fabricated messages to the Abwehr. Most agents of the Abwehr tapped out radio messages with a transmitting key, as shown here; others relayed information using secret inks or in meetings in neutral countries.

English air space undetected and flew over the countryside of Cambridge-shire. Near the village of Willingham, the dispatcher gave a farewell shove to his well-dressed passenger, clad in a close-fitting tweed suit, and Schmidt parachuted down into a field with a pack that included a two-way radio.

After a raw night in the open, he hid his gear under a bridge and hiked into Willingham, where he used the water pump to bathe his ankle, which he had twisted while landing. Then he bought a watch in a shop to replace the one he had shattered leaping from the plane and had breakfast in a café. By the time he finished eating, his suspiciously non-British presence had been reported to the local home guard, who took him into custody, skepti-cally examined papers he carried identifying him as a refugee named Harry Johnson, and turned him over to the police in Cambridge. They in turn drove him to an MI-5 detention camp for suspected spies near London. The driver went out of his way to show Schmidt Londoners calmly going about their business in Trafalgar Square, shattering the illusion fostered by the Abwehr that he would find the city paralyzed by German air raids.

At the camp, Schmidt confronted nine MI-5 interrogators who warned him that he was outside the realm of civilian law and subject to execution at any moment. They insisted he sign a confession and reveal the names of other agents. Schmidt met their demands with long, stony silences, punctuated by words of defiance. The Germans would soon invade Britain, he assured his captors at one point, and they would then be his prisoners.

This battle of wills continued for over a week. In between interrogations, Schmidt was returned to the cell block, where the jailers reminded captives of their possible fate if they failed to cooperate. "The chap next door has just been shot," a defiant prisoner might be told. "I gather you are next." There was little point in torturing Schmidt, because what MI-5 wanted was not just his confession but his full cooperation. A spy who turned double agent simply to escape a beating from men he despised was all but useless.

Finally, after 13 days, Schmidt gave in and agreed to play scripted messages back to Germany on his transmitter, which had been retrieved from hiding. "It was simply a matter of survival," he said afterward of his sudden conversion. "Self-preservation must be the strongest instinct in man." To make sure he did not relapse into hostility, Tar Robertson took the man whom MI-5 now called Tate under his wing and invited him into his home, where Robertson and his wife found him polite and personable. Before long, Masterman noted, Tate was "one of our most trusted wireless agents."

Tate's cooperation was essential because any dispatches sent to Germany by British radio operators on his transmitter would have been recognized as fraudulent. Any experienced Morse-code operator naturally develops a unique way of sending Morse signals, often called a fingerprint. Although another operator can try to copy the fingerprint, such a feat requires considerable study and practice. Agents were also trained to use secret passwords or to insert spelling errors at certain points in the message. These indicators also confirmed their identity to informed listeners.

Once Tate had been won over, he made no attempt to alter his fingerprint or otherwise alert the Abwehr to the fact that his dispatches were contrived. All told, his reports did much to exaggerate the strength of British

Shortly after his arrest in May 1941, German agent Karel Richter points out his hidden parachute to British investigators. The 29-year-old Richter, who had been lured to England by a request from Wulf Schmidt for a radio part, was caught almost immediately; refusing to change his allegiance, he was sentenced to death and hanged that December.

defenses. Among other false reports, Tate sent the Abwehr inflated production figures for British warplanes and discouraged German planners from targeting England's vulnerable south coast for invasion by warning of drifting mines and invisible tank traps there.

At any hint of skepticism in the German ranks, meanwhile, Ritter was quick to pronounce Schmidt "absolutely reliable," much as he often vouched for the credibility of Johnny. Like other Abwehr spymasters, Ritter recruited and maintained his own network of agents, and his status and income depended on their reputation. He thus had a vested interest in touting their loyalty and seeing that they received the funding they needed to expand their operations—money that ended up in the coffers of MI-5 and helped pay for Double Cross.

For their part, the British had to convince the Abwehr that it was getting its money's worth from its spies. Sustaining that illusion proved especially difficult in the case of two agents who were sent not just to gather intelligence but also to commit sabotage. Before dawn on April 7, 1941, a German seaplane touched down off the west coast of Scotland and set two young men afloat in an inflatable rubber dinghy. Each brought with him a bicycle, a suitcase containing a two-way radio, and a kit filled with detonators and other explosive devices.

After beaching their craft, the agents immediately drew attention to themselves by walking up to a fisherman's cottage and banging on the door with the butt of a revolver. They told the startled occupant that they had just arrived from Norway and asked directions to the nearest military camp. After pointing the way, the fisherman ran to a telephone booth and notified the local police. Several hours later, a constable spotted the two men riding their bicycles on the wrong side of the road and stopped them for questioning. They freely admitted that they were enemy agents, recruited by the Germans in Norway and trained as saboteurs. One was tall and lanky and identified himself as Tor Glad. The other was short and chubby and went by the name of John Moe; he was partly of British extraction and seemed eager to cooperate.

Delighted by this windfall, MI-5 gave Moe the code name Mutt and dubbed his partner Jeff, after a pair of comic strip characters of similarly contrasting stature. Mutt breezed through his interrogation as if applying for a job, answering every question fully and candidly, reminiscing fondly about his early days in London, and even offering references who could vouch for his character. Like others who became trusted double agents for MI-5, Mutt may have agreed to spy for the Abwehr with the thought of gaining entry to Britain and switching sides.

Jeff proved harder for MI-5 to control. Lonely and moody, he disliked supervision. One evening, he gave his handlers the slip and spent the night with a nurse he befriended. In August, after further indiscretions, he was sent to an internment camp on the Isle of Man. Subsequently, Mutt led not just a double life but a triple one, for he took on Jeff's identity and operated both transmitters, having mastered his partner's transmitting fingerprint.

It was not enough for Mutt simply to send reports back to Germany.

He was supposed to commit sabotage, and while he could easily claim that he and Jeff were doing so, the Abwehr would grow suspicious without supporting evidence. Accordingly, MI-5 obtained permission from the Double Cross Committee to conduct domestic acts of sabotage that would attract attention without doing much damage. Mutt's handlers set out to enhance his credentials as a saboteur that November with Plan Guy Fawkes—so called for a British holiday marked by bonfires and fireworks. The idea was to trigger an explosion and fire in a food storage facility; the incident would be noticed by the press but readily controlled.

This staged calamity nearly degenerated into a comedy of errors. Two elderly fire guards on duty at the depot were sleeping so soundly that it proved difficult to wake them and draw them away from the site where the bomb had been placed. Then a local policeman happened by and threatened to arrest several men from MI-5 who were seemingly up to no good. In the end, however, the bomb went off and the fire caused the necessary stir before being snuffed out. The Germans were sufficiently impressed to send Mutt several additional installments of money and sabotage equipment—ironically, much of it confiscated from European resistance groups, who had in turn been supplied by the British.

By late 1941, the Double Cross Committee was overseeing a large and diverse roster of double agents. Among the spies in Britain who turned against their German paymasters at MI-5's bidding were those code-named Rainbow, a young man from Portugal who played piano in a dance band and plied the Abwehr with deceptive reports on bomb damage for payment of 1,000 pounds a year; Sweet William, a clerk in the Spanish embassy who gave MI-5 access to the diplomatic pouch used to funnel secrets from London to Madrid; and the Snark, a Yugoslav woman employed as a servant in London who fed the Germans trifles, inflating their notion that Londoners were hungry and demoralized.

Most of these operatives were retired by MI-5 after a year or two without being recognized for their contributions—recognition that would have been a mixed blessing for those who had earlier performed real services for Nazi Germany. Even in Masterman's belatedly published book, most were identified only by code names. But a few of these shadowy figures eventually told their own stories in later years, including two of the most talented and trusted double agents on MI-5's roster—a Yugoslav known as Tricycle and a Spaniard called Garbo. They had good reason to be proud of the double lives they led. For they had enlisted with the Abwehr for the express purpose of crossing over and helping to defeat Hitler—and they did just that by deceiving the Germans materially about Allied plans to liberate Europe.

TRICYCLE ON THE LOOSE

On August 10, 1941, a dapper man of affairs named Dusko Popov boarded a Pan American Clipper in Lisbon, Portugal, for a leisurely trip on the flying boat to New York, which would include stops in the Azores and Bermuda. Officially, the 39-year-old Popov was heading to America to serve with the Ministry of Information for Yugoslavia's government-in-exile, formed after the Germans conquered that nation. Secretly, however, Popov had agreed to spy for Germany and had just received $40,000 from his Abwehr handler in Lisbon to carry out a devious and delicate assignment in New York. Popov's task was even more devious than the Abwehr imagined, for beneath his facade as a Yugoslav official and his undercover role as a German spy, he was playing a third and genuine role as a double agent for MI-5.

Although his life was riddled with danger and deception, the well-born Popov had a knack for enjoying himself. "To survive the multiple hazards of espionage it is better not to be too serious," he wrote in his colorful memoir, *Spy/Counterspy*. In between meetings with his Abwehr contact in neutral Portugal—a hotbed of intrigue during the war, as were many nonaligned countries—he frequented casinos and romanced one or another of his many girlfriends. His escapades caught the attention of Ian Fleming, then a British naval intelligence officer, and Popov may have been one of the models for Fleming's fictional hero, James Bond.

Popov may have coped better than others with the pressures of his double life because he was fully committed to the Allied cause and free of conflicting loyalties. Unlike Arthur Owens, he never truly belonged to the Abwehr. In the summer of 1940, a German friend of his named Johann Jebsen had recruited him in Belgrade for the Abwehr. Popov immediately reported to the local British Passport Control Office—which provided cover for British spymasters in various European capitals—and was urged to play along with the Germans. Entering Britain legally through Portugal, he enlisted as a double agent with MI-5 and promptly recruited two subagents, both of whom were supposedly snooping for Germany but really working for the home team. Popov's grateful handlers gave him the code name Tricycle.

During his flight to New York, according to his memoirs, Tricycle was joined in Bermuda by John Pepper, an officer with MI-6. "I'm just sort of a flying nursemaid," Pepper remarked, explaining that he would introduce Tricycle to the FBI's top brass in New York, who had recently nabbed dozens of German spies there and would be glad to meet with an agent sent to America by the Abwehr to help rebuild its network and collect military secrets. "And as my first chore," Pepper added, "I'll introduce you to the great American institution of dry martinis."

"Very kind of you," Popov replied with Bond-like savoir-faire when Pepper returned from the plane's bar with two chilled glasses, "but I can manage my own introductions."

Pepper performed another service for Popov when the flight reached New York. As a British official, he could pass through Customs with ease; consequently, he took charge of Popov's briefcase, which contained material so sensitive that it was thought no U.S. agency other than the FBI could be trusted with it. Affixed to a telegram among papers in his briefcase were microdots—tiny dots of film the size of punctuation marks. These microdots represented the latest German advance in the process of micro-

Dusko Popov

Pictured above in 1941, Yugoslav playboy—and British double agent—Dusko Popov was by most accounts brave, colorful, charming, and irresistible to women.

"I never took life, myself, or other people too seriously."

—Dusko Popov

Ian Fleming

A naval intelligence officer in the war, Ian Fleming went on to later fame as the creator of James Bond. Fleming and Popov met briefly, but claims that Bond was based in part on Popov remain unresolved.

photography, which had been used for some time to reproduce lengthy documents on small, easily concealed frames of microfilm. Each microdot Popov carried contained a document within a frame so tiny that the text could be read only through a microscope. Even close scrutiny of an agent's papers might fail to uncover these precious specks of film.

The FBI would benefit greatly by learning about microdot technology and knowing what to look for when agents searched suspected German spies. But the gift was all the more valuable considering the information contained on those microdots—a list of questions for Popov to investigate concerning America's defenses. Many of the questions related to the U.S. naval base at Pearl Harbor, and to answer them, he had been instructed to visit Honolulu. In the summer of 1941, only one nation potentially hostile to the United States had a rival fleet in the Pacific powerful enough to threaten Pearl Harbor—Japan. Plainly, Japan was gauging American strength there as a possible prelude to attack and had asked for help from Germany, Japan's Axis partner.

After arriving in New York, Popov checked into the swank Waldorf-Astoria and stepped out to run a few errands. When he returned, he found that someone had searched his suitcases. No longer were they aligned with the faint pencil marks he had made to indicate their position, and the hair he had placed between them was missing. He attributed the intrusion to a mere overzealousness on the part of the FBI.

When Popov met with the local FBI chief the next day, he was amazed by the man's casual response to the questions concerning Pearl Harbor. "It all looks too precise, too complete, to be believed," the chief remarked. "If anything, it sounds like a trap." He expressed greater interest in the microdot process. Popov sought permission to visit Hawaii, but New York could offer him no guarantees without instructions from FBI director J. Edgar Hoover in Washington. When Popov proposed visiting the capital to speak with Hoover himself, he was told not to do so.

In the meantime, Popov indulged himself with typical extravagance and rented a penthouse apartment on Park Avenue. His FBI contact was amazed at his new digs and doubted that Mr. Hoover would approve of such luxurious surroundings. Hoover would be visiting New York in two weeks, Popov was told, and would meet with him then. Popov did not relish the idea of passing the days idly in his penthouse under FBI surveillance. "If I bend over to smell a bowl of flowers," he complained, "I scratch my nose on a microphone." So he drove his girlfriend to Miami for a vacation—only to be approached by two FBI agents who accused him of violating the Mann Act by crossing state lines with a woman for immoral purposes. Threatened with arrest if he refused to send his companion away, Popov put her on a plane and drove back to New York alone to await his showdown with the director.

From the start of their encounter Hoover was an angry man, Popov later recalled, writing that he looked "like a sledgehammer in search of an anvil." The director eyed his target contemptuously and started pounding

TINY MESSAGES IN A DOT

Although several nations used minuscule photographs to send secret messages during the war, microphotography was a particular specialty of the Germans. Even before 1939, communications experts in the Abwehr intelligence service had found a way to shoot typed documents with regular 35-millimeter film, then photograph the negatives through a lens system similar to a microscope, reducing each image to the size of a pinhead. The resulting microdot could be hidden under a postage stamp or could take the place of a period in a document. Upon receipt, the dot would be enlarged through a reverse process to a readable size.

The theory was sound, but there were a number of practical problems. Because the microdots were printed on extremely thin optical glass, creating one required either a full photographic laboratory or a six-foot-long, 4,200-pound optical bench. The solution came in 1940, when a professor by the name of Zapp at the University of Leipzig, who was working under contract for the Abwehr, developed the Zapp Cabinet, a portable—although still cumbersome—microdot processing unit. The device, which produced a positive rather than negative image, also had the advantage of printing on thin, clear plastic, which allowed dots to be placed in a wider range of hiding places. Quickly supplied to German embassies and consulates in neutral countries around the world, Zapp Cabinets provided one of the war's most secure methods of communication. Although British censors managed to detect some microdots passing through Bermuda, the majority of the infinitesimal messages got through.

NAVAL INFORMATION

Reports on enemy shipments (material foodstuffs—combination of convoys, if possible with names of ships and speeds).

Assembly of troops for oversea transport in U.S.A. and Canada. Strength—number of ships—ports of assembly—reports on ship building (naval and merchant ships)—wharves (dockyards)—state and private owned wharves—new works—list of ships being built or resp. having been ordered—times of building.

Reports regarding U.S.A. strong points of all descriptions especially in Florida—organisation of strong points for fast boats (E-boats) and their depot ships—coastal defence—organisation districts.

HAWAII—AMMUNITION DUMPS AND MINE DEPOTS

1. Details about naval ammunition and mine depot on the Isle of Kushua (sic) (Pearl Harbour). If possible sketch.
2. Naval ammunition depot Lualuelei. Exact position? Is there a railway line (junction)?
3. The total ammunition reserve of the army is supposed to be in the rock of the Crater Aliamanu. Position?
4. Is the Crater Punchbowl (Honolulu) being used as ammunition dump? If not, are there other military works?

AERODROMES

1. Aerodrome Lukefield.—Details (sketch if possible) regarding the situation of the hangars (number?), workshops, bomb depots, and petrol depots. Are there underground petrol installations?—Exact position of the seaplane station? Occupation?
2. Naval air arm strong point Kaneche.—Exact report regarding position, number of hangars, depots, and workshops (sketch). Occupation?
3. Army aerodromes Wicham Field and Wheeler Field.—Exact position? Reports regarding number of hangars, depots and workshops. Underground installations? (Sketch.)
4. Rodger's Airport.—In case of war, will this place be taken over by the army or the navy? What preparations have been made? Number of hangars? Are there landing possibilities for seaplanes?
5. Airport of the Panamerican Airways.—Exact position? (If possible sketch.) Is this airport possibly identical with Rodger's Airport or a part thereof? (A wireless station of the Panamerican Airways is on the Peninsula Mohapuu.)

NAVAL STRONG POINT PEARL HARBOUR

1. Exact details and sketch about the situation of the state wharf, of the pier installations, workshops, petrol installations, situations of dry dock No. 1 and of the new dry dock which is being built.
2. Details about the submarine station (plan of situation). What land installations are in existence?
3. Where is the station for mine search formations (Minensuchverbaende)? How far has the dredger work progressed at the entrance and in the east and southeast lock? Depths of water?
4. Number of anchorages (Liegeplaetze)?
5. Is there a floating dock in Pearl Harbour or is the transfer of such a dock to this place intended?

SPECIAL TASKS

Reports about torpedo protection nets newly introduced in the British and U.S.A. navy. How far are they already in existence in the merchant and naval fleet? Use during voyage? Average speed reduction when in use. Details of construction and others.
~~~~d are exact details about the armoured strengths

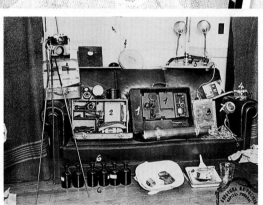

Even a document like the example at left—excerpted from a British wartime translation of Dusko Popov's Pearl Harbor questionnaire—could be hidden as a microdot on an envelope pattern like the one shown here. A Zapp Cabinet, designed to produce microphotographs in the field, appears at the center of the photograph above, as part of a darkroom discovered by Argentine authorities in 1945 in the German embassy in Buenos Aires.

Longtime FBI director J. Edgar Hoover, shown above leaving the White House after a lunch with President Roosevelt in 1937, enthusiastically hunted Nazi spies and saboteurs in both the United States and South America during the war. The strong-willed director's encounter with Dusko Popov resulted in frustration on both sides.

away, "You come here from nowhere and within six weeks install yourself in a Park Avenue penthouse, chase film stars, break a serious law, and try to corrupt my officers." He regarded turncoats like Popov as inherently untrustworthy. "You're begging for information to sell to your German friends," he said, "so you can make a lot of money and be a playboy."

When Popov attempted to explain his methods as a double agent, Hoover bellowed to an aide sitting in on the interview, "That man is trying to teach me my job."

"I don't think anyone could teach you anything," Popov retorted as he stalked out, with a hearty good riddance from Hoover. Leaving the meeting, Popov could only recognize defeat. His efforts to reach a meeting of the minds with Hoover had been doomed from the beginning.

In his book, Popov blasted Hoover for squandering the tip on Pearl Harbor and handing the enemy "a victory of incalculable proportions." But there was plenty of blame to go around for this lost opportunity. The British could have chosen a better messenger than Popov to brief the prickly and prudish Hoover. And the FBI director was not the only security chief to overlook the questionnaire's significance. Intelligence officers with the navy and army received reports on Popov's revelations at the end of September—more than two months before the Japanese attacked Pearl Harbor.

Considering Hoover's contribution to this collective intelligence failure, he might have been expected to keep quiet about the microdot incident. Instead, he took credit for uncovering the secret German technique, sending President Roosevelt a memo to that effect in January 1942 without mentioning the questions on Pearl Harbor. Several years later, in an article for *Reader's Digest,* Hoover asserted that the FBI had captured the microdots from a German spy. "We knew he was the playboy son of a millionaire," Hoover wrote in a thinly veiled reference to Popov. "With meticulous care we examined his possessions from toothbrush to shoes." A keen-eyed laboratory agent spotted the tiny dots, Hoover alleged, and the rest was history.

Popov remained in America for more than a year after his run-in with Hoover. He begged his FBI contacts for something convincing to feed the Abwehr, but all he got were stale items from military journals and press releases. When he returned to Lisbon in October 1942, he tried to shift the blame by assuring his Abwehr handler that $40,000 had not been nearly enough to organize an effective spy network in an atmosphere as hostile as the United States. "You send me there with no help whatsoever," he complained, "no contacts, a few miserable dollars, although Berlin considered it a lot, and you expect me to produce results."

The Abwehr may have been disappointed by his performance, but it needed his services now more than ever. With America's entry into the war, the balance of power had shifted in favor of the Allies, and they were laying plans for offensive action. The Abwehr trusted in agents like Popov, who had access to Britain, to uncover those plans and give Germany a fighting chance.

Tricycle and others played on that trust mercilessly in the months to come, teasing their German contacts with hints of attacks in Norway or France to divert attention from the real campaigns that would soon unfold in North Africa and Sicily. Operation Double Cross was entering its critical phase, and the planners at MI-5 relied increasingly on their best performers—tested players like the unflappable Tricycle and an ingenious master of deception called Garbo.

GARBO TAKES THE STAGE

In the summer of 1941, shortly before Tricycle left for the United States, a 29-year-old Spaniard named Juan Pujol arrived in Lisbon to carry out one of the strangest spy capers of the war. A staunch opponent of Fascism, Pujol had approached officials at the British embassy in Madrid earlier in the year and offered to spy for Great Britain. The British turned him down, concerned that using Spaniards as spies might antagonize Franco, who leaned toward Germany but remained officially neutral.

Pujol, however, was unwilling to give up. He soon called the German embassy in Madrid, hoping that if he went to work for the enemy, the British might accept him as a double agent. He was directed by phone to a café, where a "fair-haired gentleman, with blue eyes, dressed in a light suit and carrying a raincoat over his arm" would be waiting for him. Pujol assured the contact he met there, who introduced himself as Federico, that he held a British visa and could enter England legally. In truth, he had no such papers. At a series of meetings, Federico instructed Pujol in the sorts of intelligence the Abwehr wanted from England and sent him on his way with a bottle of invisible ink, three thousand dollars, and the code name Arabel.

Unable to enter England, Pujol traveled to Lisbon, where he tried without success to offer his services once more to the British. Undeterred, he proceeded with the unlikely scheme of filing reports to the Abwehr from Lisbon that supposedly originated in England. He hoped the phony dispatches might bring him enough credit as a spy to make him attractive as a double agent.

To conceal the fact that he was still in Portugal, he sent his Abwehr overseers the key to a safe deposit box in a Lisbon bank and told them he had arranged to have his reports from England deposited there regularly by a co-operative KLM pilot on the London-to-Lisbon run. His next task was to concoct eyewitness accounts of a country he had never seen. Armed with a map of Great Britain, a Baedeker tourist guide, a railway timetable, and various books and newspaper accounts, he marshaled the essential facts and filled in the blanks with his vivid imagination. He was also aided by a certain natural credulity on the German side. "He always reported what the Germans expected to hear," Masterman later wrote. "Since many of his guesses were startlingly near to the truth, he was more and more readily believed."

His reports seemingly consisted of inconsequential letters from England describing the sights. Between the lines, however, he penned his real messages to the Abwehr in invisible ink. In his first reports, he claimed that he

> "I would sit down and write letters in Catalan hour after hour, leaving wide spaces between the lines so that I could then insert whatever Tommy and I had concocted in between in invisible ink."
>
> —Juan Pujol

In a wartime photograph that may have been used for training, a woman searches a German-language letter for secret inks by brushing on a developing agent. Both Dusko Popov and Juan Pujol used such inks to report to the German Abwehr.

had been offered a job with the BBC and had recruited three sub-agents. In reality, all three were completely imaginary, a quality known in the trade as "notional."

Over time, Pujol grew bolder and more inventive. In early 1942, he relayed a fictitious report from one of his notional agents—William Gerbers, who was supposedly based in Liverpool—that a convoy of five ships had left that port city to relieve the besieged British island of Malta in the Mediterranean. A short time later, the British intercepted enemy signals revealing that the Germans had credited this false dispatch from agent Arabel, Pujol's Abwehr code name, and were diverting U-boats and torpedo planes to deal with the nonexistent convoy.

A spy who could stir up this sort of tempest was just what the planners of Double Cross needed, and they set out to find him. They soon concluded that Arabel was none other than Juan Pujol, spurned earlier at their embassies in Madrid and Lisbon. Unfortunately, no one at either place had heard from him recently. Meanwhile, Pujol was coming under pressure from his Abwehr handlers, who demanded "weightier reports on troop sitings and movements." As it turned out, his bosses did not blame him for the Malta incident—such disappointments were common in wartime and were not always the fault of the source. But Pujol assumed they were losing faith in him. "The farce was coming to an end," he wrote in *Operation Garbo*, a 1985 account he composed with British author Nigel West when West located him decades after the war. "I therefore decided to abandon the whole operation and disappear from Europe altogether."

Before throwing in the towel, Pujol made one final attempt to offer his services to the Allies through the American embassy in Lisbon. The official he spoke with promptly notified the British, who at last handed Pujol the prize he coveted—an invitation to work as a double agent for MI-5 in Britain. Arriving in the country he had long fantasized about, Pujol found the reality something of a shock: "My first recollection of England on that calm clear day in April 1942, as I walked down the steps of the plane, was of the terrible cold—cold outside and icy fear inside." Among those on hand to offer him a warm greeting, however, was Tomas Harris of MI-5's Iberian section, who spoke Spanish and would serve as his principal case officer.

To some skeptics at MI-5, Pujol seemed too good to be true. Thorough questioning erased any lingering doubts as to his loyalty, however, and he was supplied with documents identifying him as a translator for the BBC, validating the fiction he had concocted for the Abwehr. He then divulged

METHODS OF CHARGING EXPENSES AND
REFERENCES TO MONEY.
────────────────────────────────────

Letter No. 10. 31.10.41.
    (a) Personal expenses.   Hotel, tramways, etc.,
        at £2 per day.

    (b) Agents at £2 per day each.

    (c) Hire of typewriter.

    (d) Post and paper

    (e) English books.

    (f) English lessons.

    (g) Drinks and taxis.

Letter No. 11. 3.11.41.
    Detailed list of cost of all agents' journeys.

Letter No. 15. 24.11.41.
    I need a reserve fund of money here.

Letter No. 29. 7.2.42.
    (a) Am only given £10 bonuses to cut down expenses.
        (Given each month)

    (b) Travelling expenses are paid to them apart.

Letter No. 52. 30.5.42.
    Money can be sent to the National Provincial Bank,
    Swiss Cottage Branch, in name of Juan P. GARCIA,
    as representing payments of commissions.

Letter No. 65. 12.7.42.
    If you don't consider my plan for sending money to the
    Bank a good one you must study alternative means and
    let me know.

Cover letter 12.7.42.
    (a) I shall need about £200 per month for self, wife
        and child.

    (b) This does not include incidental expenses.

his most closely guarded secret—he had a wife and young son in Portugal, whose existence he had concealed up to this point from both sides for fear of involving his family in the treacherous game he was playing. The two were immediately transported to London. All that remained was for MI-5 to furnish him with a code name. In the opinion of his new handlers, he was one of the world's great actors, so they dubbed him Garbo, which, as a woman's name, would better mask his identity if word leaked to the enemy.

Pujol later gave Tommy Harris equal credit for defining Garbo's role as a supposed German agent, "a creation that afforded us both great pleasure." The two men set out to expand upon Pujol's small roster of notional subagents so that he could plausibly provide the Germans with misinformation from around the British Isles and beyond. They soon had to dispense with one of Pujol's original inventions, William Gerbers of Liverpool, to whom the false lead on the Malta convoy had been attributed. Gerbers was sure to arouse German suspicions if he failed to report the real buildup taking place in Liverpool for the invasion of North Africa in November 1942. That was a secret the British could not reveal, so earlier in the fall, Garbo reported that Gerbers had been hospitalized. In November, Garbo sent his Abwehr contact a clip from the Liverpool *Daily Post* announcing

Gerbers's death and specifying a private funeral, "No flowers please."

Garbo soon compensated for this sad loss by informing the Germans that Gerbers's widow had been in on her husband's secret and could think of no better way of honoring his memory than by spying for the Reich herself. She was not the only woman on Garbo's growing list of subagents—none of whom, of course, actually existed. He claimed to be romancing a secretary in the War Office with access to top secrets and boasted to the Abwehr of his success: "Although in her early thirties she is clearly unaccustomed to attentions from the opposite sex. This makes her all the more accessible to mine. Already she is delightfully indiscreet."

Another make-believe informant who supposedly provided Garbo with sensational material for his reports was a former seaman described by Garbo as a "thoroughly undesirable character," who demanded hefty payments from the Abwehr for his services but had valuable contacts in various ports. The sailor was said to have organized these equally imaginary informants into an efficient spy ring, making them subagents of Garbo's notional subagent. Garbo soon had so much news to pass along from his fictitious sources that he proposed a radio link to speed the flow. His Abwehr handlers obligingly sent Garbo instructions for coding messages that allowed MI-5 to decipher all their latest dispatches.

By 1943 Garbo ranked as one of MI-5's top performers, with Masterman and others on the Double Cross Committee reviewing his every move. He figured prominently in their plans to deceive the Germans as to the target and timing of the massive Allied landing planned for 1944, which would open a second front in western Europe within close range of England. Already Garbo was sending the Germans reports of buildups in various parts of Britain that suggested a possible Allied landing much earlier, sometime in the summer of 1943—perhaps in Norway, or in Brittany, or at Calais. For now, the objective was to keep German forces there from being redeployed to the eastern front, where the Russians were making great strides.

These deceptions failed, however, because the Germans doubted that the Allies were ready to strike and recognized as bluffs the paltry military measures taken that summer to make an invasion seem imminent. Once again, Garbo evaded suspicion at Abwehr headquarters by eliminating one of his notional subagents, whom he blamed for exaggerating the likelihood of a landing in 1943 and dismissed from his service that November. He also reported that another of his imaginary informants, a serviceman whose reports had been similarly misleading, had been reassigned from Britain to active duty in North Africa, where he was supposedly killed in action.

MI-5 and the Double Cross Committee learned useful lessons from this clumsy dress rehearsal in deception. In 1944, they would work closely with the armed forces to ensure that efforts by their double agents to mislead the Germans as to the time and place of the Allied invasion were backed by credible evidence. Once the stage was set for that great bluff and all the props were in place, Garbo, Tricycle, and the other Double Cross masters of deception would be ready once again to work their magic, waging a vital shadow war of lies and misdirection.

Before an August 1945 rendezvous in Spain, double agent Juan Pujol, alias Garbo (second from left), pauses for a snapshot. A ledger of claimed "expenses" shows how Juan Pujol Garcia (his full name) extracted money from his German handlers that could then be used to support the Double Cross system.

"Fiction suitably presented is often more easily credible than truth."

—Sir John Cecil Masterman, on Pujol's success

Under the scrutiny of an instructor, American OSS agents train with British and French comrades; the trainees shown here were destined for anti-German guerrilla operations in France, Belgium, and the Netherlands.

THE OSS: A SURVEY OF OPERATIONS

William J. Donovan

Nicknamed Wild Bill for his athletic feats at Columbia—and later, for the daring that earned him the Medal of Honor during World War I—William Donovan founded America's first central agency for gathering and interpreting foreign intelligence.

Called the Woolworth by its OSS creators, the Liberator .45 was inexpensive and simple in design. Meant for resistance groups, the one-shot weapon was called "a gun to get a gun."

It is essential we set up a central enemy-intelligence organization," then-Colonel William J. Donovan wrote President Roosevelt in mid-1941. With war looming, Roosevelt agreed, creating the Office of the Coordinator of Information to gather, analyze, and interpret data essential to national security. Opened on July 11, 1941, it was staffed by Donovan and seven assistants. Two months after Pearl Harbor and the entry of the U.S. into the war, the organization was renamed the Office of Strategic Services (OSS) and greatly expanded. By December 1944, it had grown to 13,000 employees, and Donovan was a major general. Two years after the war's end, a version of the OSS would return under another name—the Central Intelligence Agency, or CIA.

Men and women, soldiers and civilians were recruited to work for different OSS divisions. In the Research and Analysis division, scholars analyzed masses of data. For Research and Development, scientists and inventors developed unorthodox weapons and explosives; the Schools and Training branch taught agents how to use them. Members of the Secret Intelligence branch gathered foreign intelligence; those in Special Operations conducted sabotage and guerrilla operations; and in the Operational Groups branch, OSS officers fought alongside resistance movements in Europe and Asia. For overseas assignments, Donovan preferred agents who were "calculatingly reckless, of disciplined daring and trained for aggressive action." At training camps—some staffed by British intelligence experts—recruits learned the intricacies of survival, sabotage, and espionage. "Had any of us lacked for a profession after the War," one agent joked, "we would have made perfect gangsters."

The work of those who operated behind enemy lines was documented by yet another OSS division—the Field Photographic branch. Many of the images here and on the following pages are from their declassified files.

At left, OSS agents at a secret airfield in England prepare for a jump into occupied France in 1944. Above, members of the 492d Bomb Group, which specialized in OSS operations, gather before flying another mission to France the same year.

OPERATIONS: EUROPE

By 1943 both the Secret Intelligence (SI) and Special Operations (SO) branches of the OSS had infiltrated German-occupied western Europe to assist the local resistance forces. While there, the SI also located some anti-Nazi Germans to train as agents. Ferdinand Appenzell—"a rather shrewd and cagey fellow," according to an OSS psychologist—and Leon Lindau parachuted into southern Germany in April 1945. Within weeks, they had pinpointed jet factories and troop and defensive positions—information vital to American forces then advancing into the area.

Sabotage was the weapon of choice for Special Operations, and German-occupied France was the arena for many SO missions in preparation for, and later in support of, the 1944 invasion of France. Small, so-called Jedburgh teams—the name, although that of a town in Scotland, was apparently a random code word—helped conduct guerrilla campaigns, parachuting all over France to fight an unconventional war. "Sometimes we attacked the enemy on the road and in their pickets," reported one Jedburgh leader. "Sometimes we blew up railway lines, bridges and trains, and sometimes we ourselves were attacked." Such organized mayhem behind German lines helped speed the liberation of France. In addition, much of Yugoslavia, Greece, and Italy was liberated by OSS-supported resistance forces before Allied armies arrived.

An OSS agent in camouflage gathers his parachute after a successful night landing behind enemy lines in France in 1944. Elsewhere in France, members of a joint OSS-British mission (right) assemble a radio, their vital link to London.

In the spring of 1944, OSS operative Peter Tompkins (above, left), General Donovan's personal representative to the Italian resistance in Rome, retrieves supplies from the cellar where he had hidden them.

Agents of a joint OSS-British intelligence mission pose with Chetnik resistance fighters in German-occupied Serbia in late 1943. The OSS helped supply the resistance groups and built up intelligence units within their forces.

To prevent reinforcements from reaching the western battlefront in late 1944, a team of OSS, British, and Norwegian saboteurs sank the German troopship Donau outside Oslo harbor.

In this sequence of photographs taken over North Burma in March 1945, an agent from OSS Detachment 101 moves to the door of a C-47 cargo plane, then parachutes toward his target: a rendezvous with Kachin guerrilla fighters in the jungle below.

Following the liberation of central Burma in the spring of 1945, an American officer of Detachment 101 presents Kachin tribesmen with shotguns in recognition of their heroism in combat.

OPERATIONS: ASIA

Despite the success of OSS operations in Europe, the agency's services were put to little use in the Pacific theater. Instead, the OSS concentrated its efforts on the Asian mainland, most notably Burma and China. Detachment 101, formed in the fall of 1942, was a Burma-based OSS unit with the goal of reopening an overland supply route to China. Agents parachuted into secret jungle camps to organize local Kachin tribesmen and lead them in ambushes of Japanese troops. So successful was this force of more than 500 Americans and 9,000 Burmese in routing the enemy that they were awarded the President's Distinguished Unit Citation. Noted one OSS commander proudly, "Several Japanese prisoners volunteered the opinion that they rated one Kachin equal to 10 Japanese." In fact, the Kachin guerrillas killed 25 of the enemy for every casualty of their own.

Such cooperation was not the hallmark of operations in China. Although an agreement had been reached in 1943 to combine American and Chinese intelligence forces, Nationalist Chinese veto power over American operations curtailed those efforts. However, a deep-cover OSS network secretly collected vital intelligence throughout the war, and by 1945, these agents were blowing up Japanese railway lines and bridges throughout China.

In Tibet to study the feasibility of building a supply route, Lieutenant Colonel Ilia Tolstoy (above, left), grandson of the Russian novelist, pauses with a fellow OSS agent and their guide before a Buddhist shrine.

SECRET DIPLOMACY

The versatile training of OSS agents enabled them to act as diplomats as well as guerrilla fighters. The threat of a Japanese invasion of Tibet led two OSS agents there in late 1942 to locate potential sabotage targets in the event of Japanese occupation. Received as ambassadors by the 10-year-old ruler, the Dalai Lama, and his advisers, they created much goodwill between Tibet and America.

In a touchier diplomatic situation, in July 1945 an OSS military mission parachuted into northern Indochina, present-day Vietnam. Procuring supply drops of arms and ammunition, the OSS team trained Vietnamese guerrillas—the Vietminh, under the leadership of Ho Chi Minh—for action against the Japanese. Members of both groups appear at right, with Ho Chi Minh second from right. The men developed a cordial relationship and often talked of Ho's hopes for a free Indochina.

Soon after the war ended, a second OSS group flew to Saigon as part of the Allied occupation force. Conflict was brewing between the French and Vietnamese, but the OSS was determined to stay neutral. After a Vietnamese worker strike in September, a French crackdown in Saigon led to open fighting later that month, and a senior OSS officer was mistakenly killed by the Vietminh. As the conflict escalated between the French and the Vietminh, the OSS withdrew from Indochina.

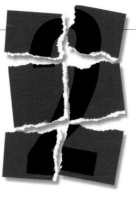

THE REICH'S
LONG REACH

aptain S. Payne Best was a busy man in the early days of September 1939. Since leaving active duty as a British army officer after World War I, he had lived comfortably in the Dutch capital of The Hague, where he dabbled in business and hobnobbed with royalty at the court of Queen Wilhelmina, sporting a monocle that made him look vaguely like one of the queen's German relatives. Neither business nor pleasure consumed him at the moment, however. Best worked undercover for MI-6, Britain's foreign espionage service. From his base in the neutral Netherlands, he ran a network of spies that reached deep inside Nazi Germany.

Best was not the agency's only man in The Hague when Hitler invaded Poland on September 1. Tucked away in the British passport office was another MI-6 officer, Major R. Henry Stevens. At 44, Stevens was a decade younger than Best but senior in rank. The two men had been working separately, but Best now joined with Stevens in a high-stakes operation aimed at nothing less than toppling Hitler from power and nipping a new world war in the bud.

That golden opportunity presented itself when a refugee from Germany named Dr. Franz Fischer offered to put them in touch with members of the German opposition. The leader of the group was said to be General Gustav von Wietersheim, commander of the 14th Panzer Corps. In late October, Best and Stevens arranged to meet secretly with Wietersheim in The Hague. Instead, three lower-ranking German officers appeared on the general's behalf. The group's spokesman identified himself as Major Schemmel. A charming man in his late 20s, his boyish face bore several faint dueling scars. He had a "quick decisive manner," Best noted approvingly, "and a ready answer to all our questions."

Schemmel began with a summary of the Polish campaign, emphasizing the losses suffered by German forces in what looked to be the prelude to a much wider and costlier war. The German general staff wanted a quick end to hostilities, he claimed, but Hitler would not oblige. Therefore, Wietersheim

The enigmatic German spymaster Admiral Wilhelm Canaris, wearing an Italian lieutenant's cap here with his own uniform coat, was a 30-year naval veteran when he took command of the Abwehr—German military intelligence—in 1935. Canaris controlled thousands of agents around the world, yet faced a never-ending battle at home with the Nazi Party's own spy service, the Sicherheitsdienst (SD).

R. Henry Stevens

S. Payne Best

and his confederates planned to take the führer prisoner and sue for peace. But first they sought assurances. "Before we take any steps against Hitler," Schemmel emphasized, "we want to know whether England and France are ready to grant us a peace which is both just and honorable."

Schemmel also wanted the British to name those with whom they might be willing to negotiate an armistice. This was a sensitive request: The answer might identify prominent Germans opposed to Hitler and secretly in touch with the Allies. Best and Stevens promised to pass the question along. Afterward, both sides enjoyed a convivial dinner at Best's house. Before leaving, the German officers were given a two-way radio and coding instructions for arranging future meetings.

Further talks between the two sides took place in early November at the Café Bacchus in the Dutch border town of Venlo. Across from the café sat the local customs post, and just down the street stood the barrier marking the German frontier. Twice, Schemmel came across to meet the British officers, making excuses for the absent general. Wietersheim had been summoned by Hitler to a meeting at Munich, Schemmel explained at the second rendezvous on November 8, but the general still wanted to confer with the British before mounting a coup. Could Best and Stevens return the next day to meet at last with Wietersheim?

The two men agreed but resolved after Schemmel left that "if the general did not come up to scratch this time," as Best put it, "we would wash our hands of the whole business." They dreaded another meeting in Venlo, which seemed to Best "a long way from home and far, far too close to Germany."

November 9 dawned chilly and gray, mirroring Captain Best's mood. The morning paper carried a bulletin describing an attempt on Hitler's life the night before in Munich, where a bomb had exploded in a beer hall and killed a number of people shortly after Hitler finished haranguing the crowd. Best wondered how the incident might affect Wietersheim's plot. Before

Complete with shaded tables on a second-floor balcony, Venlo's Café Bacchus (above) offered a pleasant site for a rendezvous. On the day they were kidnapped, Best and Stevens never made it inside.

leaving for Venlo, he and Stevens each pocketed a Browning automatic. Joining them for the drive was a Dutch lieutenant named Dirk Klop, who had helped make arrangements for Schemmel and others to cross the frontier.

As Best drove up to the café with Stevens and Klop, he noticed with alarm that the barrier on the German side of the border was raised. Schemmel was sipping coffee on the café's veranda and waved invitingly. Suddenly, a large car barreled down the road from the German side, smashing through the Dutch barrier. Several men in plain clothes stood on the running boards brandishing pistols. Two others sat precariously on the hood, firing submachine guns into the air.

The car screeched to a halt against the rear bumper of Best's vehicle, and the gunmen rushed up and collared the British officers, who were too stunned to move. "Our number is up, Best," Stevens said bleakly to his partner. Klop traded fire with the gunmen—and paid with his life. Within minutes, the attackers were back on the German side of the border, with their captives in tow.

News of the abduction left MI-6 officials stunned. As far as they knew, however, the cooperative Major Schemmel had escaped detection, and might still be plotting against Hitler in Germany. A week later, Stevens's deputy in The Hague signaled Schemmel by radio, "We are prepared now as before to continue negotiations along the lines previously agreed upon."

Schemmel's belated answer, sent on New Year's Eve with the equipment he received from the British, revealed how badly they had been fooled: "Negotiations for any length of time with conceited and silly people are tedious. You will understand, therefore, that we are giving them up. You are hereby bidden a hearty farewell by your affectionate German Opposition." He signed his message, "The Gestapo."

THE MAJOR UNMASKED

The mysterious Major Schemmel was in reality Walter Schellenberg of the SD, the Nazi Party security service, which worked hand in glove with the Gestapo *(page 50)*. Both organizations belonged to the SS, Heinrich Himmler's ruthless elite guard of soldiers, spies, enforcers, and bureaucrats whose task it was to seek and destroy all those defined as enemies of the party and its führer. Free of scruples and brimming with confidence, Schellenberg was a dangerous adversary, as Captain Best could testify. "I admit that he had completely taken Stevens and me in," Best conceded. "The man was a natural conspirator, who, as events showed, kept faith with no one."

The entire Venlo operation, in fact, had been artfully choreographed by Schellenberg. The refugee "Dr. Fischer" was actually an SD spy, assigned to the Netherlands to report on German émigrés living there. The elusive General Wietersheim was real enough, chosen for his ties to the old-school, pre-Nazi officer corps. As expected, the British had checked him out and found him a likely dissident. There was also a real-life Major Schemmel. Schellenberg had visited the base where Schemmel was stationed, studying his background and behavior so he could play the role convincingly.

Best and Stevens had ample time to ponder their appalling defeat by Schellenberg, for both spent the rest of the war in captivity, first at Gestapo headquarters in Berlin, where they underwent interrogation, and later at concentration camps. In his postwar memoir, *The Venlo Incident,* Best told of feeding his Gestapo inquisitors false leads and stale gossip. "I have never in my life come across people who could so easily be put off the scent and set chasing hares in all directions," he claimed. Nonetheless, the Germans learned more than a little about MI-6 from Best and Stevens. Schellenberg had originally hoped to discover the identities of Germans who might be plotting in earnest against Hitler with Allied support. That probe led nowhere, but seizing Best and Stevens compromised British agents and caused their networks to fall apart, depriving MI-6 of crucial sources within Germany.

Schellenberg's success—for which he received the Iron Cross first class from Hitler personally—was also a coup for his immediate superior, Reinhard Heydrich, head of the SD, overseer of the Gestapo, deputy to SS chief Himmler, and one of the most feared men in the Reich. A subordinate described him as a tall, impressive figure with "small restless eyes as crafty as an animal's and of uncanny power." Others characterized him curtly as the "Blond Beast." Heydrich would later set in motion the Final Solution—the extermination of millions of Jews and others in SS-administered death camps, a system that grew out of the concentration camps established by the Nazis in the early 1930s.

The SS served as a shadow government within the Reich, one that would readily shoulder tasks others might shy away from. The chiefs of most SS departments had rivals in the various German ministries. In the realm of espionage, Heydrich's competitor was a short, silver-haired navy admiral named Wilhelm Canaris, chief of the Abwehr, the secret service of the German military, or Wehrmacht. Canaris's slumping gait, droopy jowls, and doting affection for his pet dachshunds—his constant companions—led some observers to underestimate him. He was, in fact, a cunning man who did his best to appease the dangerous Heydrich, a former naval officer who had once

Two weeks after their capture, the front page of the Nazi Party newspaper implicates Best and Stevens, as well as a third man, Georg Elser, in a bombing attempt against Hitler. In reality, Elser, a German cabinetmaker, acted alone.

Walter Schellenberg

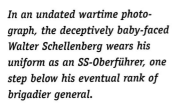

In an undated wartime photo-graph, the deceptively baby-faced Walter Schellenberg wears his uniform as an SS-Oberführer, one step below his eventual rank of brigadier general.

"The man was a natural conspirator, who, as events showed, kept faith with no one."

—S. Payne Best on Schellenberg

served under him. One of Canaris's first acts as Abwehr chief had been to cut a deal with Heydrich.

By the terms of that agreement, the Abwehr kept control of military intelligence and counterintelligence (roughly speaking, spying and spy catching), while the SD was supposed to confine itself to tracking down the regime's internal enemies. Yet Heydrich and company soon found ways of reaching beyond Germany. In the Venlo incident, for example, the SD used its authority to uncover plots against Hitler as grounds for penetrating the Netherlands and dueling with MI-6. When the Wehrmacht later seized the Netherlands, Belgium, Luxembourg, and much of France in 1940, the SD and Gestapo extended their search for political enemies to the newly occupied territory.

As their professional rivalry intensified, Heydrich and Canaris found it hard to remain cordial. They lived near each other in Berlin and sometimes even socialized, with Canaris preparing gourmet meals while Heydrich played Mozart on his violin, accompanied by Frau Canaris at the piano. At work, however, Heydrich denounced Canaris for "snooping and nosing

At a candlelit dinner for both of their services, Abwehr chief Wilhelm Canaris (second from left) and Reinhard Heydrich (third from left), head of the SD, politely mask their mutual dislike. A rising figure in the Nazi Party, Heydrich constantly sought to expand his police and spy empire (chart, below) at Canaris's expense.

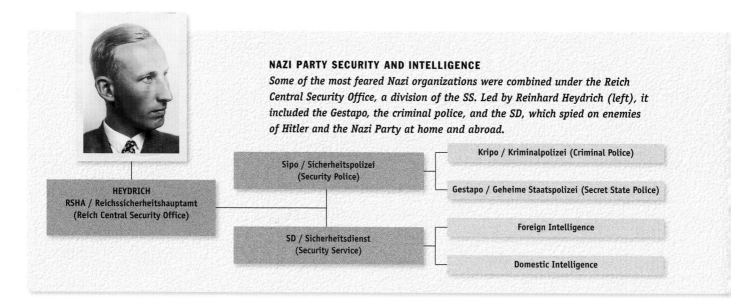

NAZI PARTY SECURITY AND INTELLIGENCE
Some of the most feared Nazi organizations were combined under the Reich Central Security Office, a division of the SS. Led by Reinhard Heydrich (left), it included the Gestapo, the criminal police, and the SD, which spied on enemies of Hitler and the Nazi Party at home and abroad.

		Kripo / Kriminalpolizei (Criminal Police)
	Sipo / Sicherheitspolizei (Security Police)	
		Gestapo / Geheime Staatspolizei (Secret State Police)
HEYDRICH RSHA / Reichssicherheitshauptamt (Reich Central Security Office)		
		Foreign Intelligence
	SD / Sicherheitsdienst (Security Service)	
		Domestic Intelligence

around," while the admiral privately termed Heydrich a "brutal fanatic."

In the long run, this nasty turf war would make an already forbidding task—competing with British, Soviet, American, and other agents at home and abroad—that much harder for the Germans. In the summer of 1941, however, as Hitler sent millions of troops storming into Russia, rival German agencies closed ranks. In an operation that began with a technical unit of the Wehrmacht, grew to include the Abwehr, and eventually brought in the Gestapo, all sides worked together effectively to shut down a spy network that broadcast secrets to Moscow from the very heart of the Reich.

THE HUNT FOR THE RED ORCHESTRA

On June 26, 1941, four days after the invasion of Russia began, a German listener at a radio monitoring station in East Prussia was scanning for messages from the Norwegian resistance when he picked up a call signal that he had never heard before: "KLK from PTX . . . KLK from PTX." What followed was indecipherable, but it was obviously the work of a "pianist," or clandestine enemy transmitter.

In the months to come, hundreds of messages from the same mysterious source were intercepted. The urgent task of locating the radio operator fell to Lieutenant Colonel Hans Kopp, chief of a Wehrmacht unit responsible for detecting signals from covert sources and identifying their origin. Once Kopp's men had a fix on the pianist, the Abwehr would deal with the culprit.

Kopp and his technicians searched for such pianists using several receivers, each with a rotating aerial that gave a rough idea of the direction from which the signal emanated. Readings from three of these direction finders in different locations could be triangulated to locate the transmitter within a given zone. But that reckoning was often maddeningly imprecise, especially when the sender was far from the receivers. After two months, the best Kopp could do was to locate the transmitter somewhere in an area extending from the southern Netherlands through Belgium into northern France.

Meanwhile, the case had taken an ominous turn. In early July the Ger-

MILITARY INTELLIGENCE—THE ABWEHR
Led by Wilhelm Canaris (left), the Abwehr, or German military intelligence, grew to a peak strength of 15,000. Within the agency, one department, or Abteilung, gathered intelligence, another sent saboteurs into Allied territory, and a third hunted enemy spies.

CANARIS
Abwehr

Abteilung I / Espionage

Abteilung II / Sabotage and Subversion

Abteilung III / Counterintelligence

mans had picked up messages from a second pianist using the same cipher as the first—a system in which numbers were substituted for letters and transmitted in groups of five. These messages originated close to home, making them easier to track, and technicians soon narrowed the location to Berlin. Cryptanalysts assigned to make sense of the contents were stumped, but they felt sure the cipher was of Russian design. The conclusion was inescapable. As German forces battled Soviet troops on the eastern front, the Soviets were receiving dispatches from a spy operating in the German capital.

For weeks, three vehicles roamed Berlin disguised as post-office vans, equipped with direction finders whose readings were then plotted through triangulation. By October Kopp's men had narrowed the location of the sender not to a single part of town, as expected, but to three areas, indicating that the operator—identified as one person by a consistent transmitting style, or fingerprint—was shifting base regularly to evade detection. Something evidently alerted the wary pianist, however, for late that month, before any of the locations could be pinpointed, the transmissions ceased.

Discouraged but not defeated, Kopp and staff refocused their attention on the original "PTX" pianist, who was still sending messages regularly from occupied territory. Indeed, those messages had increased in length after the Berlin operator left the air, suggesting that PTX was now receiving dispatches from Berlin by courier and relaying them to Moscow. Lengthier transmissions aided the direction finders, who soon narrowed the source of the signals to the Belgian capital of Brussels. In November, the Abwehr's counterintelligence branch dispatched Captain Harry Piepe to Brussels to haul in the elusive radio operator.

Piepe seemed an unlikely choice for the role of spy catcher. A short, stocky 48-year-old with a prizefighter's face and a booming voice, he stood out in a crowd and was used to confronting his foes head on, first as a cavalry lieutenant in World War I, later as an attorney and interrogator in the state prosecutor's office, and most recently as commander of an antitank company during the French campaign. He had served well in uniform, but the quickly expanding Abwehr, taking note of his legal experience and proficiency in French and English, had set him to work hunting spies in Belgium without any training. He would have to master his new trade as he went along.

Within a few weeks of arriving in Brussels, Piepe would be joined by a squad of specialists from Kopp's department in Berlin with the latest in direction-finding gear. In the meantime, he provided himself with a cover in Brussels by posing as a businessman and renting a suite at 192 rue Royale for his bogus import-export company. Next to the suite were offices of a company called Simexco. He often exchanged greetings with his neighbors in the hallway, but worried that they might overhear his conversations through the thin dividing wall. He made inquiries about Simexco and learned to his relief that the company's principals were on good terms with German authorities

Below, sandbag barricades shield a German long-range radio direction-finding station near Brest, in occupied France. Two roof-mounted rotating loop antennas at this station helped technicians determine the direction of the Soviet-controlled Red Orchestra's secret "PTX" transmitter. Combined with readings from stations elsewhere, this led German spy hunters to an area that could then be searched more precisely using mobile vans.

Harry Piepe

A German army captain turned Abwehr agent, Harry Piepe (above) disguised himself as a merchant (right) during his search for the Red Orchestra's Brussels operation.

and did business with the Todt Organization, a construction agency involved with the Wehrmacht.

Piepe soon had more pressing concerns than checking out his neighbors. By early December 1941, the direction-finding specialists were cruising Brussels in vans and reported that here, as in Berlin, signals were emanating from three locations. All the messages used the same call sign, PTX, but this time the fingerprint of the sender was different at each site, indicating that three pianists were at work in the city. Perhaps the original operator had recruited helpers to handle the increased work load from Berlin. With the discovery of two additional pianists, Piepe had a tougher task. To make a clean sweep of the operation, he would have to wait until all three transmitters were pinpointed through direction finding, then place the sites under surveillance and stage a well-coordinated raid that left none of the principals free.

Piepe's superiors in Berlin were growing impatient. The tide of war had turned against Germany on the eastern front, and they could not help but wonder if all those messages from Brussels to Moscow were partly to blame. A more experienced field officer might have withstood the heat from Berlin and laid the trap more carefully. But Piepe was new to the game. He decided to arrest one pianist—the busiest of the three and easiest to pinpoint—and force that operator to betray the others.

Fearing that the pianist might spot the direction-finding vans as they closed in on their target, the technicians switched to an ingenious new device—a suitcase-sized direction finder with a built-in aerial and an earpiece receiver. Dressed in civilian clothes, the operator could blend in with pedestrian traffic as he fixed on the transmitter. Soon the pianist's location was narrowed to a row of houses on the narrow, run-down rue des Atrébates in central Brussels. "Now at last we were ready to strike," Piepe later recalled.

Shortly before 2 a.m. on December 14, 25 German garrison troops blocked both ends of the street. Moments later, as Piepe and his agents moved in with guns drawn, a man bolted from 101 rue des Atrébates and raced down the street into the waiting arms of the troops. Piepe dashed into 101 and found a woman in bed on the first floor, trembling with fright. Hurrying up the stairs, he and his men came upon another woman as she was burning a stack of enciphered messages in the fireplace. An agent quickly pulled them from the flames and stamped out the fire with his shoe, saving the fragments, along with messages she had failed to destroy, for analysis by experts. In the next room sat the still-warm transmitter and a pile of papers filled with columns of numbers.

The woman who had been caught burning papers said she was a French citizen, but her French was barely passable. The pianist himself—the man who had tried to escape—claimed to be a Uruguayan national but spoke with a distinct Slavic accent. Neither seemed much inclined to talk. The frightened woman on the first floor, however, freely confided in Piepe, who explained to her soothingly that he was with the Abwehr, not the Gestapo, and offered her some wine to loosen her tongue.

Her name was Rita Arnould, and she was the mistress of a Soviet agent who had induced her to serve as courier for the pianist. She assured Piepe that she was a reluctant spy and tipped him off to the existence of a hidden room on the second floor that proved to be "a forger's paradise," as he put it. As Piepe examined the room, the scale of this secret operation became all too clear. Among the materials used to produce false identification papers there, he noted, were blank German documents that "could only have come from official government sources in Berlin. This implied the existence of a really vast network, with tentacles everywhere." The Abwehr's term for a spy network was *Kapelle* (orchestra). Given its Moscow connections, Piepe dubbed this far-flung organization "die Rote Kapelle"—the Red Orchestra.

Further investigation would reveal that the Red Orchestra was made up of several bands, or cells, in different countries, loosely coordinated by Moscow. In the postwar years, it would be considered a classic example of a Soviet spy network, a subject of proud Soviet propaganda and of a formal CIA study. But in December 1941, Piepe had no idea how it was organized.

Some clues came from the information provided by Rita Arnould. Arnould identified two passport photos found in the forger's room as "le Grand Chef et le Petit Chef"—the Big Chief and the Little Chief. These were not mere pianists, but conductors. The Little Chief handled operations in Brussels, and the Big Chief had wider responsibilities.

Oddly, the vital photos looked strangely familiar to Piepe. Not until later would he make the startling connection: The two men had been his Simexco neighbors from the office. "I'd passed them on the stairs a dozen times," he recalled; "we used to meet on the landing and tip our hats to one another." He added ruefully, "If you read this sort of thing in a novel, you would say that the author had laid it on too thick."

At dawn, Piepe went to Abwehr headquarters in Brussels to make a report, leaving two of his agents in charge of the house. Around noon, a man posing as a street vendor knocked at the door; he was taken into custody after a search revealed he was carrying enciphered messages. A short time later, a second visitor appeared—a portly man who produced identification in the name of Jean Gilbert, issued by the Todt Organization construction firm. He explained that there was a garage across the street with old cars that he wanted to salvage for scrap iron and had come here to ask neighbors when the place opened. The agent who questioned him told him that he would have to wait at the house until Piepe returned.

"That's impossible, utterly impossible," Gilbert objected. "I have to

Piepe's raid on the house at 101 rue des Atrébates (above) was the beginning of the end for the Red Orchestra in Brussels. A combined force of 35 men bagged the four agents at right, suspending the spy ring's transmissions for months.

A remarkable mix of personalities, those caught in the Brussels raid included Rita Arnould, a refugee from Germany; radio operator Mikael Makarov of Soviet military intelligence (the GRU); David Kamy, who had emigrated from Palestine to France; and Polish-born Sophie Poznanska, shown at far right in 1940 in Paris. Only Makarov survived internment by the Germans, who learned he was the nephew of Soviet foreign minister Molotov.

Rita Arnould

Mikael Makarov

David Kamy

Sophie Poznanska ❯

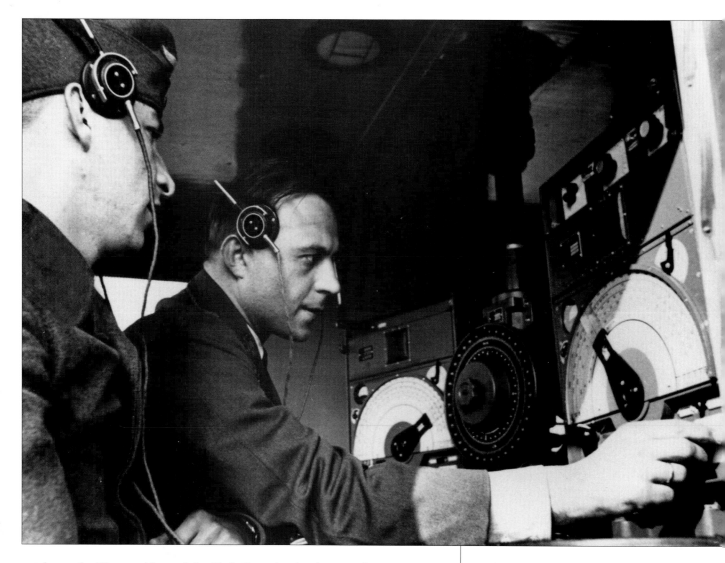

catch a train. The president of the Todt Organization is expecting my report this afternoon." Unsure what to do, the agent telephoned Piepe, who told him to release the man. It was an order that Piepe would deeply regret. For as he later discovered, the man who called himself Jean Gilbert was none other than the Big Chief, visiting Brussels to check up on the operation. Once released, he promptly slipped out of town, having warned the Little Chief and others to do the same.

Letting the man go was not Piepe's only mistake. Had he placed the house under surveillance until he located the other two operators in Brussels, he might have closed down the entire show. "We were still amateurs," Piepe admitted. "We still had to learn our trade."

He soon had help from a seasoned investigator. In January 1942, Hitler ordered the Gestapo to assist the Abwehr in silencing the Red Orchestra. A short time later, Piepe teamed up with 41-year-old Karl Giering, an SS captain who had served with the Berlin police before joining the Gestapo. Giering was as tall and thin as Piepe was short and squat. He spoke in a rasping whisper owing to the throat cancer that was slowly killing him. Despite the usual rivalry between Abwehr and Gestapo, the two men soon formed an effective team. Giering vowed to his new partner that he would break the Red Orchestra before he died.

Johann Wenzel

GRU agent Johann Wenzel (above), captured on June 30, 1942, sent reports to Moscow from Brussels by means of a GRU-supplied Nord transmitter like the one below, a bulky apparatus built partly from plywood.

With prisoners in hand, meanwhile, the counterintelligence game of wits took a grimmer turn. Giering interrogated the pianist seized in the December raid and got him to admit he was a Russian agent named Mikael Makarov, recruited and trained in Moscow by the GRU—Soviet military intelligence. The Gestapo then used what it called "intensified interrogation," or torture, to extract further information from Makarov, the woman who assisted him, and the man arrested at the house the morning after the raid. Makarov withstood the punishment and yielded nothing of value. The other man offered a false confession, claiming to be a Russian agent attached to the Soviet embassy in Paris; this story convinced the Germans, who never realized that he was actually one of the pianists in Brussels, a Palestinian Communist named David Kamy. The woman revealed little more than her identity—Sophie Poznanska of Poland—before committing suicide.

Piepe located another member of the Red Orchestra by simple logic; he figured that the forger whose workshop he had uncovered might have criminal connections. Sure enough, a check with the police led to the home of a suspected counterfeiter named Abraham Raichmann. Piepe placed Raichmann under surveillance and patiently waited for him to contact higher-ups.

Employing someone known to the police was just one of the Soviet blunders that exposed the Red Orchestra. The other two locations could not now be pinpointed because Makarov's arrest had silenced the transmissions from Brussels. But in June 1942, an operator at one of the hideouts returned feverishly to work, transmitting for such long periods that direction finders soon homed in on him. Piepe concluded that the Soviets either were ignorant of direction-finding techniques or "cold-bloodedly sacrificing radio operators." Early on June 30, he led another raid, netting the pianist and a second sheaf of messages, one of which spelled out plans for the Wehrmacht's summer offensive on the eastern front, which had begun just two days before.

Piepe interrogated the pianist, whom he described as "a short, thickset, hard-featured man, about 40 years of age, terribly working class." He revealed his true identity as Johann Wenzel, born in Danzig, but vowed to say nothing that might "betray any of his associates." Piepe took him at his word and left it to Giering and the Gestapo to apply the screws. Giering soon learned from headquarters that Wenzel was a Communist who had been recruited by the GRU in 1935. The Gestapo had been after Wenzel for years and gave him a brutal reception, torturing him for weeks until he agreed to play double agent against his Soviet handlers.

A month after netting Wenzel, Piepe's surveillance of Abraham Raich-mann finally paid off when the forger requested a blank identity card from an acquaintance in the Brussels police department, explaining he needed it for a ringleader of Red agents. Piepe then collared the ringleader when he arrived to pick up his false ID. "I have listened to some protestations of in-nocence in my time," Piepe related, "but nothing to rival his. We were com-mitting an unspeakable outrage. He was a loyal subject of Finland." Unfor-tunately, the man could not speak a word of Finnish.

With little prompting, the prisoner confessed that he was Konstantin Yefremov, a GRU officer who had taken over in Brussels after the Little Chief fled. The obliging Yefremov then betrayed what remained of the operation in Belgium, helped expose a Red Orchestra cell in the Netherlands, and offered further clues in a fast-growing case that would eventually lead Piepe and Giering to Paris in pursuit of the Big Chief.

BREAKTHROUGH IN BERLIN

The next great gain from the Brussels crackdown, however, came in Berlin itself, where investigators were finally able to close in on agents who had been performing for the Red Orchestra under their very noses. For months, Berlin's cryptanalysts had been struggling to decipher the messages sal-vaged in the first Brussels raid. Then in July, the pianist Wenzel revealed under torture that the cipher was based on key words drawn from a book known only to the senders and their superiors in Moscow. Further ques-tioning of the cooperative Rita Arnould drew from her the titles of several novels she had seen beside the transmitter in Brussels. One of those books turned out to contain the key words, identified in each message by page number, line, and the number of the word within the line. With those keys in hand, the cryptanalysts finally unlocked the vault.

The messages they deciphered revealed the damage inflicted on Ger-man forces by the Red Orchestra. Reports detailed everything from the movement of individual combat units to top-level strategy sessions of the Wehrmacht's high command, known by its German initials of OKW. "Hitler ordered capture of Odessa by 15 September," read one dispatch. "Delaying actions southern end of front seriously upsetting line-up German attack. In-formation supplied by officer in OKW."

Among those explosive messages was one that recoiled disastrously on the Soviets. A dispatch from GRU headquarters in Moscow dated the previ-ous October had expressed concern over halts in transmissions from Berlin, where the wary pianist had often remained silent for days on end. The GRU had instructed the Little Chief in Brussels to "proceed immediately Berlin three addresses indicated and determine causes failures radio links." The ill-advised message went on to divulge the precise whereabouts of the Soviet ringleaders in the German capital.

This discovery prompted an interagency meeting in Berlin that includ-ed Abwehr chief Canaris and SD officer Walter Schellenberg, who spoke for the Gestapo. The parties agreed that the Abwehr and Gestapo would con-tinue their joint pursuit of Red Orchestra cells in the occupied countries; the

Cheerful prewar portraits of key members of the Berlin Red Orchestra exposed in an intercepted message from Moscow show German citizens in good standing. The discovery that such upstanding citizens could spy on the Reich horrified Hitler and his inner circle.

"Proceed immedi-ately Berlin three addresses indicated and determine causes failures radio links."

—Intercepted Soviet message that exposed Berlin Red Orchestra

Harro and Libertas Schulze-Boysen

Arvid and Mildred Harnack

Adam Kuckhoff

Gestapo alone would go after traitors within the Reich—thus reaping credit for hauling in the spies who were of most concern to Hitler.

With the addresses provided by Moscow, the Gestapo had no trouble finding the three ringleaders in Berlin. All had histories that might have aroused more suspicion had they not been socially prominent. Luftwaffe lieutenant Harro Schulze-Boysen, tall and blond, could have been an SS poster boy. He was related to the revered Admiral Alfred von Tirpitz but as a young man had rebelled against his conservative upbringing. Imprisoned briefly in 1933 in one of the first Nazi concentration camps, he had been savagely beaten by SS guards. The experience hardened him. "I have put my revenge into cold storage," he confided to a friend. Schulze-Boysen decided on a military career in order to fight the regime from within. He now held a sensitive post at the air ministry.

Professor Arvid Harnack, the second leader, was a distinguished scholar who had married a German-speaking American named Mildred Fish. Shortly before Hitler came to power in 1933, the Soviet embassy sponsored them on a trip to Moscow, where they were recruited by the GRU. To elude suspicion, Harnack joined the Nazi Party as well as an exclusive club for Berlin's elite. His post in the Ministry of Economics gave him access to sensitive information on industrial output and trade. The third man, Adam Kuckhoff, was a noted author on Marxism, among other subjects, and had friends in high positions. He too had been spying for the Soviets since before the Nazis took power.

The Gestapo placed all three under tight surveillance, tapping their telephones and intercepting their mail. Soon investigators had identified more than 50 contacts and conspirators, including Mildred Harnack and Schulze-Boysen's wife, Libertas. Then on August 29, Schulze-Boysen placed a call to a confederate in the very bureau that had deciphered the Red Orchestra's messages. The Gestapo swung into action before that cryptanalyst could alert the ringleaders to their danger. The next day, squads of secret policemen descended on some of Berlin's most fashionable addresses and hauled the stunned occupants in to Gestapo headquarters.

There the ringleaders and their accomplices, some 60 in all, underwent relentless interrogation. Those who did not promptly confess all they knew were tortured. Libertas Schulze-Boysen eluded the first Gestapo sweep but was arrested as she boarded a train in Berlin on September 3; under questioning, she divulged the names of several others who were still free. In all, 57 more suspects were identified and thrown into the basement cells.

Appalled that so many prominent Germans had conspired against his regime, Hitler decreed the plot a "state secret," meaning that those in the know were forbidden to tell others under penalty of death. He demanded swift and merciless retribution for "the Bolsheviks within our own ranks." Yet the secret trials held in Berlin that fall revealed that they were not all Bolsheviks. Prosecutors found sufficient evidence to charge 76 of the 117 people rounded up; six had committed suicide in their cells, and the rest were released. During the trials, the disparate motives of the accused came to light.

A number of them were dedicated Communists, others simply despised the Nazis, and a few lent aid to the ringleaders for money or sex. Both Harro and Libertas Schulze-Boysen had conducted affairs with members of their circle, and Mildred Harnack, at her husband's urging, had seduced a lieutenant in the Abwehr whom she was tutoring in English and had extracted secrets from him that cost Abwehr agents their lives.

The Red Orchestra's Berlin cell was an unlikely mix of amateur and professional spies. Professor Harnack was a disciplined Soviet operative who did nothing in public to reveal his true loyalties. Schulze-Boysen and his circle, by contrast, cared less for serving Moscow than for undermining Hitler, and they freely engaged in daredevil acts of resistance like printing anti-Nazi posters and pasting them up around Berlin at night. Despite the danger of conspiring with a man who took such risks, however, Harnack and Adam Kuckhoff worked closely with Schulze-Boysen. Harnack and Kuckhoff each harbored transmitters in their homes, and Schulze-Boysen recruited the roving pianist—who had stopped sending messages after he passed direction-finding men dressed as postal workers at work in the street and heard one say to another, "Jawohl, Herr Leutnant!"

At the close of the proceedings, 15 of the accused were sentenced to prison and 15 to hard labor in concentration camps. The remaining 46 were condemned to death. At Hitler's insistence, the men were hanged slowly and the women beheaded. Almost all faced the executioner with calm dignity. Harro Schulze-Boysen wrote to his parents before his execution that his cause was worth dying for, "Such important things are now at stake on this earth that the extinction of a single human life is of small account." As Mildred Harnack went to her death, the American-born agent's last words were for her adopted country, "And I loved Germany so much!"

BAGGING THE BIG CHIEF

As the Berlin trials drew to a close, the search for other Red Orchestra ringleaders continued. Through Raichmann, the Brussels forger, Piepe and Giering learned that the Little Chief had fled to Marseille in unoccupied France. When German troops seized that sector in November 1942, the Little Chief was promptly arrested with his mistress. He identified himself as

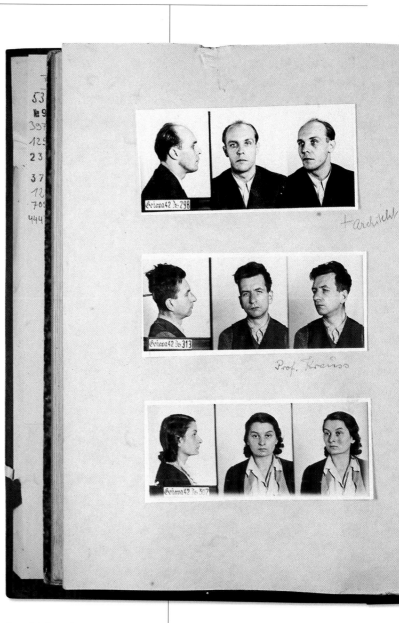

Above, grim faces of recently arrested members of the Red Orchestra in Berlin fill the pages of a Gestapo notebook.

"I regret only that I did not do more."

—Cato Bontjes von Beek, Red Orchestra member, after receiving death sentence

Captain Victor Sukolov-Gurevich, a long-time GRU agent, and offered to cooperate fully if they guaranteed his mistress's safety and allowed them conjugal visits. The bargain was struck, and Sukolov-Gurevich divulged that the Big Chief was living in Paris under the name Jean Gilbert, using the parent company of his old Simexco front as a cover.

In questioning employees of the firm, Piepe and Giering learned that Gilbert had an upcoming dental appointment on November 27. When he arrived, they burst in with guns drawn and arrested him in the dentist's chair. "The dentist was shaking, and Giering and I were in a terrible state of nerves," Piepe recalled. "The *Grand Chef* was the calmest man in the room. 'Bravo!' he said as Giering slipped on the handcuffs. 'You've done a good job.' I replied modestly: 'It's the result of two years of searching.' "

Piepe and Giering were amazed by the man's poise. They installed him in a comfortable cell, where interrogation took the form of pleasant chats over brandy and cigarettes. Obliging those who had him in their power came naturally to the Big Chief, whose real name was Leopold Trepper. Having lived for years under a Soviet regime that used terror to keep people in line, he had learned to comply and survive.

Born to poor Jewish shopkeepers in Poland in 1904, Trepper had experienced both grinding labor and galling anti-Semitism in his youth and had immigrated at the age of 20 to Palestine. There he joined the local Communist Party and met with several members of his future spy network. Arrested as an agitator by British authorities and deported from Palestine in 1929, Trepper moved to France, where he helped funnel industrial secrets to the Soviets. In 1932 he was summoned to Moscow and enrolled in an institute that trained revolutionaries for work abroad.

While Trepper was studying there, Stalin launched his murderous purges, aimed at eliminating his foes or critics from positions of power. The circle of terror eventually expanded to include ardent Communists, among them many Jews who had joined the party believing that it promised something better for their people. As the horrors continued, Trepper and other survivors obediently denounced the victims as enemies of the state. "We had become the robots and accomplices of Stalinist repression," he wrote after-

Leopold Trepper

The Soviet spy network's "Big Chief" in Brussels and Paris, Leopold Trepper (above) was an elusive fugitive who at the time of his capture by German spy hunters was attempting to fake his own death. His arrest in a dentist's office came just days before the planned bogus funeral.

❰ Margarete Barcza
❰ Victor Sukolov-Gurevich

At left, GRU agent Victor Sukolov-Gurevich strolls along a Marseille street with his mistress, Margarete Barcza, in 1942. Arrested later that year, the so-called Little Chief traded Red Orchestra secrets in exchange for their safety.

ward. In the late 1930s, he enlisted as a GRU officer and went to work in Brussels. Trepper eventually extended operations to Holland and, after entrusting the pianists in Belgium to Sukolov-Gurevich, moved to Paris. There he oversaw the collection and transmission of military secrets.

After being arrested in Paris, Trepper lured one of his agents, Hillel Katz, to a rendezvous. "Katz, the game is up," Trepper told his comrade when the Gestapo seized him at the meeting place, "we have to work with these gentlemen." Katz refused to collaborate and suffered torture. Trepper, for his part, not only betrayed Katz but also agreed to play back to Moscow messages scripted by Berlin. He later claimed that he was only doing so to monitor the German scheme and foil it, but the Soviets did not buy his story. In 1943, having lulled his German captors into keeping him on a long leash, he escaped and later returned to Moscow, hoping that his superiors there might recognize him for his services and acknowledge the mistakes that led to the destruction of his network. Instead of apologies or thanks, Trepper received 10 years in prison.

A VICTORY OVERSHADOWED BY DEFEAT

The arrest of Leopold Trepper in Paris brought the hunt for the Red Orchestra to a seemingly successful conclusion. Harry Piepe returned to his Abwehr office in a much-quieter Brussels. Karl Giering succumbed to throat cancer and died in the fall of 1943, confident that he had crushed the Soviet network. In fact, a separate cell of the Red Orchestra continued to function in neutral Switzerland, where agents radioed to Moscow military secrets received from Germany, among other places *(page 114)*.

Despite the survival of that cell, however, the near destruction of the Red Orchestra was a big victory for German counterintelligence. Canaris and his aides had little chance to celebrate, however, for the Abwehr was under mounting criticism for failures in other parts of the world. Canaris had lost one imposing rival in May 1942 when Reinhard Heydrich was assassinated in Prague by Czech resistance fighters acting on cue from British agents. But the Abwehr chief still faced a sharp challenge from the SD in the person of the rapidly advancing Walter Schellenberg, who professed friendship for Canaris while secretly plotting to take over his agency. Unlike Schellenberg, who won laurels for a few well-chosen operations like the Venlo raid and the roundup of the Red Orchestra in Berlin, Canaris shouldered many thankless tasks and suffered several devastating setbacks.

Canaris was responsible not only for hunting down enemy agents in German-occupied territory but for the more precarious task of planting German agents on foreign ground. To be sure, the Abwehr had cast its net abroad with much success before the war began and was still hauling in some impressive catches. Canaris had dozens of agents in Central and South America who provided vital information on industry and shipping. And he had good sources undercover in Egypt and other parts of the Middle East, where opposition to British rule provided openings for German infiltration.

Wearing Afrika Korps uniforms, "Sandy" Sandstetter (left) and John Eppler lounge against the captured Ford that would carry them across the Sahara.

Count László de Almásy poses by a sign on a desert road. A Nazi in real life, the explorer was later romanticized as the title character of the 1996 film The English Patient.

OPERATION CONDOR:
GERMAN EYES IN CAIRO

*Egyptian nationalist—and belly dancer extraordinaire—Hekmat Fahmy (right)
proved invaluable to Eppler in his intelligence-gathering efforts. In the photo above,
she charms a British officer and a New Zealander over drinks in a Cairo nightclub.*

In spring of 1942, a British major outside his army camp spotted two men walking out of the Egyptian desert. One of them introduced himself as Hussein Gaafar and his companion as Peter Monkaster, an American. Stranded when their car broke down, they needed to catch the Cairo train. The major obligingly arranged a lift.

Had he been more suspicious, he might have noticed some odd facts about the pair. One suitcase they carried bulged with counterfeit banknotes; another hid a radio transmitter. Hussein Gaafar, whose given name was John Eppler, and Monkaster—in reality, a German named Sandstetter—were among hundreds of men and women around the globe working for the German Abwehr.

To reach the camp, the two men had driven 1,000 miles across the Sahara, escorted by German commandos and a guide, Count László de Almásy. Once at Cairo, they would begin Operation Condor: a mission to gather information on the British army in time for the next attack by General Rommel's Afrika Korps.

John Eppler was just the man for it. Born to German parents in Alexandria, Egypt, he spoke Arabic and knew the country well. In Cairo, he and Sandstetter soon fit in, renting a houseboat on the Nile and posing as playboys. Besides entertaining British officers, they recruited an agent—Hekmat Fahmy, a belly dancer who hated British dominion over Egypt and who formed a liaison with Eppler.

At first, the spies met with little success. That seemed to change when a British officer told Fahmy that he was carrying a key dispatch. The dancer lured him to her houseboat, seduced and drugged him, and called Eppler. In the officer's briefcase, Eppler found a British order of battle stamped "Most Secret." Excitedly, he copied the document and went back to his own boat. There, however, he and Sandstetter could not reach a German desert radio station.

Before they could try again on a different night, Condor came to an end. Acting on a tip from another of Eppler's girlfriends, British police surrounded the boat and captured both Abwehr agents—along with Fahmy. The crucial document remained unknown to the Germans, its fate a perfect example of the fortunes of war.

Spying on enemies on their home turf was another matter, however. Canaris was blissfully unaware that all the German spies reporting to him from Britain were actually serving as double agents for MI-5 *(pages 14-33)*. But other reversals for the Abwehr were all too obvious to Canaris and his demanding führer. As war raged in Europe, two German espionage operations in the United States—the first conducted while the United States was still officially neutral—had failed spectacularly. The disasters left Canaris under heavy fire.

Nikolaus Ritter, the same intelligence officer who recruited several of the Abwehr agents subsequently turned by the British Double Cross Committee, was responsible for the first of these failures. On paper, Ritter was a superb choice. Before joining the Abwehr's air intelligence branch, he had lived for 10 years in the United States. Moreover, he had scored a prewar intelligence coup in the United States in 1937 by obtaining blueprints for the top-secret Norden bombsight, which allowed warplanes flying at high speeds to deliver payloads with pulverizing accuracy.

It may have been that success that encouraged Ritter to try something similar in 1939 when a reluctant recruit named William Sebold fell within his grasp. A German-born American citizen, Sebold disembarked at Hamburg that February to visit his mother and ran afoul of Gestapo agents, who induced him to spy for Germany, using as leverage a police record he had acquired before emigrating. Any spying Sebold might do in America would

In a picture taken by an FBI dock photographer in October 1937, Abwehr officer Nikolaus Ritter (above, left) heads down Manhattan's Pier 86 to U.S. soil, where he would soon acquire plans for a sophisticated airplane bombsight. Although the FBI knew of other German spies, it had not yet identified Ritter as a foreign agent; this photograph was taken as a matter of routine.

A Spy with Flair

Espionage came naturally to Frederick Albert Duquesne, a flamboyant South African whom the Abwehr considered one of its most valuable agents in America. Naturally theatrical, he used at least 40 aliases and changed identities like a chameleon. He was also vain enough to purchase and wear a chestful of secondhand military awards *(above)*. "You couldn't believe anything Fritz said," his sister-in-law once cautioned. "But he said it all so perfectly, you thought it was all true."

In the espionage arena, however, Duquesne was a cautious agent who insisted on meeting his Abwehr case officer, William Sebold, outdoors. When Duquesne finally felt safe enough to meet at Sebold's office, federal agents caught him on film proposing a scheme to turn candy-coated gum into miniature bombs. Four days afterward, alarmed by his apparent switch from espionage to sabotage, the FBI arrested Fritz Duquesne.

count as military espionage, so the Gestapo dutifully handed him over to the Abwehr, who assigned him to Ritter. Ritter deemed Sebold a good prospect and put him through the Abwehr's seven-week spy school in Hamburg, where he became an accomplished pianist, prepared to send signals across the Atlantic by shortwave radio.

After completing the course, Sebold received orders to return to America under a false name and passport and make contact with four agents in New York, carrying microfilm messages for each concealed in his watch. He would then transmit to Germany by radio the most urgent dispatches he received from those agents (other messages would travel by courier). This would put Sebold at the heart of a growing spy ring in New York, where a number of Abwehr agents found haven among the city's 600,000 German-American residents, the vast majority of whom were loyal to the United States. Ritter told Sebold that Germany was acting in self-defense in spying on America. "We have no choice," he explained. But Sebold himself had a choice, albeit a dangerous one. Shortly before embarking for the United States, he slipped into the American consulate in Cologne and explained his plight. He was told to stay calm and play along until contacted by the FBI.

When Sebold's ship docked in New York in early 1940, three FBI agents met him in his cabin. He handed over the microfilm for them to copy, then followed his Abwehr instructions and opened an office on Broadway and 42nd Street for the bogus Diesel Research Company for meetings with German agents. FBI agents bugged the office and placed a camera behind a two-way mirror. Sebold then contacted the four agents on his list and passed along the microfilm messages, which queried the agents on such vital matters as arms shipments to Britain that could be targeted by German U-boats.

Sebold's contacts included Lilly Stein, an Austrian-born model who served as a recruiter and courier for the Abwehr; Everett Roeder, an engineer who helped produce components for bombsights; and Hermann Lang, who had furnished the Norden bombsight plans to Ritter two years earlier and still worked at the Norden plant. The fourth agent was in a class by himself—62-year-old Frederick Duquesne *(left)*, a fiery Boer from South Africa who was driven by deep hatred for the British. In addition to spying for the Abwehr in New York, the eccentric Duquesne proposed wild schemes for sabotage.

Soon reports from Duquesne, Lang, and others were flowing into Sebold's office, where they were sifted and censored by the FBI before being radioed to Germany. The Abwehr was delighted to receive such intelligence immediately by radio, rather than waiting weeks for couriers to arrive by ship, and instructed other agents in the New York area to contact Sebold at his office and pass their information through him. "This is like shooting fish in a barrel!" chortled one FBI agent behind the fake mirror as the hidden cameras recorded one visiting spy after another.

In late June 1941, the FBI closed the trap and arrested Lang, Duquesne, and 31 other German agents in what J. Edgar Hoover touted as "the greatest spy roundup in U.S. history." Back in Berlin, Admiral Canaris studied the list of those apprehended and noticed that Sebold's name was missing. "Where is Tramp?" Canaris asked, referring to the roving agent by his code name.

The answer became horrifyingly clear when Tramp surfaced as star witness for the prosecution in the spy trials, testifying for two days not only about espionage operations in New York but also about his forced recruitment by the Gestapo and his Abwehr training under Ritter. The jury saw hours of film of the defendants passing secrets in Sebold's office. All 33 either pleaded guilty or were found guilty, with Duquesne and Lang receiving the harshest sentences—18 years in prison each.

Ritter was beside himself with rage at Sebold's double cross. "The bastard!" he bellowed. "The traitor!" A colleague ventured to contradict him, pointing out that Tramp was no traitor, having faithfully served "his new fatherland." Indeed, Ritter had gambled hugely on the forced recruitment of an expatriate and lost all. The fiasco crippled the Abwehr's operations in the still neutral United States and helped solidify American opinion against Germany.

Six months later, the two countries were at war. Hitler, ever eager to strike the first blow, ordered a broad campaign of sabotage in America. Lacking agents in place to carry out such an ambitious scheme, Canaris reluctantly authorized a daring infiltration that exploited the capacity of German U-boats to reach American shores undetected and made Ritter's recent foray look almost tame by comparison.

SABOTEURS ON THE SPOT

Shortly before midnight on June 12, 1942, the German submarine *U-202* surfaced off a deserted beach near the Hamptons on the eastern tip of Long Island. Concealed by thick fog, four men slipped over the side into a rubber dinghy and paddled to shore. There they took off their German naval uniforms—worn to keep them from being tried as spies if they were arrested while landing—and changed into civilian clothes, burying the uniforms in the sand along with four heavy wooden boxes they had brought with them.

Just then a flashlight pierced the fog and a voice called out, "What's going on here?" John Cullen, a 21-year-old rookie seaman, was making his nightly patrol from a nearby Coast Guard station. A man approached him, smiling, and identified himself as George Davis. "We're fishermen from Southampton and ran aground," he explained. Then one of his companions shouted something in German. The unarmed Cullen was thoroughly alarmed.

Davis grabbed him. "I don't want to kill you," he said, pushing a wad of bills into Cullen's hand. "Take this and have a good time. Forget what you've seen here." The coastguardsman backed away into the darkness, then turned and ran for the station to alert his mates. By the time an armed patrol returned, the intruders were gone. But their buried uniforms were

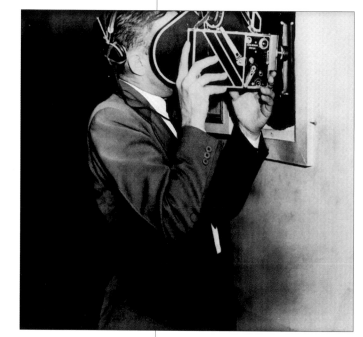

Above, an FBI employee secretly films double agent William Sebold as he meets with a German spy. Hermann Lang, one of 33 agents caught in the trap and arrested in 1941, appears at right in a series of FBI photographs; as the agency had planned, a clock and calendar are visible beside him.

"This is like shooting fish in a barrel!"

—FBI camera operator

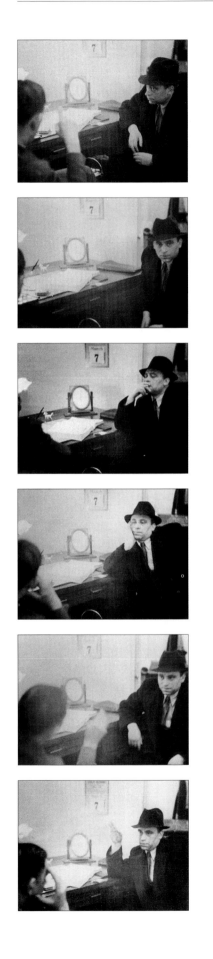

quickly uncovered, as were the wooden crates—filled with explosives, timers, and incendiary devices, many of them disguised to resemble harmless objects like lumps of coal or fountain pens. Evidently, the suspects meant to return for this gear once they found shelter. They had made their way to a nearby station on the Long Island Railroad, where a ticket clerk recalled four strangers catching an early train into New York City. The Coast Guard notified the FBI.

These four would-be saboteurs constituted the vanguard of Operation Pastorius, named for Francis Pastorius, a pioneering German immigrant to America. Four days later, a second U-boat surfaced before dawn off the east coast of Florida, and another team of four Germans came ashore on a beach 25 miles south of Jacksonville and moved inland without being detected. Both teams had been selected and trained by Lieutenant Walther Kappe of the Abwehr, who had lived for some time in the United States and been active in pro-Nazi groups there. The eight men he chose for the operation were all former residents of the United States, and two were American citizens.

Unlike William Sebold, these recruits were offered incentives rather than threats. Kappe promised them good jobs in Germany when they returned. They went through a two-month course in subversion and sabotage at Quentz Lake, a secluded Abwehr training ground near Berlin. Over breakfast, the recruits conversed in English and read recent issues of *Life* and *The Saturday Evening Post* to brush up on American culture. They spent several hours a day in the laboratory, mastering explosives, and two evenings a week at a nearby tavern, where Kappe first plied them with drinks, then peppered them with questions about their assumed identities.

By the spring of 1942, they were ready for action. Kappe gave each leader $70,000 and the others several thousand dollars each. They carried fake documentation and a handkerchief inscribed with the addresses of two Abwehr contacts in invisible ink. Kappe directed them to attack strategic targets like arms factories, reservoirs, and hydroelectric plants and to spread terror by targeting stores, hotels, and railway stations. If any team member wavered in his duty, the others had orders to kill him.

Canaris had doubts about the mission, remarking that it would "cost these poor men their lives." But no one anticipated just how quickly and completely the plan would unravel. The weak link in Kappe's chain turned out to be the leader of the Long Island team, Georg Johann Dasch, alias George Davis, who had lived in America for more than 15 years. Perhaps Dasch harbored sympathy for the U.S., as he later claimed, or perhaps he just lost his nerve after pondering the likelihood of being caught and executed.

When Dasch and his three team members reached Manhattan, they split up, with Dasch and agent Ernest Burger taking a room in one hotel and their two confederates checking into another. Dasch took Burger out for a day of shopping and sightseeing and informed him over dinner that he had a plan to get them out of the fix they were in. Burger realized that Dasch intended to betray the operation.

"I told him right to his face that I knew exactly what he wanted to do," Burger related. "His answer was that if I knew that, I would have to kill him."

FEDERAL BUREAU OF INVESTIGATION
UNITED STATES DEPARTMENT OF JUSTICE
J. EDGAR HOOVER, DIRECTOR

EIGHT GERMAN SABOTEURS

GEORGE JOHN DASCH ERNEST PETER BURGER RICHARD QUIRIN HEINRICH HARM HEINCK

EDWARD KERLING HERBERT HANS HAUPT WERNER THIEL HERMANN OTTO NEUBAUER

The FBI's speedy capture of the entire Pastorius team (above) owed much to the aid of one of the saboteurs, Georg Dasch. Part of a four-man contingent brought to Long Island by submarine, Dasch confessed the plot to authorities soon after their arrival.

At left, FBI agents dig up boxes buried on a beach by the four German saboteurs who landed in Florida in 1942 as part of Operation Pastorius. Among the materials inside were explosives, percussion caps, and timing devices; planned sabotage targets ranged from canals in St. Louis to the New York City water supply.

Burger smiled disarmingly and made it clear he had no intention of obeying Kappe's order. A short time later, Dasch called the FBI's New York office, introduced himself as Franz Pastorius, newly arrived from Germany, and promised to contact the bureau's Washington office shortly with information of special interest to J. Edgar Hoover.

True to his word, Dasch took a train to Washington, checked into a hotel, and promptly called FBI headquarters. Before long he was spilling his story to a team of agents and a stenographer. He listed the objectives of both teams and provided the names and likely whereabouts of his coconspirators. All eight agents were soon in custody, having failed to carry out a single act of sabotage.

News of the arrests drew banner headlines. Many Americans favored a swift military trial for the defendants, and authorities preferred to keep details of the operation secret. By order of President Roosevelt, a military tribunal was convened to try charges against civilians for the first time since the Lincoln assassination, and the press was barred from the proceedings.

All eight men were quickly found guilty. Dasch, who had expected to be hailed as a hero for exposing the plot, received 30 years at hard labor, and Burger, who had later cooperated with authorities, got a life sentence. The remaining six were condemned to death and went to the electric chair on August 8th, less than two months after they stepped ashore.

The Pastorius debacle epitomized the waning fortunes of the Abwehr and Admiral Canaris. By late 1942 Germany was losing ground militarily, and many blamed faulty intelligence. Canaris grew distracted and listless. "He made an old, tired, and war-weary impression," observed one SS officer. Canaris had also become increasingly alarmed by Hitler's brutal policies and erratic behavior. Returning from one meeting at which the führer flew into a rage, he confided to an aide, "I've seen a madman." Doubts about the admiral's loyalty increased after two high-ranking Abwehr officers were arrested by the Gestapo in April 1943 for conspiring to overthrow Hitler.

The last straw for Canaris and his agency came in early February 1944 when a top Abwehr agent in Istanbul defected to the British, compromising the entire German spy network in Turkey. A few days later, on February 12, Hitler ordered the creation of a "unified German secret information service," under control of the SS. Admiral Canaris was forced into retirement. In June, the Abwehr ceased to exist, and those who retained their jobs found themselves part of the same organization as the Gestapo. Heading this unified secret service for the SS was the ever ambitious and opportunistic mastermind of Venlo, Walter Schellenberg.

PLOTS TO KILL HITLER

No one paid much attention in August 1939 when a German cabinetmaker named Georg Elser began frequenting Munich's famous Bürgerbräukeller, site of Adolf Hitler's first attempt to seize power, the abortive Beer Hall Putsch of 1923. Elser, a Communist sympathizer, knew that Hitler would return to the beer hall on November 8, 1939, to mark the anniversary of the putsch as he had in years past by addressing veterans of the uprising. If Elser had his way, that speech would be Hitler's last.

Each night, Elser hid in the cavernous beer hall as the place was closing, then went quietly to work, removing a piece of the paneling behind the speaker's rostrum and slowly gouging a hole in the masonry underneath. In early November, Elser put a bundle of stolen explosives in the hole and set a homemade timing device to detonate on the eighth at 9:20 p.m. Hitler was set to begin speaking at 8:30, and Elser figured the long-winded führer would be in the middle of a tirade when the bomb went off.

But shortly before the event, Hitler decided to start at eight and end by nine, returning to Berlin that night. After delivering the address *(left)*, he departed hastily and was on his way to the train station when the bomb exploded, collapsing the ceiling and killing nine people.

By Hitler's own reckoning, it was the seventh assassination plot he had survived. He saw this latest escape as further proof that he was blessed by fate, but he tightened security and cut back on public appearances. Henceforth, any serious attempt on his life would have to be an inside job.

In fact, there were a number of high-ranking Germans

German police and firemen pick through the rubble of the blast at Munich's Bürgerbräukeller on November 8, 1939, which killed nine people in the beer hall and injured 60 others shortly after Hitler finished addressing the party faithful. Elser's bomb had been hidden in a column behind the podium.

FATE OF THE CONSPIRATORS

Elser (right), who spent more than five years in detention before being executed, was the last person entirely unknown to Hitler to make an attempt on his life. The key players in subsequent conspiracies—shown on the following pages in roughly the order in which they joined the opposition to Hitler—were all well-connected members of the military or government, and nearly all paid with their lives.

Name: Georg Elser
Title: Civilian (cabinetmaker)
Fate: Executed at Dachau, 1945

Hitler shakes hands at Army Group Center headquarters near Smolensk, where dissident officers led by Henning von Tresckow, then still a colonel, smuggled a bomb aboard Hitler's plane before he left on March 13, 1943. Opposition to Hitler was heightened here by the recent disaster at Stalingrad, where he refused to allow German troops to retreat from a hopeless position.

Name: General Ludwig Beck
Title: Chief of the army general staff
Fate: Committed suicide, 1944

Name: General Franz Halder
Title: Chief of the army general staff
(Beck's successor)
Fate: Quit the resistance, survived the war

Name: General Erich Hoepner
Title: Commander, Panzer Group 4,
on the eastern front
Fate: Executed, 1944

Name: Major General Henning von Tresckow
(*above, center*)
Title: Staff officer, Army Group Center
Fate: Committed suicide, 1944

Name: Lieutenant Fabian von Schlabrendorff
(*above, far right*)
Title: Aide to Tresckow
Fate: Imprisoned until war's end

At a ceremony for wounded veterans in Berlin (above) on March 21, 1943, Hitler narrowly avoided a second assassination attempt by von Tresckow's clique, one of whom planned a suicide attack with a bomb concealed in his coat pocket. Hitler rushed through the visit and left before the would-be assassin could get near him.

with access to Hitler who secretly wished him ill. The hunt for such conspirators prompted the Venlo raid that nabbed British agents Best and Stevens one day after the beer hall blast. Interrogation of the two MI-6 men, however, failed to reveal the names of leading Germans intent on toppling Hitler, since few were in league with the British or other foes of the Reich. Indeed, they saw themselves as patriots, defending Germany against a dangerous dictator.

As early as 1938, army chief Ludwig Beck conspired with his deputy and successor, Franz Halder, to oust Hitler before he ignited a major conflict by invading Czechoslovakia. But that scheme collapsed when the British and French let Hitler have the country without a fight. Such diplomatic triumphs—and lightning German victories early in the war—reduced the threat of a coup. When German forces met with devastating setbacks in late 1942, how-

ever, General Beck and other military and civilian leaders began plotting in earnest to kill Hitler and seize power.

An opportunity arose when Hitler visited the headquarters of Army Group Center near Smolensk on the eastern front in March 1943 (*opposite*). He was preceded there by Abwehr chief Canaris, who never backed an assassination plot, yet opposed Hitler and harbored conspirators in his spy agency. Several of them accompanied Canaris to Smolensk and passed explosives and time-delay fuses to an accomplice, Colonel Henning von Tresckow.

As Hitler was preparing to fly home, Tresckow asked an officer in the führer's entourage to deliver two bottles of brandy to a friend. The officer agreed and boarded Hitler's plane with a harmless-looking package given to him by Tresckow's aide, Fabian von Schlabrendorff, who had triggered the bomb to explode in 30 minutes. The plane took

off promptly, but the "brandy" package failed to detonate. Hitler remained ignorant of this plot and another failed assassination attempt in Berlin a week later.

In 1944 a wide circle of conspirators that included General Beck and Field Marshal Erwin von Witzleben, commander of the Berlin military district, hatched a plot to assassinate Hitler, take control of Berlin, and arrest Nazi officials. Volunteering to kill Hitler was Colonel Claus Graf von Stauffenberg, a distinguished veteran who had lost a hand and an eye in combat in North Africa. As chief of staff of the Reserve Army, he and aide Werner von Haeften were summoned to the Wolf's Lair, Hitler's field headquarters in East Prussia, for a briefing on July 20, 1944.

Before Stauffenberg entered the conference room there, he and Haeften slipped into an empty lounge. Working together, they broke the acid capsule on the timer of one of two packets of explosives hidden in Stauffenberg's brief-

In these July 1944 photos, Stauffenberg stands at attention at far left while a general greets Hitler at the Wolf's Lair on the 15th, five days before Stauffenberg planted a bomb that wrecked a room (center). Hitler escaped with minor injuries and addressed the nation by radio that evening (above), confirming that he was alive and dooming the coup attempt.

case. The bomb was set to go off in just 10 minutes, and a sergeant sent to summon Stauffenberg was at the door. In his haste, he discarded the second packet of explosives and hurried to the meeting with the briefcase.

The conference had already begun when Stauffenberg entered the room. Hitler nodded to him as he took a seat close by and placed the briefcase under the table. As quickly as he dared, Stauffenberg excused himself on the pretense of making a phone call and left the premises. Moments later, an explosion rocked the building behind him.

Convinced that no one inside could have survived the blast, Stauffenberg and Haeften drove off and caught a plane to Berlin. They arrived there to find reports filtering in from the Wolf's Lair that Hitler was still alive. Four others in the conference room had been mortally wounded, but Hitler, once again, had escaped, shielded by one of the table's thick wooden supports, which stood between

Name: General Hans Oster
Title: Abwehr chief of staff
Fate: Executed, 1945

Name: General Friedrich Olbricht
Title: Chief of staff of the Reserve Army
Fate: Executed, 1944

Name: General Karl Heinrich von Stülpnagel
Title: Military governor of France
Fate: Executed, 1944

On July 21, 1944, one day after Colonel Stauffenberg's bomb attack at the Wolf's Lair, Hitler's trusted henchman, SS Major Otto Skorzeny (foreground, taller figure), walks purposefully through the courtyard of army headquarters in downtown Berlin, now firmly in the hands of SS troops. Stauffenberg and three other coup plotters were executed by firing squad here on the night of July 20.

him and the bomb. Had the briefcase contained both packets of explosives, he would probably have been killed. Instead, he survived to rally his supporters in Berlin. By midnight, loyal SS troops were in control of the capital.

Retribution was swift and merciless. Stauffenberg died before a firing squad, and General Beck shot himself, as did several others involved. Nearly 200 more suspects—mostly army officers—were rounded up, tortured, and condemned to death in a show trial. "They are not to receive the honorable bullet," Hitler raged. "I want them to be hanged like common traitors and strung up like butchered cattle." A camera crew captured their death throes as they dangled on cords from meat hooks and slowly strangled under their own weight. Hitler reportedly watched the films.

Throughout Germany, hundreds of people unconnected to the plot—including innocent relatives of Stauffenberg—were rounded up by the SS and executed or sent to concentration camps. German resistance to Hitler was virtually wiped out. No further attempts on his life would be made before war's end, when he himself undertook what countless would-be assassins had failed to accomplish.

Two prominent Germans who had ties to the conspirators but refrained from plots to kill Hitler nonetheless paid with their lives. Field Marshal Erwin Rommel, once the führer's favorite commander, was forced to commit suicide in October 1944 for privately advocating Hitler's removal from power. And Canaris, now no longer Abwehr chief, was arrested on July 23 by his old SS nemesis Walter Schellenberg, tortured, and imprisoned for months before being put to death on April 9, 1945. The night before he went to the gallows, he tapped a message in code to a prisoner in the next cell. His words expressed convictions shared by many of those executed for opposing Hitler, "My time is up. Was not a traitor. Did my duty as a German."

Name: Colonel Albrecht Ritter Mertz von Quirnheim
Title: General staff

Name: General Erich Fellgiebel
Title: Commanding officer, Signal Troops
Fate: Executed, 1944

Name: Lieutenant Werner von Haeften
Title: Reserve Army officer
Fate: Executed, 1944

Roland Freisler sentences accused conspirators in the July 20 plot to death in his so-called People's Court in Berlin. Freisler, a fervent Nazi, often berated and humiliated the defendants, was killed in court during an Allied bombing raid in February 1945.

BREAKING
THE CODES

 n February 27, 1941, Lieutenant General Oshima Hiroshi, Japan's newly appointed ambassador to Germany, arrived at the Berghof, Adolf Hitler's retreat high in the Bavarian Alps, to present his credentials to the Führer. Despite Hitler's professed disdain for non-Aryans, he offered a glowing welcome to Oshima, who had recently helped maneuver Japan into strengthening its military ties with Germany and Italy. So supportive of Hitler that correspondent William Shirer called him "more Nazi than the Nazis," Oshima had served in Berlin before and saw the expansionist Reich as a model for imperial Japan.

When Hitler greeted Oshima, he had no reason to suspect that this firm friend of Germany would unwittingly betray some of its most precious military and diplomatic secrets. Oshima himself would have been horrified to learn that from the moment he assumed his post and began sending dispatches back to Tokyo over a commercial radio circuit, he became in effect an enemy informant. He never imagined that his messages—each of which was enciphered on a machine made for diplomatic use that the Japanese regarded as invulnerable to decryption—were being read with enormous interest not only in Tokyo but also in Washington. Intercepted and recorded, the messages posed puzzles that were regularly solved by the U.S. Army's Signal Intelligence Service (SIS), which had succeeded in building Purple, a machine that mimicked the Japanese device. So dazzling was this feat that the Americans dubbed the resulting intelligence Magic.

This breakthrough transformed Oshima and all other members of the Japanese diplomatic corps who used the cipher machine into unknowing spies for the Americans and their future allies. In April 1941, two months before Hitler launched his invasion of Russia, Oshima radioed a dispatch to Tokyo detailing plans for that massive offensive as revealed to him by Reichsmarschall Hermann Göring. Oshima's message spelled out "the number of planes and numbers and types of divisions to be used,"

Adolf Hitler greets Lieutenant General Oshima Hiroshi, Japanese ambassador to Germany, in February 1939 as German foreign minister Joachim von Ribbentrop looks on. An ardent admirer of Hitler, Oshima gladly returned to Germany in 1941 for a second term as ambassador—unaware that American code breakers were reading his confidential messages from Berlin.

recalled an SIS translator who had turned the Japanese text into English. "I was too excited for sleep that night."

Just a few weeks after this coup, in early May, the staff at SIS received a nasty surprise in the form of intercepted messages from the foreign minister in Tokyo to the Japanese ambassador in Washington. "It appears almost certain that the United States government is reading your code messages," the foreign minister warned, adding that this was told "very confidentially to Ambassador Oshima by the Germans as having been reported to them by a fairly reliable intelligence medium."

The news sent shock waves rippling through intelligence circles in Washington. If the Japanese altered or replaced their machine, it could take the Americans months or even years to catch up. The suspense lasted for two agonizing weeks, until another intercepted message to the Japanese embassy in Washington revealed that officials in Tokyo retained absolute faith in their cipher machine and blamed any breach that might have occurred on human error or misconduct. Henceforth, the foreign minister insisted, only one trusted man at the embassy would be allowed to operate the machine. Believing that their technology was inviolable, the Japanese continued to use the machine to encipher diplomatic messages throughout the war.

This decision gave the Americans and the British continuing access to the communications of Japanese diplomats, including the supremely well informed ambassador Oshima in Berlin, whose radio traffic with Tokyo during the fall of 1941 offered strong hints that Japan might soon enter the conflict. On November 30, Tokyo advised Oshima that "there is extreme danger that war may suddenly break out between the Anglo-Saxon nations and Japan," adding that "this war may come quicker than anyone dreams." Unfortunately for the Americans who were tapping into this traffic, the messages did not specify precisely when or where that conflict might begin.

A week later, on December 7, the Japanese bombed Pearl Harbor and quickly went on to attack American forces in the Philippines and the British at Singapore. When Hitler subsequently honored his pact with Tokyo by declaring war on the United States, America entered the conflict on both fronts, and Oshima became one of the Allies' prime sources of information on enemy plans in Berlin as well as in Tokyo.

In the years ahead, Oshima made a number of unwitting contributions to the Allied war effort. Perhaps his greatest disclosure was an extensive report he dispatched after inspecting German defenses along the French coast in late 1943, as the Allies were drawing up plans for the invasion of Normandy. In describing fortifications along Germany's Atlantic Wall and the deployment of forces there, he

The cipher machine that included the restored piece shown here was used at the Japanese embassy in Berlin by Ambassador Oshima and staff and confiscated when Allied forces occupied the city in May 1945.

From: Berlin.
To : Tokyo.
9 July 1941

#878

A person close to Foreign Minister Ribbentrop advises us in confidence, the following report on the progress of the German-Soviet war:

1. One of the revelations as a result of the German-Soviet war to date, is the amazing weakness of the Soviet air force. On the other hand, the Soviet (land forces) put up an unexpectedly strong resistance to attack.

Possibly it is due to the fact that - - - - - -at the outbreak of the war, but whatever the cause, Germany has now complete control of the air. Although the Soviet air force has managed to drop a few bombs in Finland and Rumania it has been unable to make a frontal air attack on Germany proper.

There were a few points of interest on the Soviet bombers, but in general, it may be said that in both plane construction and in the flyers themselves, the Soviet Union is far outclassed. Combat planes in particular were of exceedingly inferior construction.

2. It is true that the land forces put up a fairly stiff resistance. However, this resistance is not so strong as to force Germany to change her original plan of action nor her aims. Everything is proceeding according to schedule which is strengthening the belief that they will continue to do so in the future.

3. As far as Germany is concerned - - - - - - -(remainder of message not received).

19509

(D) Navy Trans. 7-15-41 (C-NR)

JD-1: 3652

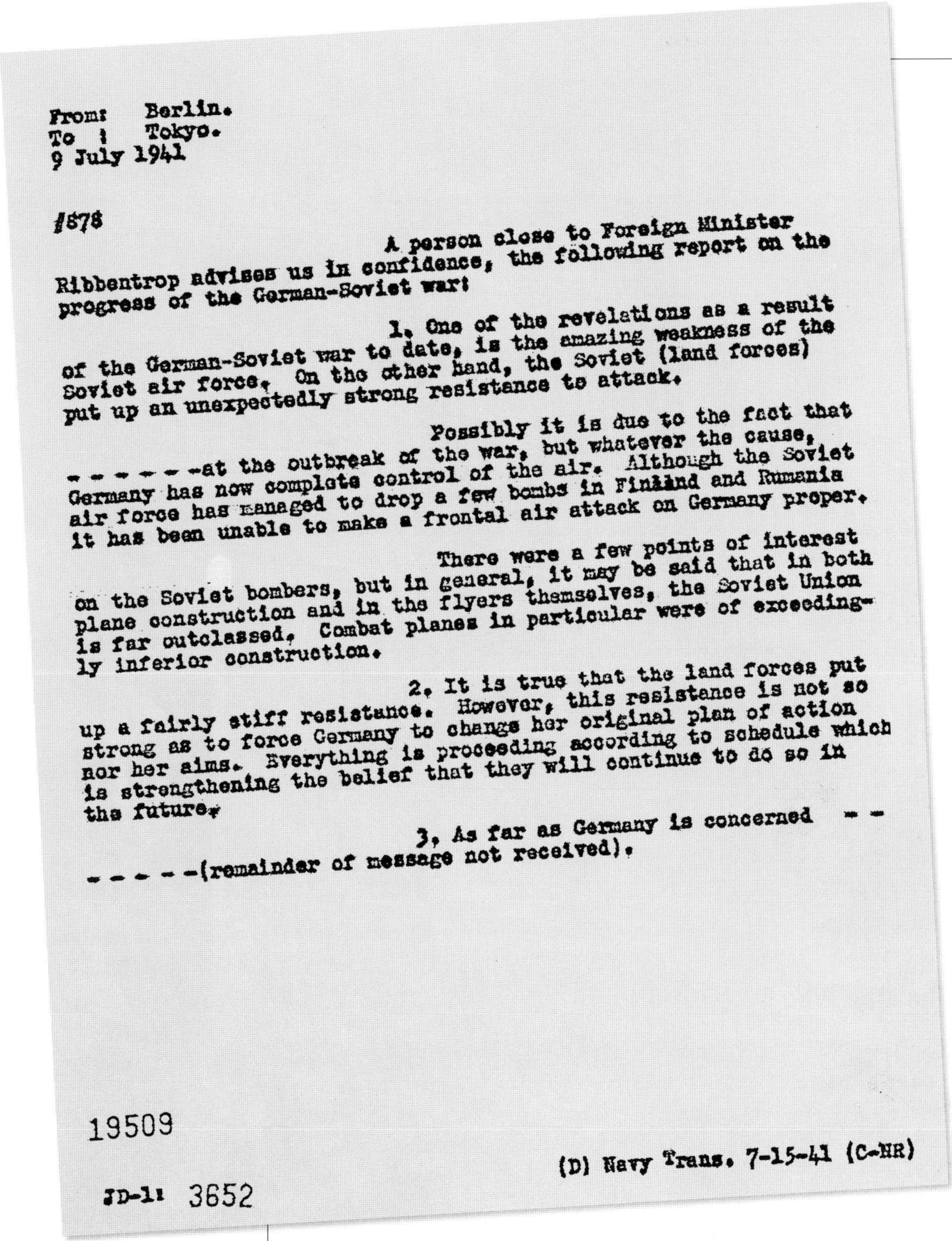

Solved by American cryptanalysts, a message sent by Oshima to Tokyo in July 1941 reveals that the German invasion of the Soviet Union is "proceeding according to schedule." Oshima's radio dispatch was intercepted by the Americans, who picked up only part of the message.

confirmed that the coast of Normandy was relatively lightly defended: Hitler expected the invasion farther north, across the Strait of Dover, and had concentrated his forces to meet that threat. Oshima's revelations through Magic helped convince a skeptical Winston Churchill that a landing at Normandy was feasible and brought the Allied leaders firmly into line behind that well-chosen objective.

Oshima Hiroshi lived long enough to see Germany and Japan defeated and reconstructed, but he never learned of his own role in betraying Hitler's intentions. By the time he died in 1975, at the age of 89, the huge part that code breaking had played in determining the war's outcome was still little understood, either in Japan or elsewhere. The sheer scope of the Allied success in cracking enemy messages was one of the biggest secrets of the war, and its full extent was just now coming to light.

REVEALING THE WIZARDS

The silence that once cloaked Magic—and the similar and equally significant British achievement in solving the puzzles posed by the German Enigma machine, resulting in the intelligence known as Ultra—was all the more remarkable considering how many people participated in such programs during the war. Some 10,000 Americans worked for the army's SIS, and many others labored for the navy's code-breaking outfit in Washington, Op-20-G. Across the Atlantic, roughly 12,000 Britons worked at Bletchley Park, the nerve center northwest of London that produced the Ultra decrypts. The organization at Bletchley had a quaint and somewhat deceptive name—the Government Code and Cypher School (GC&CS).

As that title implied, those known loosely as code breakers, or more precisely as cryptanalysts, dealt with two distinct kinds of puzzles: codes and ciphers. A code works by words—replacing a word or phrase with a group of letters or numbers. A coded message identifying London as the target of a bombing raid might substitute for "London" the letter group ARBL, for example, or the number group 3964.

A cipher, by contrast, works by letters. Each letter of the original message may be replaced by a single letter or a group of letters and numbers. A simple cipher might substitute *x* for *e* and *j* for *n* each time those letters appear in a message, for example, so that the word *enemy* would be enciphered XJXBA. But so simple a system is easily solved. Machines such as the

Frederick W. Winterbotham

The Man Who Unveiled Ultra

Britain's F. W. Winterbotham, shown at top right in 1942, spent much of his life undercover. After spying on Germany with the help of pilot Sidney Cotton, he handled the wartime intelligence known as Ultra—a term he coined to describe ultrasecret decrypts of German Enigma messages. But in 1974, this former guardian of secrets turned gentleman farmer *(right)* caused a stir by divulging the code-breaking feats at Bletchley Park in his book *The Ultra Secret.* Some colleagues objected to errors in his memoir—and others to the very idea of unveiling Ultra. One Ultra veteran, Walter Eytan, was at first so taken aback that he refused to read it, but his wife saw a review and finally learned what her husband had been doing "at a place called Bletchley."

Enigma encipher a letter differently each time it appears in the text, so that *enemy* might come out PJAVR.

To complicate matters for code breakers, enemies sending sensitive messages during the war sometimes encoded the text and then enciphered the coded text. And alert services often changed their codes as well as the settings for their cipher machines. Keeping up with those changes was a never-ending challenge that drove some cryptanalysts to their wits' end.

Code breakers were the key figures in Magic and Ultra, but many other specialists contributed as well. They included radio operators at listening stations around the world who intercepted a vast array of Morse signals at various frequencies; traffic analysts who determined the origin and transmission location of those signals; a host of clerks and technicians; translators who converted messages from German, Italian, or Japanese into English; intelligence analysts; and liaison officers responsible for cautiously passing on the decrypts.

All those involved in these top-secret projects swore oaths of silence. Arthur Benson, who helped provide Ultra dispatches to Winston Churchill, had lunch every few weeks during the war with his sister, a cryptanalyst. Not until years later did either sibling realize the other had been involved in any way with wartime intelligence. So critical was code breaking to the security of the United States and Great Britain in the postwar period that the secret of the wartime decryption of Enigma was maintained long after the struggle ended.

Finally, in the 1970s, British authorities, knowing that surplus Enigma machines were no longer in use anywhere in the world, concluded that disclosing some of those secrets 30 years after the fact could do little harm—and might be a public-relations coup. In 1974, F. W. Winterbotham, the officer in charge of distributing Ultra dispatches to Allied commanders during the war, received official permission to publish *The Ultra Secret*, a book that gained worldwide attention *(sidebar, opposite)*. In writing the book, Winterbotham worked from memory. He was also not fully informed on all aspects of Ultra and its history. As a result, his account overlooked the part that French intelligence and Polish cryptanalysts had played before the war in helping to solve the Enigma, and it also fostered some misconceptions about how Ultra was used.

Nonetheless, the book did shed considerable light on one of the war's last great mysteries, and it led to further disclosures as well. Soon historians were rewriting their accounts of the war to acknowledge the enormous impact of cryptanalysts on some of its major battles and campaigns. Yet the revelations left people wondering why the Allies had not reaped even greater benefits.

The answers lay partly in the difficulty of keeping up with the ever-changing enemy codes and cipher settings and partly in the failure of commanders to make the most of the intelligence that they did receive. Furthermore, some Allied codes had been broken by the Germans and Japanese, although the Axis powers failed to match the cryptanalytical accomplishments of their opponents. The war would certainly have been

"I was shocked to the point of refusing to read the book when someone showed me a copy, and to this day I feel inhibited if by chance the subject comes up."

—Walter Eytan, on *The Ultra Secret*

far costlier for the Allies without their phenomenal code-breaking campaigns—efforts that began long before the start of the conflict and involved some of the finest scientific minds of the 20th century. "To the question, why did not Ultra shorten the war," F. H. Hinsley, a British historian and Ultra veteran concluded, "the answer is that it did."

SOLVING THE ENIGMA

Many years before World War II, farsighted intelligence officers for the world's major powers understood that a key to obtaining enemy plans in the next war lay in uncovering the secrets of the cipher machines increasingly used by rival nations to protect their communications. Among the pioneers in this new branch of technological espionage was Captain Gustave Bertrand of the Deuxième Bureau, the famed intelligence service of the French army. In the fall of 1930, Bertrand set up a special unit to steal or purchase information that might help French cryptanalysts cope with baffling messages such as those enciphered by the Germans on military versions of the Enigma machine, which was sold in the early 1920s as a commercial device to conceal business communications.

Operating in Paris out of a shabby office on the Left Bank, Bertrand and staff came up with little of significance until the summer of 1931, when a tantalizing letter arrived. It was from a German named Hans-Thilo Schmidt, who offered to sell instructions for use of the Enigma machine employed by the German army. Bertrand arranged for a German-born agent who went by the code name Rex to meet Schmidt at the Grand Hotel in Verviers, Belgium, not far from the German border, and assess his offer.

The well-bred Schmidt seemed an unlikely traitor. His mother was a baroness, his father was an eminent professor, and his older brother was chief of staff of the signal corps and former head of the Cipher Office at the Ministry of Defense. Schmidt himself, a failed businessman, had to settle for a job as a clerk at the Cipher Office, and he obtained that position only with his brother's help. Now in his mid-40s, he could see just one way of improving his fortunes—by selling the secrets entrusted to him. He needed cash to live in the style to which he felt entitled, and he did not mind betraying an institution that placed his brother so high above him.

Rex reported to Bertrand that Schmidt and the documents he was peddling appeared genuine. A week later, Bertrand arrived in Verviers with a photographer and closed his first deal with the German spy over whiskey and cigars in Schmidt's room at the Grand Hotel. For 10,000 marks, or about $4,000, Schmidt allowed Bertrand and his assistant to photograph the documents. Schmidt later returned the papers to their proper files in Berlin.

Bertrand continued to press Schmidt for more documents because the first batch he showed to cryptanalysts failed to achieve the immediate results he hoped for. A French expert concluded that the documents were of no use in solving Enigma. Undeterred, Bertrand obtained permission to share the intelligence with cryptanalysts in other nations concerned about Germany's future intentions. The British concurred that Schmidt's offer-

Gustave Bertrand

Hans-Thilo Schmidt

French intelligence officer Gustave Bertrand purchased classified material that helped solve the Enigma from Hans-Thilo Schmidt, a low-paid clerk in the German Cipher Center who had failed in the soap manufacturing business and made ends meet by peddling some of his country's most precious secrets.

ings were of little help. Not until Bertrand met with Polish intelligence chiefs in Warsaw that December did he know for sure that he was on to something big. The Poles were delighted with the gift and eagerly awaited further revelations from Bertrand's source. Only in Poland had cryptanalysts advanced far enough toward a solution of Enigma to make full use of what Schmidt had to offer.

Wedged between two troublesome giants, Germany on the west and the Soviet Union on the east, the Poles had every incentive to eavesdrop on their neighbors. And when the German armed forces began using the Enigma to encipher their messages, Polish intelligence officers were quick to respond to the challenge. Before cipher machines, cryptanalysts had to be linguists, because codes are based on linguistic elements. Now they needed to be mathematicians to solve the machines' complex riddles. The Polish Cipher Bureau had recently recruited three gifted young mathematicians from the university at Poznań, situated in formerly German territory ceded to Poland at the end of the last war. Like other students there, the recruits were fluent in German.

Of the trio, the most brilliant was a quirky young man in his mid-20s named Marian Rejewski, whose genius went largely unnoticed until instructors from the Cipher Bureau singled him out at a special night class they conducted for prospective cryptanalysts at the university. He was something of a loner, which was just as well, for he would spend much time alone, puzzling over the Enigma in a small room overlooking the tomb of the Unknown Soldier in Warsaw's Saxon Square.

In recent years the Poles had purchased a commercial Enigma and intercepted and photographed a more advanced German-military version of the device, accidentally sent through Polish customs. Thus they knew the machine's basic setup. When an Enigma operator pressed a letter on the machine's typewriter-like keyboard, an electronic impulse passed through its wired code wheels, or "rotors," and lit up a different letter on a display that resembled the keyboard *(pages 88-89)*. The machine at the receiving end performed the same operation in reverse. If the sender pressed *o* and illuminated *k*, the receiver would press *k* and illuminate *o*.

Solving the problem posed by the latest and most advanced Enigma used in Germany was no simple task, because the Germans were constantly improving their system to render it more secure. Furthermore, even if the Poles had been given such an Enigma, in theory they would not have been able to read messages enciphered on it unless they knew which settings the sender had used; there were far too many possibilities for trial and error to succeed. The machine then in use by the Germans had three rotors, which had to be placed in the machine in the proper order. Each rotor had 26 possible settings. In addition, movable cables on a plugboard further complicated the process. To decipher a message, the receiver had to use the same placement and setting for the rotors as the sender had. Given this array of complications, the number of possible settings soared into the quadrillions—or more than an entire squad of code breakers could run through manually in many lifetimes.

AN ENIGMA FOR
CODE BREAKERS

Thanks to the Enigma cipher machine, the German military by 1930 boasted the world's most secure communications system. In years to come, however, rival code breakers broke into that system at great effort and used the machine to help defeat Germany.

Introduced in 1923, the Enigma was touted as a way of protecting business documents against the "inquisitiveness of competitors." Pressing a letter on the keyboard sent an electrical impulse through the wiring and lit up a different letter on the lamp board *(diagram, opposite)*. To reverse the process and decipher the message, a receiver had to have an identical machine and use the same setting as the sender. That meant inserting the rotors in the same order and placing them in the same starting positions (each rotor had 26 positions, for the letters of the alphabet).

The German military improved the Enigma by adding a plugboard up front with movable cables connecting different points, vastly increasing the number of possible enciphering permutations. Confident that foes could never find the right settings, the Germans had tens of thousands of Enigmas in use by war's end, with settings that changed daily. Their misplaced faith in the machine—whose settings were derived by Allied code breakers using ever more sophisticated computing devices—proved disastrous for Germany.

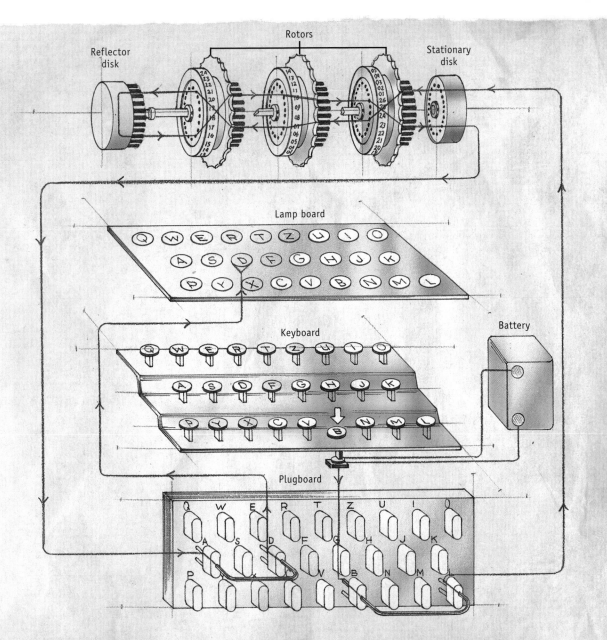

Reflector disk

Rotors

Stationary disk

Lamp board

Keyboard

Battery

Plugboard

The diagram above shows how Enigma enciphered one letter as another; this example reflects one of many rotor combinations and involves just two plugboard cables. When B is pressed on the keyboard, a battery-powered impulse travels through a cable on the plugboard from B to L before entering the stationary disk at top, followed by a series of rotors. In each rotor, crossed wires transpose impulses from one of 26 contact points, representing the letters of the alphabet, to different positions. The impulse is transposed several times as it passes through the rotors, rebounds in the reflector disk, and goes back through the rotors. Reaching the plugboard as A, it registers on the lamp board as D. Each time an Enigma operator pressed a key, the first rotor advanced one position, changing the path for the next letter, so that the next B, in this example, would not be turned into D. The second and third rotors also advanced, but less often. With each part of the machine adding to the number of possible permutations, the challenge of solving intercepted messages was heroic in scale.

Understandably, the Germans felt they had the perfect cipher machine. But they failed to reckon with devastating breaches of security like that exploited by Hans-Thilo Schmidt or with the determination of the Poles.

Even before Rejewski had the benefit of Schmidt's revelations, he and others at the Cipher Bureau had identified a telltale feature of the Enigma intercepts. Each dispatch began with six letters representing the three-letter rotor setting for that particular message, chosen at random by the sender and enciphered twice on the machine using the basic setting for all messages that day, as given in a book distributed to authorized Enigma users. This repeated encipherment of the same three letters was meant to enable the recipient to correct for any transmission errors. But it also offered Rejewski vital clues into the keying being used, as did the senders' frequent choice of predictable settings like *abc* or *qwe,* the first three letters on the keyboard. With these clues, he reduced the operating principles of the Enigma to a series of complex equations. He was not able to solve those equations, even with the first set of documents provided by Schmidt, however, because there were too many unknowns.

Everything fell into place for Rejewski in December 1932 when he received further disclosures from Schmidt, courtesy of Bertrand: critical documents revealing the keys, or settings, used by Enigma operators for the months of September and October. This divulged not only the basic rotor settings for each day but also the prescribed changes in rotor order for those months as well as the arrangement of the cables on the plugboard, a mystery that Rejewski had been unable to fathom. "Thanks to my having these keys," he remarked in an interview after the war, "the number of unknowns in the equations was reduced." By the end of the year, he recalled, Enigma was solved. "Now all that had to be done was to build the machine."

A Polish electrical firm called AVA produced a replica of the current German machine in short order. But Rejewski and company could not rest on their laurels. The Germans soon recognized that operators were using easily guessed rotor settings and put a stop to that foolishness. And in the mid-1930s, as Hitler expanded his army and readied it for offensive action, the German Cipher Office mandated daily changes in the rotor positions, greatly magnifying the task of decryption.

Rejewski and his colleagues, who had been reading German messages frequently since 1933, now found it increasingly difficult to find the right settings. Their burden might have been eased had they been let in on fresh secrets that Bertrand had obtained from Schmidt and had passed along to the directors of the Polish Cipher Bureau. But bureau officers withheld the material, reasoning that such help would not always be available and their wizards might do better in the long run without cribbing from German documents.

Sure enough, the cryptanalysts and their technical assistants came up with ingenious ways of accelerating the frustrating process of checking one setting after another to find one that worked. One of Rejewski's colleagues, Henryk Zygalski, devised large perforated sheets resembling huge punch cards. When placed one atop another and laid over a light table, they allowed light through at a few holes on an alphabetical grid, indicating settings that might unlock the meaning of the messages for a given day. Preparing those so-called Zygalski sheets was time consuming, however, so the Poles speeded the search by wiring one Enigma to another and using the machine to race through settings until it found a winner.

This mechanization process culminated in 1938 with the invention of a marvel the Poles called a *bomba,* or "bombe," consisting of six Enigmas wired together. The machine ticked as it operated and shut off automatically when it reached a possible solution. If that setting failed to reveal the day's messages, the Poles started the bombe ticking anew and tried again. The machine was not infallible, but it often arrived within hours at a solution that the designers of Enigma had confidently estimated would take code breakers eons to find. By November 1938, six bombes were busily at work in Warsaw.

In the months to come, however, the Germans raised the ante for cryptanalysts. They supplied operators with five different rotors, three of which would be inserted into the machine as prescribed each time it was reset, and increased the number of plugboard connections from six to ten. To read Enigma messages in a timely manner, the Poles would now need 60 bombes, not six. This was beyond their means, and in any case, they were in imminent danger of being invaded by Germany. The Poles decided to turn over everything they had on Enigma to their British and French allies, before it was too late.

In late July 1939, Gwido Langer, head of Polish intelligence, hosted an

> ## "Now all that had to be done was to build the machine."
>
> —Marian Rejewski, after solving the Enigma

extraordinary conclave of Allied cryptanalysts and intelligence officers at a walled compound deep in the Kabacki woods, south of Warsaw. Bertrand was among those representing France. From Britain came Alastair Denniston, head of the Government Code and Cypher School, and Dillwyn Knox, a brilliant linguist and cryptanalyst in Denniston's outfit who had labored on Enigma with limited success. After the visitors told of their difficulties, Langer, relishing the moment, lifted the covers off several mysterious objects on a table to reveal Enigmas.

"Where did you get these?" asked an astonished Bertrand.

"We made them ourselves," replied Langer proudly.

Denniston and Knox could scarcely contain their admiration and envy. But an even greater surprise awaited them in the next room: the bombe. The Poles gave the French and British each a set of blueprints for that device and a working Enigma.

Little more than a month later, German tanks rolled over the Polish border. Rejewski and his colleagues escaped with several Enigmas to France, having destroyed everything else at the Cipher Bureau that might reveal their breakthrough to the invaders. They continued to work covertly as cryptanalysts in France until late 1942, when the Germans seized the rest of that country. Rejewski then fled with others on the team to Britain. Nothing they accomplished during the war could surpass what they had achieved before it began. Through the great gifts they bequeathed to their allies, they hastened the defeat of the forces that had crushed their homeland.

BUILDING A BETTER BOMBE

For Alastair Denniston, the bequest from Poland was a godsend. By 1939 his once cozy "Cypher School" in London had more than 200 employees. Only about 30 of them were code breakers, however, and of that number few could claim any mathematical or technical expertise. Most were wordmen like Denniston himself, a master of the German language who had distinguished himself as a naval cryptanalyst during World War I, before cipher machines revolutionized the field. A few of Denniston's brightest stars, notably Dillwyn Knox, had recently made headway against less-sophisticated versions of the Enigma used by the Italians and others, but they could do nothing with the latest dispatches from Germany.

Indeed, the British would have been hard pressed to take advantage of the gifts from Poland had not Denniston recognized belatedly that his organization needed recruits of mathematical genius and set out to find them by offering courses much like the one the Poles had conducted in Poznań a decade earlier. The purpose was not simply to teach pupils code breaking but to identify prodigies who would soon surpass their instructors at solving cryptanalytical puzzles.

Among the prospects who attended the courses as war loomed was a shy, disheveled, 27-year-old named Alan Turing,

As sketched below, the bombe invented by the Polish cryptanalysts used six sets of Enigma rotors (only one set is shown in detail here) to sift through a vast number of possible Enigma machine settings and find those used by the Germans to encipher their daily messages. Turning on shafts driven by a motor, the rotors stopped when a possible solution was achieved.

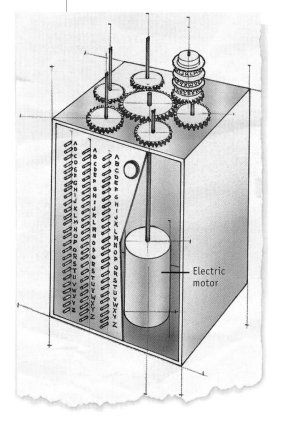

Electric motor

Dillwyn Knox

Alastair Denniston

Classicist Dillwyn Knox, whose experience translating fragmentary Greek texts helped prepare him for code breaking, was one of many expert linguists at Britain's Government Code and Cypher School. The code-breaking unit was headed by Alastair Denniston, himself a former German teacher.

who spoke with a terrible stammer and had a habit of picking his fingers raw. A Fellow at King's College, Cambridge, he had recently published a visionary paper in which he demonstrated that a machine capable of making a fundamental distinction—between 0 and 1—could perform the most complex of calculations. This concept became known as the "universal Turing machine" and earned him recognition in later years as the intellectual father of the computer. Turing's contribution to the evolution of the computer was not just theoretical, however. He was an inspired engineer, and together with other wizards recruited by Denniston and his staff to deal with Enigma, he would devise cryptanalytical computing machines that considerably improved upon the Polish bombe.

Bletchley Park, the secure country estate in Buckinghamshire where Turing and company worked their wonders, had grounds spacious enough to accommodate dozens of prefabricated Nissen huts, each housing people with a specific function *(pages 98-99)*. For lodging, the staff roomed in local pubs or in houses in surrounding villages.

Turing arrived there on September 4, one day after Britain declared war on Germany, to enroll full time with the GC&CS for a modest stipend of £600 a year. Like others on the premises, he was sworn to secrecy. His landlady at the nearby Crown Inn thought ill of him for doing nothing worth mentioning at Bletchley while others his age were enlisting to fight. Whether the army would have wanted him was another matter. He was plagued by hay fever and bicycled to work in pollen season wearing a gas mask. His bicycle chain tended to fall off, but instead of repairing it, he counted the number of pedal revolutions that produced the effect and got off in time to make adjustments. He locked his tea mug to radiators to prevent its being stolen and buried his cash in the woods around Bletchley to protect it in case of invasion—and then forgot where he had stashed it.

The eccentric Turing found good company at Bletchley. One of his close collaborators there—and his nearest rival for pure analytical genius—was Gordon Welchman, a humorless character described even by friends as a "solemn old stick." Like Turing, he applied his wits to areas well beyond his academic specialty, algebraic geometry, and devised new machines and new ways of processing information that helped Bletchley master the Enigma more rapidly.

Welchman's superiors were not sure what to do with him when he arrived at Bletchley. So they set him to work on a seemingly minor task, analyzing the external aspects of German radio messages—frequencies, directions, call signs, and introductory elements such as addresses, taken from Enigma intercepts. In studying these data, Welchman developed on his own the method called traffic analysis, which had been worked out independently by other intelligence services as well. This approach involved analyzing the external characteristics of a message before solving it, to determine its origin and destination and so, perhaps, its likely contents.

Traffic analysis yielded enormous benefits for code breaking. Welchman found that radio dispatchers in the various branches of the German military had standard ways of addressing one another and standard phras-

Alan Turing

Gordon Welchman

es that cropped up repeatedly in their communications. Simply by knowing where the message was coming from, one could surmise that there were certain "probable words" in the text.

Cryptanalysts had long been using probable words to break codes and ciphers. The great achievement of Turing, with a powerful assist from Welchman, was to apply this concept to the circuitry of a new and better bombe, one that narrowed the time-consuming hunt for a setting capable of solving a given message. By mid-1940, the first of many such Turing bombes at Bletchley was up and ticking, allowing the British to break some German messages within hours and others within days, depending on how long it took them to identify the origin and nature of the messages and derive the probable words or phrases, known as cribs.

As the decryption effort accelerated, officials at Bletchley wrestled with the problem of sharing the results without letting the Germans know their codes had been broken. F. W. Winterbotham devised a secure system for distributing intelligence through liaison units to commanders in the field and chose the term Ultra (for Ultra Secret) to classify the decrypts. The ultimate test for Ultra was whether commanders received the news in time to make use of it. For the duration of the war, the wizards and their machines would work around the clock to solve the latest Enigma puzzles and produce decrypts before developments on the battlefield rendered them obsolete.

ULTRA AT WAR

By August 1940, when German warplanes set out to destroy British air defenses as a prelude to invasion, the Luftwaffe's Enigma messages were being solved routinely at Bletchley. Unlike the other German armed services, which revised their Enigma settings more often, the Luftwaffe would long adhere to one basic key, or menu of settings, known to the British as Red. Luftwaffe operators were also far less careful in following guidelines for use of the Enigma machines, and that sloppiness helped the code breakers as well. Peter Calvocoressi, who worked as a translator in Bletchley's Hut 3, recalled that cryptanalysts handling Luftwaffe intercepts in Hut 6 eventually became so accustomed to Red that they seldom needed more than a few hours to solve the daily puzzle: "We in Hut 3 would get a bit techy if Hut 6 had not broken Red by breakfast time."

Ultra was not a major factor in the air war that came to be called the Battle of Britain, however. During the campaign, Luftwaffe commanders used Enigma-encrypted radio messages to issue advisories of forthcoming attacks but communicated specific battle orders by wire—an option not often available to German forces in other theaters during the war. Ultra divulged the locations of Luftwaffe squadrons and their strength but seldom if ever revealed precisely when or where air strikes would occur.

Ultra did alert the British to major shifts in German strategy, however, such as Hitler's decision in the fall of 1940 to postpone his expected invasion of Britain, which never materialized. Furthermore, Ultra revealed that the Luftwaffe planned to use a system of intersecting radio beams to guide its pilots to bombing targets at night. This led to a method for jamming those beams that sometimes succeeded in deflecting bombers from their targets.

"The geese who laid the golden eggs— and never cackled."

—Winston Churchill
on the Bletchley Park code breakers

By 1941 the British had weathered the worst of the Blitz and were challenging German and Italian forces for control of North Africa. Code breaking figured prominently in that sprawling desert campaign, which depended heavily on radio communications and required field commanders to signal their intentions well in advance to maintain their supply lines and the cohesion of their forces. General Erwin Rommel, whose wily moves as commander of the Afrika Korps earned him the title of the Desert Fox, made rapid gains against the British in 1941, thanks in part to the work of German code breakers who read messages to Washington from the American army attaché in Cairo, detailing British plans. Any advantages Rommel gained from such decrypts, however, were more than offset by the intelligence British commanders gleaned from Ultra in the later, climactic stages of the campaign.

By July of 1942, rebounding from a British offensive, Rommel had advanced westward across the desert as far as El Alamein, only about 65 miles from Alexandria. But he was near the end of his supply tether, and the British knew it. Cryptanalysts at Bletchley had succeeded in recent months in mastering the Enigma key used by the German army. That key called for changes in the settings every eight hours, but once code breakers had determined the systematic nature of those changes, they were able to provide decrypts of messages to and from Rommel's forces within 24 hours of interception. Further revelations came from the ever obliging Luftwaffe, whose liaison officers worked closely with Rommel and dispatched reports that were promptly read by the code breakers.

Among the decrypts that did Rommel the most damage were those divulging messages he received from his superior officer in Italy, Field Marshal Albert Kesselring of the Luftwaffe, now serving as commander in chief of German forces in Italy and North Africa. His staff sent Rommel precise information on Axis convoys bound for North Africa, specifying their cargo and their shipping dates—all enciphered on a Luftwaffe Enigma. Bletchley sped the decrypts to the RAF and the Royal Navy, which targeted those convoys and sank fully half the vessels carrying supplies to Rommel in 1942.

Ultra not only helped strip Rommel of supplies but also revealed his battle plans to his British counterpart, General Bernard Law Montgomery, who took command at El Alamein in early August. The ever confident "Monty" assured his troops at the time that he knew what Rommel was up to—a statement that British intelligence chiefs considered far too close to the truth to be uttered publicly. In fact, Montgomery knew from Ultra that Rommel was planning a night attack at El Alamein at the next full moon, in late August. He also learned from the same source that his German adversary was feeling very ill after 19 months in the desert. Subject to a variety of woes that included low blood pressure, a severe nasal infection, fainting spells, and a possible case of gastritis, Rommel almost had to yield command shortly before the attack occurred. When German forces went into battle on the night of August 30, they came up against meticulously prepared defenses and fell back a few days later after heavy losses, leaving them vulnerable to a counterstrike.

Montgomery bided his time, secure in his knowledge that Rommel's

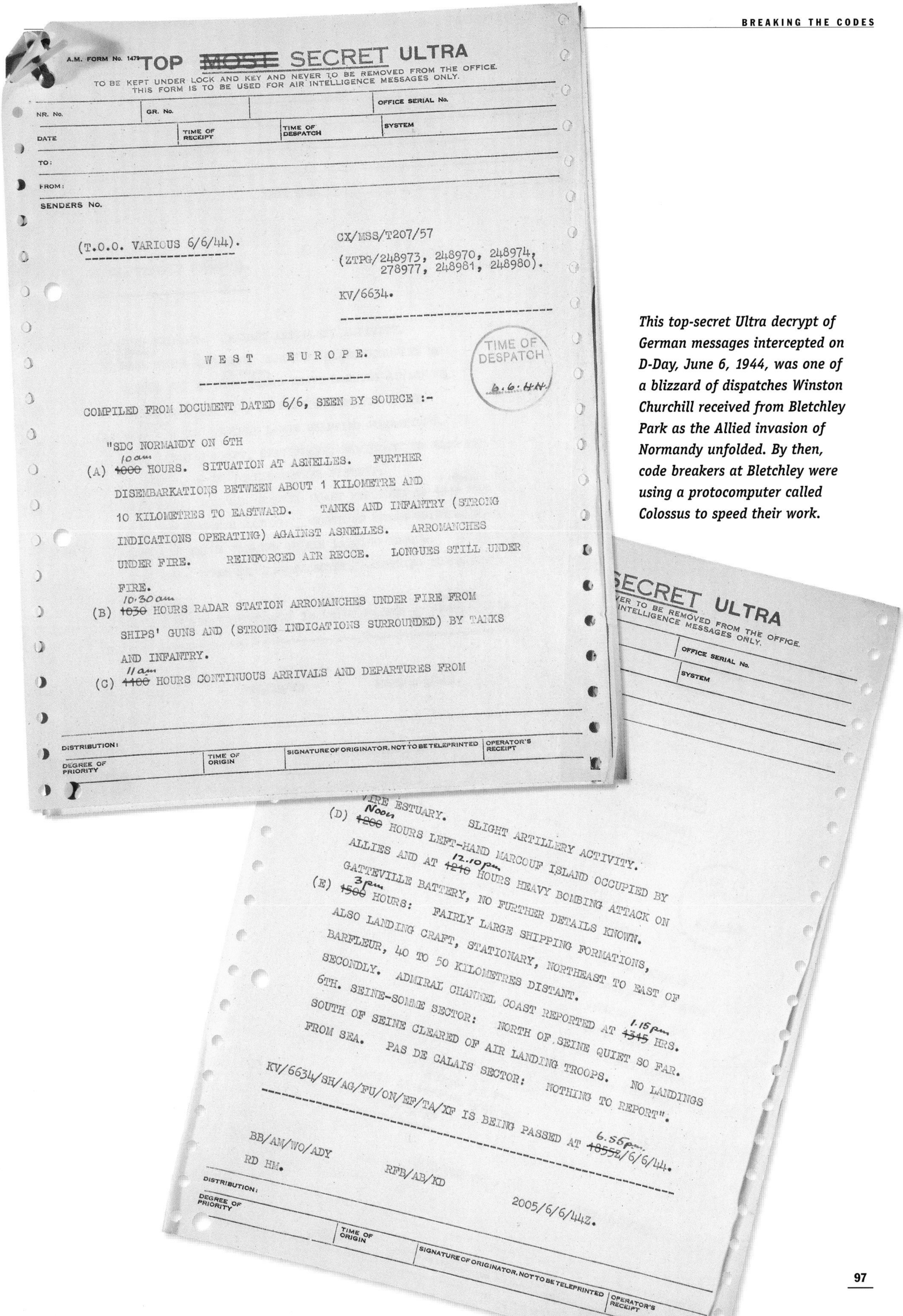

A.M. FORM No. 1479 **TOP** ~~MOSE~~ **SECRET ULTRA**

TO BE KEPT UNDER LOCK AND KEY AND NEVER TO BE REMOVED FROM THE OFFICE.
THIS FORM IS TO BE USED FOR AIR INTELLIGENCE MESSAGES ONLY.

| NR. No. | | GR. No. | | | OFFICE SERIAL No. | |
| DATE | | TIME OF RECEIPT | TIME OF DESPATCH | SYSTEM | | |

TO:

FROM:

SENDERS No.

(T.O.O. VARIOUS 6/6/44).   CX/MSS/T207/57

(ZTPG/248973, 248970, 248974,
278977, 248981, 248980).

KV/6634.

W E S T   E U R O P E.

TIME OF DESPATCH
6.6.44

COMPILED FROM DOCUMENT DATED 6/6, SEEN BY SOURCE :-

"SDC NORMANDY ON 6TH

(A) ~~1000~~ *10 am* HOURS. SITUATION AT ASNELLES. FURTHER
DISEMBARKATIONS BETWEEN ABOUT 1 KILOMETRE AND
10 KILOMETRES TO EASTWARD. TANKS AND INFANTRY (STRONG
INDICATIONS OPERATING) AGAINST ASNELLES. ARROMANCHES
UNDER FIRE. REINFORCED AIR RECCE. LONGUES STILL UNDER
FIRE.

(B) ~~1030~~ *10.30 am* HOURS RADAR STATION ARROMANCHES UNDER FIRE FROM
SHIPS' GUNS AND (STRONG INDICATIONS SURROUNDED) BY TANKS
AND INFANTRY.

(C) ~~1100~~ *11 am* HOURS CONTINUOUS ARRIVALS AND DEPARTURES FROM

| DISTRIBUTION: | | | SIGNATURE OF ORIGINATOR, NOT TO BE TELEPRINTED | OPERATOR'S RECEIPT |
| DEGREE OF PRIORITY | | TIME OF ORIGIN | | |

SECRET ULTRA
...VER TO BE REMOVED FROM THE OFFICE.
...INTELLIGENCE MESSAGES ONLY.

| OFFICE SERIAL No. |
| SYSTEM |

...IRE ESTUARY. SLIGHT ARTILLERY ACTIVITY.
(D) ~~1200~~ *Noon* HOURS LEFT-HAND MARCOUF ISLAND OCCUPIED BY
ALLIES AND AT ~~1210~~ *12.10 pm* HOURS HEAVY BOMBING ATTACK ON
GATTEVILLE BATTERY, NO FURTHER DETAILS KNOWN.
(E) ~~1500~~ *3 pm* HOURS: FAIRLY LARGE SHIPPING FORMATIONS,
ALSO LANDING CRAFT, STATIONARY, NORTHEAST TO EAST OF
BARFLEUR, 40 TO 50 KILOMETRES DISTANT.
SECONDLY. ADMIRAL CHANNEL COAST REPORTED AT ~~1345~~ *1.15 pm* HRS.
6TH. SEINE-SOMME SECTOR: NORTH OF SEINE QUIET SO FAR.
SOUTH OF SEINE CLEARED OF AIR LANDING TROOPS. NO LANDINGS
FROM SEA. PAS DE CALAIS SECTOR: NOTHING TO REPORT".

KV/6634/SH/AG/FU/ON/EF/TA/XF IS BEING PASSED AT ~~1855~~ *6.56 pm* /6/6/44

BB/AM/WO/ADY
RD HM.   RFB/AB/KD

2005/6/6/44Z.

| DISTRIBUTION: | | | SIGNATURE OF ORIGINATOR, NOT TO BE TELEPRINTED | OPERATOR'S RECEIPT |
| DEGREE OF PRIORITY | | TIME OF ORIGIN | | |

This top-secret Ultra decrypt of German messages intercepted on D-Day, June 6, 1944, was one of a blizzard of dispatches Winston Churchill received from Bletchley Park as the Allied invasion of Normandy unfolded. By then, code breakers at Bletchley were using a protocomputer called Colossus to speed their work.

INSIDE BLETCHLEY PARK

One morning in 1942, Diana Payne of the Women's Royal Navy Service (WRNS) arrived with 21 other so-called Wrens to begin work at Bletchley Park. "It was a hideous Victorian mansion standing in grounds with several large huts," Payne later recalled. The Wrens were led into one of the huts, where they were informed brusquely that they would be toiling in shifts on a top-secret project with little hope of promotion and, she added, "given until lunchtime to decide whether we could face the ordeal." One Wren backed out, but Payne and the others dutifully signed the Official Secrets Act and joined a code-breaking staff at Bletchley that had mushroomed from a few hundred people at the start of the war to 7,000 by 1942. As pictured here, the recruits worked at various intelligence tasks on a 581-acre estate that resembled a small city by war's end *(above)*.

Payne and her fellow Wrens had good reason to maintain secrecy, for they were assigned to operate Bletchley's all-important bombes. Working eight-hour shifts for 28 days at a stretch, they received instructions from code breakers and adjusted controls on "monster" machines, which sometimes malfunctioned and gave them electric shocks. Like many at Bletchley, from the elite cryptanalysts on down, they felt the strain of toiling relentlessly at tasks that left no room for error and suffered from nightmares and nervous exhaustion. While on leave, they were not allowed to discuss their work with family or friends. Payne was so tight lipped about her duties that relatives considered her "something of a failure." But Allied hopes for victory rested in part on the secret and unstinting labors of Payne and thousands of others at Bletchley.

INTERCEPT CONTROL, HUT 6

In the scene at right, staffers in Hut 6 receive and record intercepts of coded messages sent by the German army and air force and relayed from far-flung Allied listening stations. Hut 6 code breakers then broke the messages, working around the clock in three shifts.

COLOSSUS

At left, Wrens tend to Colossus, Bletchley's protocomputer. The machine's innovative electronic circuitry allowed it to perform calculations even faster than Bletchley's bombes, which remained in operation until war's end.

PRIORITY TEAM, HUT 3

At right, analysts in Hut 3, responsible for interpreting the messages solved in Hut 6, pore over decrypts to gauge their significance and determine which should have priority in transmissions to commanders.

supply situation and his health were both deteriorating. Rommel was away in Austria receiving treatment when the British attacked at El Alamein on October 23. The stricken general hurried back to the front and resumed command, but he failed to repulse Montgomery, who knew his enemy's weaknesses to the letter and relentlessly pressed his advantage until his forces finally broke through in early November, sending Rommel packing and dooming German forces in North Africa to defeat. Ultra's hefty contribution to this pivotal victory remained a closely guarded secret. All the credit for outfoxing the Fox went to Monty.

Code breaking also played a key role in the Battle of the Atlantic, the crucial struggle for control of the sea lanes linking Britain to the United States. The decryption of radio messages helped both the Allies and the Axis find and destroy scores of enemy vessels that might otherwise have eluded detection in the vastness of the Atlantic. Early on, the Germans broke the code used by Allied merchant ships, whose messages revealed where they were going and made them easy prey for U-boats. But those same U-boats, prowling in so-called wolf packs, were themselves dependent on radio links to coordinate their attacks and so were critically vulnerable to code breaking.

The German navy was keenly aware of that risk and labored diligently to protect its Enigma messages against decryption. Instead of relying on one basic key for the whole service as the Luftwaffe did, the navy assigned different keys to its

Coventry's Unavoidable Fate

Few postwar stories about code breaking caused more controversy than the erroneous report that Winston Churchill had learned from Ultra intercepts of German plans to bomb Coventry on the night of November 14, 1940—but decided against defending the city to protect the Ultra secret. Ultra did in fact warn Churchill of an air raid, timed to coincide with the full moon at midmonth. But the target was not known, and not until late on November 14 did the British learn by tracking the radio beams used to guide German bombers that the objective was Coventry. By then, it was too late to evacuate the city, but the RAF sent up fighters and tried in vain to jam the guidance beams. Undeterred, German bombers blasted the city that night, killing or wounding 1,200 people, destroying more than 50,000 homes, and reducing Coventry's famed cathedral to rubble (right).

various branches and sectors. The most vital of those keys, called Hydra, served U-boats and surface ships in the Atlantic. Traffic analysis provided Bletchley with some information, but code breakers made little progress on Hydra until mid-1941, when the Royal Navy seized Enigma documents aboard two captured German weather ships and salvaged an entire Enigma machine from the disabled sub *U-110*. Hitherto, wrote Peter Calvocoressi, Bletchley had produced the "merest sniff of naval Ultra." Before long, naval cryptanalysts in Hut 8 were churning out decrypts that laid bare the enemy's assets in the Atlantic.

This breakthrough allowed Allied convoys to steer clear of prowling wolf packs, so reducing their depredations by late 1941 that the Germans began to suspect a leak. They responded in early 1942 by equipping U-boats with Enigmas that contained four rotors instead of three and all but defied decryption. The code breakers at Bletchley Park were back at square one, and Allied convoys were virtually helpless. In the last half of 1942, U-boats sank nearly 500 ships. It looked for a time as if Germany might win this battle—and with it, perhaps, the war itself.

Once again, however, the cryptanalysts in Hut 8 got the break they needed from a daring salvage effort by the Royal Navy. In late October 1942, officers and men from the destroyer HMS *Petard* boarded the German sub *U-559* in the Mediterranean after forcing it to the surface with depth charges, and they retrieved cipher documents from the doomed vessel at the cost of two lives. That haul helped Bletchley solve the riddle and regain access to wolf-pack signals. The Allies exploited this breakthrough to the hilt, rerouting convoys and targeting U-boats with new antisubmarine weapons. In May 1943 the German navy temporarily conceded defeat and withdrew its battered wolf packs from North Atlantic waters. It was one of the two greatest victories for code breaking during the war—rivaled only by the secret American efforts that produced Magic and that eventually undermined Japan's bid to dominate the Pacific.

The British got their first glimpse of what American code breakers had wrought in February 1941, when a team of four cryptanalysts, two from the U.S. Army and two from the navy, arrived at Bletchley with a gift that rivaled the one offered by the Poles two years earlier. The American visitors were junior officers, but their consignment for the British was top grade—one of the so-called Purple machines that the Americans would use to read messages between Tokyo and Washington as well as those to and from Ambassador Oshima in Berlin. The British had concentrated their code-breaking efforts on cracking Enigma and reading German messages. Now, they could interpret any "Purple" Japanese diplomatic signals they managed to intercept—messages that might contain hints about Japanese designs in Southeast Asia, where British forces were at risk.

Officials at Bletchley Park were of course delighted with this gift and made the Americans welcome. They declined to reciprocate fully, however, by offering an Enigma to the Americans in return. They were simply not prepared to share all they had with allies who had yet to enter the war.

Perhaps Bletchley would have been somewhat freer with information if the visiting delegation had included the officer who headed the team responsible for producing Purple: William Friedman, technical chief of the army's Signal Intelligence Service and one of the world's foremost cryptanalysts. Friedman's absence was no slight on the part of the Americans. Shortly before the delegation left for England, he had suffered a nervous breakdown that his physician attributed "to prolonged overwork on a top-secret project." Indeed, Friedman's team had been laboring tirelessly on Japanese ciphers for the better part of a decade.

Friedman had come to code breaking by a circuitous path. After graduating from Cornell in 1914 with a degree in genetics, he had been hired to develop new strains of wheat at Riverbank, a research center near Chicago owned by the eccentric millionaire George Fabyan. Among Fabyan's pet projects was an attempt to prove that the works of Shakespeare had in fact been written by his contemporary Francis Bacon, who Fabyan thought had left proof of his authorship in the form of enciphered messages in the text. Friedman became involved in the project and eventually concluded that there was nothing to the idea, but his time was not wasted. Through the project he met his future wife—and found his calling as a cryptanalyst. Soon he was publishing papers on the subject that helped transform code breaking from an art into a science.

Before taking charge of the newly formed SIS in 1930, Friedman had worked for the army signal corps as a civilian employee for several years; there he had kept close track of cipher machines, purchasing a commercial Enigma machine for analysis in 1927 for a mere $144. He was not at all surprised when intercepts in the early 1930s indicated that the Japanese had introduced a cipher machine of their own design for diplomatic purposes. SIS dubbed this the Red machine and set out to solve the puzzle it posed. (It was sheer coincidence that the Bletchley Park team later gave the name Red to an Enigma machine key as well.) By then, Friedman had recruited three young mathematicians to cope with such challenges. It was the Depression era, and good jobs were hard to come by. One of the recruits, Frank Rowlett, was so ignorant of cryptanalysis that he thought the position related to crypts or burials, but he took it anyway. Friedman was an avid instructor and soon brought Rowlett and the others up to speed.

MAKING MAGIC

Friedman's team was small compared with the navy's code-breaking unit, Op-20-G. While the army's SIS attacked the ciphers developed for Japanese diplomats, Op-20-G concentrated on the codes and ciphers used by the Japanese navy, the U.S. Navy's great competitor in the Pacific. Language training contributed to the unit's success. Under a program for "language officers," a promising young navy cryptanalyst, Lieutenant Joseph Roche-

The Royal Navy destroyer Bulldog tows a captured U-boat, the U-110 (upper left), back to port in May 1941, shortly after a Bulldog crew boarded the doomed sub, retrieving an Enigma machine and vital related documents.

William Friedman

Master cryptanalyst William Fried-
man, shown above by himself in
a portrait from his later years,
stands at top center in 1935 with
the code breakers he directed at
the U.S. Army's Signal Intelligence
Service. Under Friedman, recruits
like Frank Rowlett (far right)
solved the Japanese cipher machine
called Purple and were hailed
as magicians for producing the
intelligence trove known as Magic.

fort, was sent to Japan for three years to study the language. That particular investment later yielded big dividends when Rochefort headed the navy's superb code-breaking team at Pearl Harbor.

By the mid-1930s, Op-20-G had solved the code then being used by the Japanese fleet. But when Friedman went to the chief of that unit for a briefing, seeking tips that would help his team deal with Red and discover the contents of Japanese diplomatic cables, he was snubbed, leaving him wondering for a time whether the rivalry between the services outweighed America's competition with Japan.

Forced to rely on their own devices, Friedman's team spotted a fatal flaw in the Red machine: It substituted a vowel for a vowel and a consonant for a consonant. Using this as their wedge, members of the group pried into the system and eventually cracked it. As they discovered, the Red machine yielded to general cryptanalytical techniques similar to those Rejewski had applied so successfully in his work for the Polish Cipher Bureau.

By cracking Red, Friedman's unit had achieved parity with Op-20-G, and the two code-breaking outfits began to cooperate—thanks in part to Captain Laurence Safford, a veteran cryptanalyst who returned from duty at sea in 1936 to take charge of Op-20-G. The two chiefs agreed not only to share their secrets but also to divide the labor of solving and translating the many diplomatic messages to and from Tokyo, with Op-20-G handling the duty on odd calendar days and SIS performing it on even ones.

A new challenge arose in early 1939, however, when the Japanese began installing an entirely new cipher machine at their embassies around the world. Friedman's team dubbed the device Purple and shouldered the task of solving its riddles. Meanwhile, Op-20-G worked to break naval codes in use by the Japanese fleet, whose radio operators encoded their messages before enciphering them.

The Japanese were not careful enough, however. They gave the SIS team a huge break by phasing in their new machine and sending the same messages to diplomats using Purple as to those still relying on Red, allowing the cryptanalysts to use Red decrypts to attack Purple. This alone did not permit SIS to reconstruct the new machine, because its operating principles were radically different from Red's. In mid-1939, after puzzling over the data for months, Frank Rowlett invited Leo Rosen, an electrical engineer from MIT, to join the Purple team. Rowlett explained the substitution patterns he and others had detected in the Purple cipher and asked Rosen to come up with a mechanism that could produce those patterns. Rosen concluded that the Japanese had used telephone stepping switches—devices that route calls dialed from one telephone to another without needing switchboard operators.

This was a big step forward for Friedman's team. Still, it took them another year of intense effort to figure out just how those stepping switches were arranged and wired on Purple and construct an analogue. Friedman never spoke of his work at home, but his wife heard him pacing the kitchen floor, night after night and month after month. Finally, in September 1940, he had the pleasure of showing off the results of his team's heroic effort to Captain Safford of Op-20-G in a scene reminiscent of the unveiling of the Polish Enigmas to Allied cryptanalysts the year before.

"My God," said Safford when he saw the army's Purple machine. "Where'd you steal it?"

"We built it ourselves," replied Friedman.

Safford was so impressed that he would later call the army's solution of the Purple machine "the greatest cryptanalytic achievement of all time." The wizards at SIS were soon being referred to as magicians, leading to the term Magic for the intelligence their breakthrough produced.

No amount of Magic could avert conflict with Japan, however. By late November 1941, decrypts of Japanese diplomatic traffic made it abundantly clear to the chiefs of staff in Washington that Japan was preparing to wage war in the very near future. A few of the decrypts hinted that Pearl Harbor might be among the possible targets, including a message from Tokyo to the Japanese consul in Honolulu in late September seeking details on the locations of warships and aircraft carriers there. But Magic provided many other indications that the Japanese were eyeing targets that were closer to their home islands and easier for their forces to reach, including the American-defended Philippines and various British possessions in Southeast Asia.

Little of this Magic was reaching Pearl Harbor itself. As a security measure, the list of those allowed to see the diplomatic decrypts had been pruned over the summer, and the naval commander at Pearl Harbor, Admiral Husband Kimmel, was denied access. Kimmel did have a naval code-

breaking team at hand, headed by Commander Joseph Rochefort. But the diligent Rochefort and his staff were still struggling with Japan's complex naval codes and had little material to work with in the crucial days of early December, when radio operators with the Japanese strike force sent to attack Pearl Harbor remained silent. The only warnings received at Pearl were vague and repetitive advisories from Washington that failed to rouse the commanders and their forces to a state of readiness.

Back in the nation's capital on Sunday morning, December 7, intercepted diplomatic messages provided two belated warnings. Around daybreak, SIS puzzled out the 14th and final section of a long message from

Wreckage litters an American airfield at Pearl Harbor on the fateful morning of December 7, 1941. The surprise Japanese attack, which propelled the U.S. into the war, raised questions in Washington as to why warnings from Magic intercepts that Tokyo was preparing for hostilities seemingly went unheeded in Hawaii.

Joseph Rochefort

Commander Joseph Rochefort headed the naval team at Pearl Harbor that decoded plans of the Japanese fleet in 1942, setting the stage for the American triumph at Midway. Admiral Chester Nimitz nominated Rochefort for the Distinguished Service Medal, but a feud within the Department of the Navy cost him his post. He was not awarded the medal until after his death.

Tokyo to Ambassador Nomura Kichisaburo in Washington spelling out Japan's rejection of American proposals in last-ditch talks between the two powers and concluding that "it is impossible to reach an agreement through further negotiations." Another message instructed him to "please submit to the United States Government (if possible to the Secretary of State) our reply to the United States at 1:00 p.m., on the 7th, your time." To specify the hour at which to sever relations suggested that hostilities might begin then—and 1 p.m. in Washington was around dawn in Hawaii, an ideal time for a surprise attack.

Colonel Rufus Bratton, who was in charge of routing the decrypts, received this one in Washington around nine in the morning, immediately recognized its import, and placed a call to the army chief of staff, General George Marshall, who was out for his morning ride. When Marshall saw the decrypt later in the morning, he ordered that General Walter Short, commanding the army forces at Pearl Harbor, be warned at once. Foul-ups in executing Marshall's order, however, resulted in the warning being sent as a commercial telegram.

By the time the messenger arrived by motorcycle at the military message center in Honolulu, it was already midafternoon, and more than 400 Japanese warplanes from a fleet of six aircraft carriers commanded by Admiral Yamamoto Isoroku had long since rained destruction on Pearl Harbor. The navy's biggest assets—its three aircraft carriers—had left Pearl Harbor recently and escaped harm. But two battleships and two destroyers had gone down and 13 other warships had been badly damaged in an attack of devastating precision that caught hundreds of American aircraft on their runways and claimed the lives of nearly 2,400 servicemen.

REDEMPTION AT MIDWAY

"Forget Pearl Harbor and get on with the war!" Those words from Commander Joseph Rochefort to his navy code breakers at the battered naval base in Honolulu summed up the determination of American intelligence officers to put the lost opportunity behind them and be ready the next time Japan attacked. In truth, however, no one could forget Pearl Harbor. In 1942 the army went a long way toward remedying the situation by expanding and relocating the SIS to its own version of Bletchley Park at Arlington Hall, a few miles from the Pentagon. Several thousand SIS code breakers, interpreters, analysts, and clerks labored there under strict secrecy to extract and exploit every last bit of Magic from Japanese diplomatic and military intercepts.

Messages to and from diplomats would not help the depleted Pacific Fleet track the movements of the potent Japanese navy, however. In the aftermath of Pearl Harbor, that critical task fell to Rochefort and his team of code breakers in Honolulu. They could not be faulted for failing to warn of Yamamoto's well-disguised and brilliantly executed strike. But Rochefort vowed that the man who succeeded Kimmel as commander in chief of the Pacific Fleet, Admiral Chester Nimitz, would never lack for intelligence. As Rochefort later remarked, "I took it as my job, my task, my assignment that I was to tell the Commander-in-Chief today what the Japanese were going to do tomorrow."

Rochefort presided at the start of the war over a staff of some two dozen cryptanalysts, translators, traffic analysts, and radio listeners. They were soon augmented by fresh recruits, including the entire band of the sunken battleship *California,* who escaped with their lives but lost their instruments. Like many musicians, they made good code breakers.

All these men were packed into two air-conditioned basement rooms with steel doors in the 14th Naval District Administration Building at Pearl Harbor, working 84-hour weeks in 12-hour watches, rarely emerging into the tropical sun. "Had I not witnessed it," wrote J. W. Holmes, who served as liaison officer between Rochefort's unit and Nimitz's staff, "I never would have believed that any group of men was capable of such sustained mental effort under such constant pressure for such a length of time." Commander Rochefort, Holmes added, left the basement rarely, to change clothes or bathe: "For weeks the only sleep he got was on a field cot pushed into a crowded corner; always nearly fully dressed, he was ready at a moment's notice to roll out and jump into carpet slippers and an old, red smoking jacket."

Although Rochefort and his staff had IBM tabulating and sorting machines to help them with their calculations, they faced a daunting task, and one fundamentally different from the challenges tackled by the Magic team. Rather than using cipher machines, as the Japanese diplomatic service did, operators for the Japanese navy first encoded the plain text using a book that provided five-digit code numbers for more than 30,000 words, phrases, letters, and numbers: They then enciphered the coded text by subtracting from each code number a five-digit number listed in a cipher table, which contained more than 100,000 such entries. To allow receivers to decipher the message, they indicated the page, column, and line of the cipher table at which the numbers began.

This manual form of encipherment would have been nearly impossible for Rochefort and his team to break had the Japanese changed the table on a monthly basis. But such changes were not easily made by a widely dispersed navy in wartime, and the Japanese ended up using the same table and code book for several months. Over that time, the listeners at Pearl Harbor made so many intercepts that the cryptanalysts came across instances in which operators had used the same sequence of numbers from the cipher table. Those revealing coincidences, and the use of informed guesses as to what some of the five-digit numbers might mean based on traffic analysis, enabled Rochefort and company to reconstruct portions of the cipher table and the code book.

This was slow and painstaking work, unrelieved by the dramatic breakthroughs associated with solving cipher machines. By May 1942, however, Rochefort had the ability to read as much as 25 percent of the text in any given intercept. He and his staff then filled in the gaps, and he was able to brief Nimitz in astonishing detail on Yamamoto's plans.

Rochefort's revelations were as alarming as they were revealing.

"Had we lacked early information of the Japanese movements, and had we been caught with carrier forces dispersed, the Battle of Midway would have ended differently."

—Admiral Chester Nimitz

Yamamoto would stage a diversionary strike on the Aleutian Islands off Alaska to distract American attention from his principal objective. Then he would attack a target identified in Japanese messages by the letters *AF*—probably the American-occupied atoll of Midway, situated 1,300 miles northwest of Hawaii, or close enough to serve as a base for operations against Pearl Harbor. Knowing that Nimitz could not afford to lose Midway, Yamamoto would lie in wait for the Pacific Fleet as it steamed out and would destroy it with a task force that included four aircraft carriers. Even with full knowledge of Yamamoto's plans, Nimitz would face a huge challenge. One of his three carriers, the *Yorktown,* was limping back to Pearl after suffering severe battle damage in the Coral Sea, further limiting his forces. He had to be sure that AF was indeed Midway before he committed what remained.

To confirm the identification, Rochefort cabled the base at Midway to transmit an uncoded radio message that its water purifier had broken down. Almost immediately, a Japanese listener monitoring American communications reported, as hoped, that AF was short of fresh water.

A Japanese heavy cruiser lies shattered and smoldering after being attacked by U.S. warplanes during the Battle of Midway on June 4, 1942. News of the intelligence coup that led to the American victory at Midway leaked to the public three days later when the Chicago Tribune ran an unauthorized front-page article headlined "Navy Had Word of Jap Plan to Strike at Sea."

Reassured, Nimitz deployed his forces. To guard the Aleutians, he sent 13 destroyers and five cruisers. To the base on Midway he sent fighters and bombers, which would make the first attack on the Japanese fleet. Then he ordered the carriers *Enterprise* and *Hornet* to depart their stations in the Coral Sea for Midway, leaving a cruiser behind to imitate their radio signals so that their absence would not be noticed. The battered *Yorktown* faced an estimated 90-day repair period at Pearl Harbor, but a crew of 1,400 welders, fitters, and electricians restored her in 48 hours with a herculean effort and saw her off to Midway on May 31.

Fortunately for Rochefort, the Japanese naval code and cipher table, months overdue for change, remained in place until May 28. By then, his team had come up with the dates for the attacks: June 3 for the Aleutian diversion and June 4 for Midway. Furthermore, the code breakers were able to tell Nimitz the course of Yamamoto's all-important carrier force, enabling him to position his own carriers for an ambush about 175 miles from Midway at 6 a.m. on the 4th.

In the end, it scarcely mattered that the warships sent to block the Aleutian attack were out of position and failed to stop the Japanese from landing a small force there a few days after the diversionary bombing attack occurred as scheduled. The crucial battle took place the following day, off Midway, and even with Yamamoto's plans in hand, Nimitz and his forces found themselves in a desperate struggle. Early on, an entire wave of American torpedo planes was virtually annihilated in a fruitless assault on the Japanese carriers. Warplanes from those carriers later spotted the *Yorktown* and inflicted such a beating on the patched-up ship that she would never fight again. But sheer guts and determination carried the day for the Americans, who renewed their assault with fresh waves of dive bombers. All four Japanese carriers went down—a staggering loss for the Japanese fleet.

This great American victory, coming just six months after the disaster at Pearl Harbor, proved to be the turning point in the Pacific war, ending the threat to Hawaii and giving the United States the time it needed to construct a fleet vastly superior to Yamamoto's, which never recovered from the carnage at Midway. As General Marshall remarked of that contest, it was "the closest squeak and the narrowest victory," and no one who knew what Rochefort's team had accomplished doubted that their work had been the decisive factor. "Had we lacked early information of the Japanese movements, and had we been caught with our carrier forces dispersed," Nimitz told his officers afterward, "the Battle of Midway would have ended differently."

For Yamamoto, code breaking spelled not only defeat but, ultimately, death. On April 18, 1943, American fighter planes on a mission code-named Vengeance, guided by a decrypt spelling out Yamamoto's itinerary, attacked and destroyed a plane carrying the Japanese admiral to a base on the Solomon Islands. That strike marked the demise of a master strategist whose blueprint for victory had overlooked one crucial factor—the phenomenal capacity of code breakers to penetrate and foil the best-laid plans.

A GALLERY OF SPIES ❯

Behind the scenes, a great espionage drama was played out during the war by a diverse cast of characters who took to spying for various reasons. Some of the secret agents profiled on the following pages, including Germany's Richard Sorge (right), were motivated by ideological principles or patriotism; others spied for profit or thrills. All were gifted actors who disguised their true loyalties and crossed international lines at some risk. The American-born entertainer Josephine Baker (page 122), for example, served her adopted country of France by smuggling intelligence on the Germans to Allied agents in Spain. Perhaps the greatest incentive for these spies was the knowledge that they were performing in an exclusive arena where the efforts of a few daring individuals could make a world of difference.

A GALLERY OF SPIES

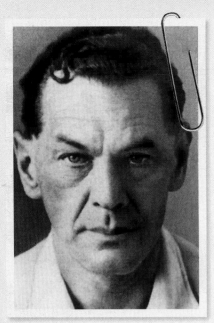

RICHARD SORGE

CODE NAME: **RAMSEY**
SPIED FOR: **SOVIET UNION**
SPIED ON: **JAPAN AND GERMANY**

May 11, 1941, marked the beginning of National Spy Prevention Week in Japan. By encouraging people to report to police all meetings between Japanese citizens and foreigners, officials hoped to uncover an elusive spy ring operating in Tokyo. They also sought to raise awareness with signs proclaiming "Beware of Spies!" and "Spy Prevention—Something Anybody Can Do!"

For Richard Sorge, a 45-year-old reporter in Tokyo for the *Frankfurter Zeitung,* one of Germany's leading newspapers, this clumsy counter-espionage campaign served as a timely warning. He canceled his rendezvous that week with Ozaki Hotsumi, adviser to the Japanese premier. Sorge and Ozaki had long met monthly at some of Tokyo's fanciest restaurants, where Sorge

indulged his passion for Japanese food while taking in the latest disclosures from Ozaki about Japan's war plans and its dealings with its Axis partners in Berlin. Sorge then passed that intelligence along—not to his readers back in Germany, but to his masters in Moscow. Unbeknown to officials in Tokyo and Berlin, Sorge was at the very center of the spy ring that the Japanese were trying to flush out. For years, he had been betraying German and Japanese secrets to the Soviet Union. And Ozaki, who harbored Communist sympathies, was

among his chief accomplices.

By spying for the Soviets, Sorge was returning to his roots. Born in Russia in 1895 to a Russian mother and a German father, he moved to Berlin with his parents as a child and fought for Germany during World War I. Afterward, he enrolled at the University of Hamburg, where he became one of many young radicals who responded to Germany's economic turmoil by embracing Communism at the same time that others turned to fascism. Although Sorge remained a German citizen, he felt deeply

GERMAN CORRESPONDENT RICHARD SORGE
SECRETLY REPORTED TO MOSCOW FROM TOKYO.

attached to the land of his birth and returned there to teach in Moscow, where he caught the eye of Soviet spymasters. In the late 1920s, he obeyed instructions to ward off suspicion by resigning from the Communist Party, a standard practice for foreign Soviet agents. He then left Moscow as an agent for the GRU—Soviet military intelligence.

By 1933 Sorge was working as a German journalist in Japan. It was a perfect screen for espionage, giving him access to diplomats at the German embassy in Tokyo as well as Japanese officials. The Germans assumed that he had renounced his Marxist past, and he reinforced that impression by joining the Nazi Party. But Sorge remained a rebellious and reckless figure. He had a weakness for alcohol and a sharp temper, sometimes arguing violently with Nazi zealots at the embassy. He was also an audacious womanizer who kept a wife in the Soviet Union and a live-in mistress in Japan while carrying on an affair with the wife of his confidant, German ambassador Eugen Ott, who never suspected Sorge of political treachery.

For all his indiscretions, however, Sorge was among the most valuable agents the Soviets ever had. Spy Prevention Week in 1941 may have forced him to postpone meetings with his Japanese contacts, but it did not deter him from filing an urgent report. On May 12, Sorge radioed to Moscow that Germany planned to invade the Soviet Union in late June. Stalin ignored this warning, however, fearing that Sorge's report was part of a conspiracy to undermine the nonaggression pact with Hitler and prod the Soviets into war with Germany.

On June 22, as Sorge had predicted, Germany launched a massive offensive against the Soviet Union. Caught off guard, Stalin hoped to stop German forces short of Moscow by transferring Soviet troops from Siberia, which would weaken his defenses against Japan. He had to know if the Japanese were preparing to join the Germans in attacking the Soviet Union. In August, Sorge confirmed that Japan

had no such plans. Stalin shifted forces from the Far East to the German front, where they helped stem the tide and prevent the fall of Moscow.

By early October, Sorge was signaling that a war between Japan and the United States was inevitable and imminent. By then he was also requesting permission to leave Japan;

he was under severe strain, and Tokyo authorities were cracking down on suspected Communists. So prized were his reports, however, that Moscow denied his requests. On October 15, Ozaki Hotsumi was arrested—and three days later Sorge was hauled in. Subjected to relentless interrogation, he finally confessed to spying and was sentenced to death. The execution was long postponed, however, as the Japanese repeatedly offered to trade Sorge as part of a prisoner exchange. The Soviets bluntly replied: "The man called Richard Sorge is unknown to us."

Richard Sorge was executed by hanging on November 7, 1944, an hour after Ozaki met the same fate. Not until after Stalin's death did the Soviets acknowledge Sorge's crucial contribution to the war effort by honoring him as a hero.

MOSCOW BELATEDLY HONORED SORGE FOR HIS SERVICES BY ACCORDING HIM A COMMEMORATIVE STATUE AND POSTAGE STAMP.

RUDOLF RÖSSLER

CODE NAME: LUCY
SPIED FOR: SOVIET UNION
SPIED ON: GERMANY

Long after Richard Sorge ceased reporting from Tokyo, intelligence officers at GRU headquarters in Moscow continued to receive detailed dispatches on German war plans from covert sources that included a mysterious circle in Switzerland known as the Lucy ring. In some cases, decisions made by the German high command in Berlin were radioed by the Lucy ring to Moscow in less than 24 hours, enabling the Soviets to anticipate enemy moves on the eastern front with a precision that stunned the Germans fighting there.

Just how much the Soviets knew about German plans became chillingly clear to troops of the 24th Panzer Division one night in 1942 as they prepared for what they thought would be a surprise attack, only to hear this greeting trumpeted from loudspeakers in the distance: "Panzergrenadiers of the 24th, we shall not be south of

Voronezh the day after tomorrow as your leaders have assured you. You needn't try to encircle us—we won't be there. Save your bread, your ammunition and your gasoline, for we are going to besiege you. The luckiest will be those who have kept a bullet to blow their own brains out."

Such threats were not always fulfilled, but they left the Germans feeling betrayed and exposed. Not until after the war would they learn that much of the damage was done by one of their own—a German émigré named Rudolf Rössler. His ring may have been code-named Lucy because he operated out of Lucerne, Switzerland, having moved there with his wife in 1933 after Hitler came to power. A determined foe of the Nazis, he started a publishing company in Lucerne and, under the pen name Hermes, wrote articles displaying an uncanny

SWISS OFFICIALS FOUND A TRANSMITTER HIDDEN (*AT X ABOVE*) IN THE CLOSET OF ALEXANDER FOOTE.

knowledge of Hitler's plans well before the war. In 1936, for example, Rössler predicted Germany's occupation of the demilitarized Rhineland zone a month in advance.

Just where Rössler obtained such information would remain a mystery. When a GRU agent asked him early in the war to share his intelligence with Moscow, Rössler agreed on condition that he not reveal his sources. The GRU generally discounted reports from anonymous sources, but they found what Rössler had to offer too good to pass up, providing him with a radio operator, a British Communist named Alexander Foote. Rössler's prodigiously productive spy ring outlived other Red Orchestra operations that radioed German military secrets to Moscow, continuing to provide reports on German plans and troop movements into early 1944.

In May 1944 Swiss officials arrested Rössler and others in his ring, perhaps to protect them from German agents who were after them. (Rössler had earlier obliged the Swiss by advising them on Hitler's intentions in regard to their country.) Rössler and company were soon released, and he died a free man in Switzerland in 1958. The shadowy figures who supplied the material he passed to Moscow may have been prominent Germans opposed to the Nazi regime. True to his stated principles, however, Rössler never named his sources.

AMY THORPE PACK

CODE NAME: **CYNTHIA**
SPIED FOR: **GREAT BRITAIN**
SPIED ON: **VICHY FRANCE, ITALY**

Legendary for using her charms to pry secrets from foreign officials, Amy Thorpe Pack has been likened to Mata Hari. Unlike the ill-fated Mata Hari, however, who flirted with figures on both sides during World War I and accomplished little as a spy before being executed by the French, Pack was a shrewd agent who remained faithful to the Allied cause and served it well.

Born in 1910 to a socially ambitious mother and a U.S. Marine Corps officer, Amy Thorpe—known to acquaintances as Betty—made her debut at 18 in Washington, D.C., and attracted a flock of suitors with her seductive smile, hazel eyes, and auburn hair. At 20, she settled on Arthur Pack, a British diplomat almost twice her age, and after their wedding became a citizen of her husband's country as well as her own.

By 1937 the couple was stationed in Warsaw and their marriage was faltering. Amid rising international tensions, Betty Pack volunteered her services to the head of the Polish branch of MI-6, Britain's overseas spy agency. Poland and Britain were not yet aligned against Germany, and she helped London read Warsaw's diplomatic intentions by seducing several men, including an official at the foreign ministry. "Our meetings were very fruitful," she remarked of one informant. "I let him make love to me as often as he wanted, since this guaranteed the smooth flow of political information I needed."

After separating from her husband in January 1941, Betty Pack returned to the United States, where she was given a new role by spymaster William Stephenson of MI-6, who coordinated British security efforts with the Americans. He assigned her the code name Cynthia and sent her to Washington undercover as a journalist. There she rented a house in Georgetown and hosted parties that included Cabinet members and diplomats.

Her first big assignment was to obtain naval cipher books from the Italian embassy. She accomplished this within weeks by embarking on an affair with a longtime admirer, 60-year-old Admiral Alberto Lais, naval attaché at the embassy. As she later confided in her memoirs, Lais limited his attentions to affectionate caresses but was prepared to do almost anything in exchange for that privilege. At one point he brought her a silver trinket box, which gave her a chance to reveal what she would like even better—the naval ciphers. Pack said that

AMY THORPE PACK, SHOWN AT HER WEDDING AT AGE 20, WAS CONSIDERED A PRIZE CATCH.

the admiral was not willing to hand her the books himself but that he gave her the name of a low-paid embassy secretary, who allowed her to photograph and return the documents for a price. This information was credited with helping the Royal Navy defeat Mussolini's fleet off Cape Matapan in the Mediterranean in late March 1941.

Pack's next challenge was to infiltrate the French embassy in Washington, which represented the pro-German Vichy regime. Once again, she fulfilled her assign-

PACK SEDUCED CHARLES BROUSSE (LEFT)
AND ALBERTO LAIS (RIGHT) IN HER
GEORGETOWN NEST.

ment by seducing an older man. In this case, he was the French press attaché, Charles Brousse, who deceived both his wife and his embassy superiors during the course of their torrid affair. Pack told him that she was a spy, and Brousse, who resented the Nazis, supplied her with cables, letters, files, and other classified material. Brousse balked, however, when Pack asked for the naval cipher books kept at his embassy. He pointed out that he had no access to those ciphers, and the books were locked securely in a safe at night in the office of the naval attaché.

In response, Pack proposed a daring plan. She and Brousse would befriend the embassy's night watchman and tell him they wanted to use the embassy at night for a romantic rendezvous. Then, while supposedly engaged in a tryst, they would let in a safecracker, who would extract the cipher books, to be photographed and returned before dawn. Following two abortive attempts to pull off the heist, Pack

THE OSS CHIEF WANTED A "CERTAIN YOUNG LADY"
NAMED PACK TO ACCOMPANY BROUSSE TO FRANCE.

and Brousse finally succeeded the third time, but not without a scare. Hearing an approaching watchman, the two hastily removed their clothes. When the guard looked in on them during his rounds, he caught Pack's naked profile in the gleam of his flashlight, murmured his apologies, and hurried away.

This escapade helped Allied code breakers keep tabs on Vichy France as American troops prepared to land in North Africa in 1942. Duly impressed, OSS chief William Donovan, who worked closely with Stephenson, arranged for Pack to pose as Brousse's stepdaughter and return to France with him and his unsuspecting wife on an espionage mission. The plan was scrapped, however, when Brousse's wife found the two in bed together and refused to go along with the charade.

That was not the end of the affair, however. Around the time that Pack's husband died in 1945, the Brousses divorced. With the war years behind them, Betty and Charles got married and settled down in a castle in France, where they remained until her death in 1963.

OFFICE OF STRATEGIC SERVICES
WASHINGTON, D. C.

December 22, 1942

SECRET

Mr. Frederick B. Lyon
Executive Assistant to Assistant Secretary Berle
State Department
Washington, D. C.

Dear Mr. Lyon:

At my request, I understand that Mr. Kimbel has discussed with you a matter concerning a certain young lady to be permitted to go to Hershey and later to proceed with the French to France in the diplomatic exchange. I should greatly appreciate your making it possible for this to be accomplished.

Sincerely,

William J. Donovan
Director

JOHN CAIRNCROSS

CODE NAME: **CARELIAN**
SPIED FOR: **SOVIET UNION**
SPIED ON: **GREAT BRITAIN**

Few young Britons had wider access to state secrets during the war than John Cairncross. A rising star in the foreign office when the conflict began, the 26-year-old Cairncross served as secretary to Lord Maurice Hankey, the cabinet minister overseeing Britain's intelligence services, and went on to handle Ultra decrypts at Bletchley Park and work for MI-6. His British superiors admired his work, but no one was prouder of his performance than his Soviet handlers, who had recruited the promising Cambridge University scholar around 1937 to spy for the NKVD, the Soviet state security agency that vied with the GRU and reported directly to Joseph Stalin.

In later years, when his espionage activities for Moscow were exposed, Cairncross was labeled the "fifth man" of the notorious Cambridge spy ring, agents recruited as prospects in the 1930s at Cambridge University who went on to burrow deep into Britain's intelligence establishment. Cairncross admitted to spying, but he denied that he was part of any ring. Of the five Cambridge spies, he was clearly the odd man out. The other four—Harold "Kim" Philby, Guy Burgess, Donald Maclean, and Anthony Blunt— were all privileged members of British society who embraced Communism. Cairncross, by contrast, was a Scottish ironmonger's son who attended Cambridge on a scholarship; he claimed he was never a committed Communist and that he passed intelligence to the Soviets only during the war to help them defeat Hitler. After an investigation in the 1960s, officials concluded that he had done little harm to the nation's interests and should not be prosecuted.

Shortly before Cairncross died in 1995, however, revelations began emerging from the KGB—the successor to the NKVD—that contradicted his claims. Not only had he started spying for the Soviets when Stalin and Hitler were still allies, but he also continued to provide Moscow with secret reports until 1951, well into the Cold War.

Furthermore, the harm done by his wartime espionage was not limited to Germany. While working at Bletchley Park, he indeed passed along Ultra decrypts that helped the Soviets defeat German forces in such crucial contests as the Battle of Kursk in 1943, something Cairncross proudly admitted. What he failed to acknowledge, however, was that he also divulged to Moscow secret British research that spurred the development in the United States of the first atomic bomb in 1945, a feat that the Soviets soon duplicated thanks to hefty contributions from several spies like Cairncross. As early as 1941, reported a top NKVD man, Cairncross was providing Moscow with "valuable and absolutely secret documents" on nuclear science in Britain. In the end, such disclosures did nothing to hasten the defeat of Germany and much to undermine the security of Great Britain and its allies in the Cold War that followed.

THE GROUNDS OF CAMBRIDGE UNIVERSITY HARBORED JOHN CAIRNCROSS AND OTHER SOVIET RECRUITS IN THE 1930s.

DONALD KENNEDY

SPIED FOR: **AUSTRALIA**
SPIED ON: **JAPAN**

As Japanese forces swept across the Pacific in December 1941, Donald Kennedy of Australia found himself in the path of the storm. Posted to the British-controlled Solomon Islands, which served as a buffer between the advancing Japanese and Australia's northeast coast, Kennedy was assigned to monitor enemy movements as part of a diverse corps of scouts called the coast watchers, organized by the Australian navy.

Manning some 100 outposts in a 2,500-mile arc embracing the Solomons and other islands, the coast watchers consisted largely of resident Australians, bolstered by officers like Kennedy—a captain in the navy—and sometimes aided by native islanders. Their chief task was to spy on Japanese forces at sea, on land, and in the air and

report by radio. But coast watchers also fought as commandos and rescued stranded Allied servicemen—among them a future American president, Lieutenant John F. Kennedy, and the crew of his *PT-109.*

Donald Kennedy began operations by roaming the Solomons in his sloop, the *Waiai,* and making contact with Australians and others in the area who might aid the Allies. Japanese forces soon descended from the north, and Kennedy and his fellow coast watchers filed reports on the invasion by radio—at the risk of being shot as spies if they were caught. After enemy fire sank the *Waiai,* Kennedy established a base for his operation at Segi, a remote harbor on the southern tip of New Georgia *(map, opposite).* There he set up headquarters in an abandoned plantation house, concealed by palms, vines, and camouflage nets.

The intelligence provided by Kennedy and other coast watchers

proved vital in 1942 when American forces landed on the island of Guadalcanal and began a long, grueling campaign to drive the invaders out of the Solomons and back toward Japan. Coast watchers radioed warnings of Japanese bomber squadrons bound for Guadalcanal directly to American commanders there, giving them time to call in fighter planes from nearby aircraft carriers to meet the threat. "The coastwatchers saved Guadalcanal," declared Admiral William F. Halsey Jr. afterward, "and Guadalcanal saved the Pacific."

Upon securing Guadalcanal, Americans moved up the island chain in early 1943 toward Kennedy's base on New Georgia. By then, he had mustered a force of some 70 native islanders, who had orders to kill any Japanese who trespassed on their sanctuary. The Japanese were unable to penetrate Kennedy's stronghold, and he became one of the most wanted and

KENNEDY *(CENTER)* WELCOMES AMERICANS TO HIS PLANTATION HEADQUARTERS WITH TEA.

SOLOMON ISLANDERS RECRUITED BY KENNEDY JOIN AMERICAN FORCES IN PATROLLING THE WATERS OFF NEW GEORGIA IN CANOES.

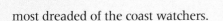

KENNEDY'S FIRST RECONNAISSANCE VESSEL, THE *WAIAI*, FELL PREY TO JAPAN.

most dreaded of the coast watchers.

After the Americans reached New Georgia, Kennedy turned over his base at Segi to the Marines and moved his outfit to nearby Vangunu Island. While continuing to spy on Japanese movements, he became increasingly involved in rescue and commando operations, making use of six vessels, most of them captured from the Japanese. One was a 10-ton schooner, the *Dundavata,* which Kennedy armed with three machine guns scavenged from wrecked American and Japanese planes and once used to ram and sink a Japanese whaleboat carrying combat troops. During the war, Kennedy was responsible for rescuing 28 downed American fliers, earning the Distinguished Service Cross from the U.S. A fellow officer hailed him aptly as "the undefeated, undefeatable man of Segi."

ELYESA BAZNA

CODE NAME: CICERO
SPIED FOR: GERMANY
SPIED ON: GREAT BRITAIN

For six months, from October 1943 to April 1944, rival spymasters in Europe puzzled over the identity and motives of a cunning agent the Germans called Cicero. The British knew from intercepts that an unidentified spy by that name was passing classified information to the Germans in Ankara, Turkey, and suspected that he was working out of the British embassy there. The Germans, for their part, knew who Cicero was but wondered what he was up to. Was he one of the best sources of stolen intelligence to come their way—or a double agent, feeding them misinformation?

The man who caused such consternation was Albanian-born Elyesa Bazna, employed as valet to the British ambassador to Turkey, Sir Hughe Knatchbull-Hugessen. It was a measure of Bazna's cunning that he ever obtained such a position. A petty criminal as a youth,

he had charmed his way into household service at one embassy after another in Ankara. He was about age 40 when he landed the job with the British that brought Bazna—whose only motive was greed—his big payoff.

Lax security made his task almost easy. The British ambassador preferred working at his residence rather than at the embassy and kept top-secret papers locked in a black box on the table next to his bed. One morning, he left his keys in the bedroom while taking his bath. Bazna, who had been awaiting such an opportunity, made a

wax impression of the keys. Thereafter, when the ambassador was occupied elsewhere with such matters as his regular afternoon sessions at the piano, Bazna would unlock the box, retreat

with the contents to his small room below the stairs, and photograph the documents under a bright light before returning them to their place.

After Bazna had photographed 52 documents, he approached the German embassy in Ankara and offered to sell the film for £20,000. (Although willing to betray the British, he retained faith in their currency.) "I was intoxicated at the thought of such a large sum of money," he later wrote. "It did not for a moment enter my head that the Germans would refuse."

Once the Germans had exam-

SIR HUGHE KNATCHBULL-HUGESSEN NEVER SUSPECTED HIS VALET WAS A SPY.

ined Bazna's film, they not only accepted his terms but also promised to pay well for further deliveries. One document he provided revealed Allied plans to press Turkey, then a neutral nation, to allow its territory to be used for military operations against Germany. Those plans were thwarted by Franz von Papen, the German ambassador to Turkey, who knew from Cicero's disclosure just what the Allies intended. Another document contained a list of British agents in Turkey. German doubts about Bazna's reliability subsided as he continued to furnish riveting material.

Bazna's contact at the German embassy was Ludwig Moyzisch, a dedicated Nazi from Austria who worked for the party's foreign espionage branch. "We always met in his car, an Opel Admiral," Bazna recalled of his meetings with Moyzisch. "He drove slowly down a prearranged street until he caught sight of me. I would get in quickly, and we would disappear among the winding suburban streets." When Moyzisch felt sure nobody was following them, he would hand Bazna his payment in exchange for the film.

Bazna hid the payments, delivered in British bank notes, under the carpet in his room, explaining later that he "enjoyed the sensation of treading on it." As his illicit earnings increased, he went on a spending spree, renting a hilltop house outside Ankara and furnishing it with lush carpets and other items no honest valet could have afforded. Above the door, he penciled the words "Villa Cicero"—an indiscreet reference to his German code name. To this hilltop "oasis," as he called it, he brought his local mistress, Mara, employed as a nanny for a British

AFTER THE WAR, BAZNA SHOWED THE PRESS HOW HE SECRETLY PHOTOGRAPHED DOCUMENTS.

COUNTERFEIT BANK NOTES OF THE SAME TYPE AS THIS ONE WERE BAZNA'S PAYMENT FROM THE GERMANS.

diplomat. She knew of Cicero's espionage but thought at first he was working for Turkey.

Bazna might have betrayed himself through such recklessness had he not quit spying when Moyzisch's secretary defected to the Allies. Fearing exposure, Bazna fled Ankara with some £200,000, confident that he was

set for life. Much to his chagrin, however, the bulk of the bank notes he received from Moyzisch turned out to be fake, produced by forgers in a German concentration camp who were compelled to work for the Nazis. Bazna was eventually arrested and served time in prison—not for spying but for dealing in counterfeit notes.

JOSEPHINE BAKER

SPIED FOR: **FRANCE**
SPIED ON: **GERMANY**

In the fall of 1939, Jacques Abtey, an intelligence officer for France's Deuxième Bureau, approached the famous black singer and dancer Josephine Baker—who had relinquished American for French citizenship two years earlier—and asked her if she was willing to risk her life for her adopted country. Abtey knew that Baker was in a good position to gather and convey secrets. But he worried that she might lack the nerve or even turn out to be another Mata Hari and betray France. A few words from Baker dispelled Abtey's doubts. "France made me what I am," she told him. "The Parisians gave me their hearts, and I am ready to give them my life."

Thus Baker became an unpaid spy. Using her embassy connections, she attended as many diplomatic parties as she could and trolled for information that might interest Abtey, who became her lover. When the Germans seized Paris in June 1940, she found herself subject to racial persecution by the Nazis and fled south to Toulouse in unoccupied Vichy France. There she met up with Abtey and plotted with him and members of the resistance to smuggle intelligence on German occupation forces out of France.

On November 23, 1940, Baker and Abtey, who was disguised as her ballet master, boarded a train for Spain. Their secret information had been copied onto Baker's sheet music in invisible ink; photographs were hidden under Baker's clothing. Neither the Spanish policemen nor the German agents at the border suspected Baker was a spy. They let her—and the drab little man carrying her suitcase—cross unimpeded into Spain. From there the two passed into Portugal, where Baker handed her concealed trove to the British.

Baker spent most of the rest of the war in North Africa, enter-taining Allied troops and occasionally carrying information for the resistance from Morocco to Lisbon. Baker died in France in 1975, having been honored by her adopted country with both the croix de guerre and the Medal of Resistance.

SENSATIONAL ON STAGE, BAKER SERVED FRENCH INTELLIGENCE BEHIND THE SCENES.

NEAR THE WAR'S END, BAKER WORKED OPENLY WITH THE FREE FRENCH.

RAOUL WALLENBERG

SPIED FOR: UNITED STATES
SPIED ON: GERMANY, HUNGARY

Sweden's Raoul Wallenberg won renown after the war for saving tens of thousands of Hungarian Jews from the Nazis. Not until 1996, however, was it revealed that Wallenberg also spied against the Germans and their Hungarian allies for the OSS.

A prominent businessman in his early 30s, Wallenberg was assigned to the Swedish legation in Budapest, Hungary, in July 1944 after a secret deal between the United States and neutral Sweden. The Americans had agreed to ease up on demands that Sweden stop trading with Germany in exchange for the appointment of Wallenberg, a fervent anti-Nazi. Wallenberg's mission was twofold—to do all in his power publicly to rescue Jews and to serve covertly as a link between the OSS and the Hungarians resisting the Germans.

When Wallenberg arrived in Budapest, thousands of Hungarian Jews were being deported daily in boxcars to death camps. But the Nazis had agreed not to harm anyone carrying a certificate of protection from a neutral country. Wallenberg had the Swedish legation print thousands of such certificates and handed out stacks of these "Wallenberg passports" at train stations and other sites where Jews awaited deportation. Then he talked or bribed Nazi officials into releasing those carrying the certificates into his custody and moved the Jews into safe houses, buildings he claimed as neutral ground by flying the Swedish flag. In December 1944, when Soviet troops reached Budapest, they found 97,000 Jews still alive—many of them saved by Wallenberg.

All the while, Wallenberg had been meeting with Hungarian resistance leaders and communicating in code with the OSS. None of this covert activity was directed against the Soviet Union. But whether or not his OSS work was known to the Soviets—the matter remains a mystery—Wallenberg became a target of suspicion. He was last seen in Budapest on January 17, 1945, riding in a car with a Soviet officer. By month's end, it is now known, he was being held as a spy in Moscow's notorious Lubyanka prison. The Soviets later claimed he died in prison in 1947 of a heart attack, although he was reportedly seen alive long after that date. In 1989 Soviet officials returned some of Wallenberg's belongings to his family. They termed his arrest and imprisonment a "tragic mistake."

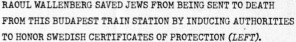

RAOUL WALLENBERG SAVED JEWS FROM BEING SENT TO DEATH FROM THIS BUDAPEST TRAIN STATION BY INDUCING AUTHORITIES TO HONOR SWEDISH CERTIFICATES OF PROTECTION (*LEFT*).

SUPPORTING
THE RESISTANCE

ew places in Europe seemed farther from the turmoil of World War II than the Shetland Islands, mere specks in the gray vastness of the North Sea. Located about a third of the way between Scotland and Norway, they were rocky and bog strewn, with wandering flocks of sheep and a thin population of farmers and fishermen—descendants of Viking warriors who had sailed from Scandinavia in longships more than a thousand years earlier and used the Shetlands as bases from which to raid distant ports. Since the days of the Vikings, little besides the fierce storms of winter had disturbed the tranquillity of these remote British islands. But in 1941, they once again became a staging ground for daring voyages—expeditions that crossed the North Sea in fair weather and foul, funneling weapons and agents to Norwegian resistance forces, who were battling the German troops that had occupied their country the year before.

Organizing this risky operation, which became known as the Shetland Bus, were Major L. H. Mitchell and Sublieutenant David Howarth from the SOE (Special Operations Executive), a covert British agency organized in 1940 and instructed by Prime Minister Winston Churchill to carry out sabotage and subversion in German-occupied territories and "set Europe ablaze." In fulfilling that explosive mandate, SOE sought volunteers from the occupied countries who were prepared to risk their lives to help liberate their homelands. Mitchell and Howarth found ready recruits among those who had fled Norway by fishing boat after the Germans seized their country. By the summer of 1941, the Shetland Bus had a fleet of six sturdy fishing boats and some 45 stalwart Norwegian seamen ready to begin shuttling supplies to resistance fighters in their homeland as soon as fall approached and the nights grew long enough to provide sufficient cover.

Their goal was to penetrate under darkness the fishing zone that extended out 50 miles from the Norwegian mainland to a line guarded by German aircraft and patrol boats; once inside that line, they

In October 1944 a German firing squad trains its rifles on Georges Blind, a member of a French resistance group, in an effort to make him talk. With a mocking smile, Blind called his interrogators' bluff—and survived. Months later, however, he vanished from a concentration camp and almost certainly died. Capture, torture, and death were constant risks for those who resisted German rule.

would be hard to distinguish from legitimate Norwegian craft, pursuing catches in the authorized zone. Even more dangerous than those German patrols were the squalls that grew more frequent as the year progressed and the nights grew longer. "The winter seas north of Shetland are some of the roughest in the world," wrote David Howarth. "This made the enterprise unique: nobody in history had ever deliberately made such long voyages in such small boats and on such stormy seas. Even the Vikings sailed in summer."

On August 30, 1941, just as the stormy season began, a fishing boat named the *Aksel* made the fleet's first run, setting out from the obscure Shetland harbor of Lunna under the command of a young Norwegian named August Naeroy. His mission was to land an SOE agent on the coast just north of the city of Bergen. The agent would then make contact with Norwegian army officers who were organizing an underground sabotage cell, provide them with funds, and arrange for the delivery of eight tons of explosives and weapons to the saboteurs by the same route at a future date.

The *Aksel* bore a false registration number, but she was otherwise authentic—a classic wood-hulled Norwegian fishing boat built for stability rather than speed, 65 feet long with a wide hold and a dependable single-cylinder engine that generated a mere hundred horsepower and emitted what Howarth described as a "loud and solemn tonk-tonk-tonk from its exhaust pipe." Naeroy, too, was the real thing, a Norwegian fisherman intimately familiar with the coastal waters of his homeland. "It was an emotional moment for all of us," recalled Howarth, "when *Aksel* tonk-tonked out of Lunna in the dark."

Naeroy was expected back within four days, and Howarth and Mitchell grew alarmed when he failed to turn up on schedule. Fearing that the crew had come to grief, they sent out search planes. Finally, on the morning of September 5, the *Aksel* came *tonk-tonking* into her Shetland base. To the puzzlement of those watching from shore, she was decorated with heather and birch boughs—a decidedly festive look. Skipper Naeroy soon dispelled the mystery. The *Aksel*, he reported, had been delayed by bad weather crossing the North Sea but had entered the fishing zone undetected and landed the agent with no trouble. At that point, Naeroy and his five-man crew decided to celebrate their success to date. They linked up with local girls, went to a dance, and later invited their companions aboard the *Aksel* for a visit. An attack of conscience finally sent them on their way. At no time had the Germans bothered them.

Except for the brush with bad weather, this rollicking start offered little hint of the trials that lay ahead for the Norwegians. As winter approached, they were lashed at sea by gale winds and mountainous waves. Meanwhile, the Germans grew more alert to the possibility of trespass and tightened their watch over the coastal waters. The secret fleet began to sustain heavy losses. In December, the *Aksel*, then under a new skipper and on the way back from landing an agent in the far north of Norway, radioed for help. A plane dispatched to find her spotted the boat sinking and her men huddled in a dinghy nearby, but a destroyer sent to their rescue found nothing by the time it arrived. The *Aksel* had most likely been attacked by a German patrol plane,

At right, a Norwegian fishing vessel carrying three agents of the Special Operations Executive leaves Britain's Shetland Islands (map, inset) on a mission to support resistance fighters in occupied Norway. Braving North Sea winters and German patrols, the boats of the Shetland Bus ferried agents and matériel to and from rendezvous points along hundreds of miles of the Norwegian coast.

" 'To take the Shetland bus' became a synonym in Norway for escape when danger was overwhelming."

—David Howarth, British officer, Shetland Bus operation

and the dinghy may have overturned in heavy seas, drowning the crew. Nor were they the only victims. By January, three of the six fishing boats had disappeared; 24 men had been lost at sea.

Yet the Bus kept running. New recruits from among the ranks of Norwegian refugees more than made up for the losses. In time, the strategy of delivering supplies in native fishing craft ceased to be effective against the wary Germans patrolling the 50-mile limit, and the boats were replaced by larger, faster subchasers donated by the American navy. Over the course of the war, the intrepid Norwegians completed 207 round trips between the Shetland Islands and their homeland. In the process, they landed 219 agents and supplied the Norwegian resistance with 314 tons of weapons, explosives, and communications gear.

In large part because of this operation, the Norwegian resistance movement flourished, helping to ensure that a garrison of nearly 300,000 German soldiers was tied up on Norwegian soil and unavailable for action against Allied forces elsewhere. The Shetland Bus brought resistance fighters in Norway not just weapons and explosives but also the morale-boosting assurance that they were not alone in their struggle. "Everyone

The small figure of an observer at upper left
reveals the huge scale of two wrecked locomotives
sabotaged by one of the French resistance guerrilla
bands known as the maquis. In the inset at right,
a maquis leader shows several fighters a British
Sten gun, typical of the weapons airdropped by
the Allies to support resistance groups.

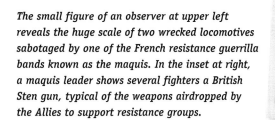

in Norway knew that the route to and from Shetland was always kept open," wrote Howarth, "and this knowledge helped to maintain their hope of ultimate freedom and their wish to fight for it."

FANNING THE FIRES OF REBELLION

At the end of 1940, the year both the SOE and its Shetland Bus operation were established, conventional fighting was over for most of Europe for years to come. From the Arctic Circle to the Mediterranean, from the cliffs of Normandy to the spires of Warsaw, the swastika waved triumphant. Northern France was in Nazi hands, while in southern France the Vichy regime retained its authority only by collaborating with the Germans. Some countries—among them Sweden, Switzerland, Spain, and Portugal—had avoided subjugation by remaining neutral. Others such as Hungary and Rumania had joined the Axis. Still others, including Yugoslavia and Greece, would soon be conquered by the Axis. By late 1941, as German forces on the eastern front approached Moscow, all of continental Europe from the Steppes of Russia to the Atlantic Ocean was either directly under Hitler's boot or rendered harmless to him by neutrality. With breathtaking speed, the Nazi dictator had forged what came to be known as Festung Europa: Fortress Europe. His armies manned the battlements; his aircraft patrolled the skies; his Gestapo agents prowled the streets, watching for signs of rebellion.

Yet despite this massive and intimidating enemy presence, the fires of resistance flickered in homes and workplaces all across occupied Europe. Many acts of defiance were impulsive and individualistic—tearing down the despised swastika, refusing to eat in a café when Germans were on the premises, scrawling defiant graffiti after dark. Other forms of resistance involved collective effort but did not necessarily require outside support. On their own initiative, opponents of German rule banded together to publish underground newspapers or to provide hiding places for Jews and for others at risk.

Resistance fighters intent on waging war against the occupying forces, however, needed assistance of the sort provided by the SOE. Would-be saboteurs required fuses and explosives as well as personal instruction in their use. Guerrilla bands, too, needed weapons and training. Resistance leaders had to have radios and contacts with outside operators in order to arrange for deliveries of supplies, identify important targets, and coordinate their operations with the overall war effort.

Such external support, begun by the British through the SOE and reinforced by the Americans through the OSS (Office of Strategic Services), came by many routes. Mediterranean sardine boats played the same daring role as the Norwegian boats of the Shetland Bus by ferrying guns and SOE agents to France from British-controlled Gibraltar. Many more deliveries went by air. In a pioneering flight before dawn on June 13, 1941, a British Whitley bomber followed lights to a drop zone on the grounds of a château near Limoges, France, then parachuted containers crammed with submachine guns, fighting knives, mines, fuses, and other deadly gear. By war's end, about a hundred thousand such containers would be dropped into France.

Agents parachuted in as well—some 700 of them arrived by this means in France alone. Others came in planes that actually set down in German-controlled territory. The SOE's favorite delivery vehicle was the Lysander, a slow, small, single-engine aircraft that needed only about 400 yards of grassy field as its runway. Flown by a specialized RAF unit, Lysanders aiding the resistance soon came to be called the Moon Squadron for their secret nighttime landings in enemy territory.

The agents themselves included not only British and American volunteers but also one-time refugees now returning to aid their occupied homelands. They were trained in such skills as parachute jumping, combat arts, sabotage, lock picking, coding and radio operations, and escape. The SOE or OSS provided agents with suitable civilian clothes, false papers, and the passwords and instructions they needed to link up with resistance groups. Agents were also offered the option of carrying cyanide capsules, to be taken if they fell into enemy hands and concluded that death was preferable to torture and the risk of betraying their colleagues.

The poison was a grim but realistic measure, for agents and resistance workers lived under the constant threat of exposure. The Gestapo and other German security forces were horribly skillful at persuading prisoners to surrender the names of confederates, addresses of safe houses, passwords, and other information that could be used to shut down a network or perhaps penetrate and take control of it.

A LINE FOR LIFE

While operations like the Shetland Bus and the Moon Squadron ferried supplies and agents into occupied Europe, so-called escape lines smuggled fugitives back out. These lines, which sprang up early in the war, were often strung out over hundreds of miles, encompassing scores of workers, all for the sole purpose of helping their "passengers" to escape. For Allied servicemen stranded in occupied territory and civilians seeking to evade Nazi authorities, they were a lifeline.

Escape lines began springing up early in the war to rescue soldiers left behind in 1940 when the British hastily evacuated their forces from Dunkirk. They grew busier as Allied bombing campaigns intensified; numerous planes were shot down, which left thousands of surviving airmen stranded behind enemy lines. Retriev-

Tuning in Hope

On June 18, 1940, as Germany overran France, General Charles de Gaulle (above) addressed French citizens over BBC radio, proclaiming, "Whatever happens, the flame of French resistance must not and shall not die." Well aware of the power of such words, Nazi occupiers sought to keep them from being heard. Throughout occupied Europe, home radios were confiscated. Possession was punishable by imprisonment and fines.

Despite the risk, many civilians anxious for war news built their own radios, often disguising them as household items like the iron and the varnish can shown here, which open to reveal small receivers. Those in the resistance also listened to the BBC for code phrases, some of which, for example, confirmed a weapons drop or announced an agent's return.

ing them not only salvaged an important fighting asset but also boosted the morale of aircrews who had to face German air defenses in the future. Many lines were aided by MI-9, a fledgling branch of British military intelligence established to support and organize escape routes *(pages 136-137)*. But for the most part, the lines were staffed by local men and women, at the ever present risk of betrayal, arrest, and the likely sequels of torture and death.

The first job of those who manned escape lines was to find wandering servicemen and other fugitives before the Germans did, then to supply them with civilian clothes and papers. Guides next led them step by step to freedom by whatever means offered—on foot or by railroad, automobile, or even bicycle, with stops along the way at safe houses. The end of the line might be an isolated border crossing into Spain, Switzerland, or another neutral country or a spot on the coast where they could be picked up by boat.

For security, most escape lines used a system of so-called cutouts along their entire length. One guide would leave his or her passengers at a designated rendezvous; the next guide would arrive later to continue the trek. In theory, none of the guides knew each other, eliminating the risk of betrayal if one was captured. Yet no escape line could function without at least a few leaders and go-betweens with extensive knowledge of the operation, and they could do terrible damage if they divulged their secrets to the enemy. The very size of the larger escape lines was against them; those who participated knew that their own capture might be simply a matter of time.

Such was the case with the O'Leary Line. One of the first and most efficient of the escape lines, it was the invention of a Scottish officer named Ian Garrow, who had been stranded in France after the evacuation of Dunkirk. Despite his imperfect French, Garrow asked for help from local resistance workers. Together, they devised a network for picking up other soldiers and airmen and conveying them out of occupied France, across the Vichy-run south, over the Pyrenees, and through Spanish territory to the safety of the British consulate in Barcelona. But in planning how others could get away, Garrow had given up his own hope of going home. He remained in France to run the line and was caught and imprisoned by the Vichy police in 1941. Garrow's escape line got the name O'Leary after his role was assumed by a Belgian-born SOE agent, Albert-Marie Guérisse, who took the nom de guerre of Patrick Albert O'Leary. Under O'Leary's direction, the number of workers on the line grew—perhaps dangerously—to more than 250.

A considerable portion of those volunteers met an ugly fate in late 1941 when one of the O'Leary Line's couriers, a man named Harold Cole, took money intended for another escape worker, then cast his lot with the Gestapo. After he gave them every name and address he knew, some 50 members of the O'Leary Line—although not the elusive O'Leary—were rounded up and executed. Cole had told his fellow escape workers that he was a British army captain who had been trapped in France after Dunkirk. In reality, he was a sergeant who had deserted before the evacuation (making off with funds from the sergeant's mess), and he had a long criminal record for housebreaking and fraud back home.

Despite Cole's damage to the line, it was later rebuilt, and it went on to additional triumphs. When O'Leary discovered that Ian Garrow was about to be shipped from a concentration camp in France to the notorious camp at Dachau, he managed to smuggle a guard's uniform to Garrow in camp and the prisoner walked out scot-free. Garrow then became a passenger on the line that he had helped to found, and he slipped safely out of France. Meanwhile, the O'Leary Line continued to escort hundreds of soldiers and airmen to Spain—only to suffer still another devastating roundup in 1943 that decimated its ranks. This time O'Leary himself was arrested, beaten, and tortured by the Gestapo and sent to the Dachau concentration camp. He managed to survive, but many others who fell captive as he did paid with their lives.

A COMET IN THE NIGHT

While the O'Leary Line got significant help from Britain's MI-9, including an MI-9 radio operator ferried in by the Moon Squadron, the most successful escape line of all was a stubbornly independent affair that came to be known as the Comet Line for the speed with which it smuggled fugitives to freedom. The line was the brainchild of a Belgian woman in her mid-20s named Andrée de Jongh, known to her friends as Dédée. She completed her first run in August 1941 when she turned up unannounced at the British consulate in Bilbao, Spain, with three passengers in tow—a British soldier and two young Belgians who wanted to fight for the Allies. She informed the consul that she had escorted her passengers all the way from Brussels to the base of the Pyrenees in southern France, where she had induced a Basque smuggler to guide them over that rugged mountain barrier into Spain.

The British consul listened in amazement as this petite woman promised to return with more passengers a few weeks hence. Next time, she said, she would bring only British soldiers and airmen. All she wanted from the British was money for food, railroad tickets, and the frontier guides—and she promised to repay those sums after the war was won.

True to her word, Dédée showed up in Bilbao two months later with more passengers. By then, MI-9 had checked into her background and interviewed the men she had helped escape. Hearing nothing but praise for her resourcefulness and courage, the British were ready to join forces with her, but Dédée insisted on running the line as a purely Belgian operation. Money would be gratefully accepted, but any further assistance was politely rebuffed; in Dédée's view, radio contact with Britain was not worth the risk.

The Comet Line was very much a family concern. Dédée had help from her mother, her sister, and her aunt, but her chief collaborator was her schoolmaster father, Frédéric de Jongh. Although Dédée accompanied the first passengers to Spain herself, no escape line could function securely or efficiently with just one guide. By the summer of 1941, Dédée was already

Albert-Marie Guérisse

British agent Albert-Marie Guérisse, a native Belgian known in the resistance as Patrick O'Leary, coldly eyes a Marseille street photographer in 1941. At the time, O'Leary had just become head of a major escape line for airmen and other fugitives after the sudden arrest of its founder— and his friend—Ian Garrow.

under suspicion by German authorities. While she was away in Spain, Gestapo agents visited her home and inquired as to her whereabouts. Her father, who was not yet a target of investigation, pretended that young Dédée had run off impulsively and that he had lost touch with her.

Warned of the Gestapo's inquiry, Dédée confined herself to guiding escapees from France to Spain. Meanwhile, her father organized a relay of guides from Brussels to Paris and set up safe houses in that city, moving there himself in early 1942 under an assumed identity to elude Gestapo agents who were closing in on the operation in Brussels. The men Frédéric de Jongh had left in charge there were soon arrested, as was Dédée's sister. But as happened time and again when resistance leaders were seized, others stepped forward to replace them.

At the southern end of the line, near the Spanish border, Dédée found an indispensable ally in a fellow Belgian, Elvire de Greef, known as Tante Go (Aunt Go), for her dog Gogo. Tante Go made arrangements for hiding,

In an act of bravado, three downed American pilots escorted by a guide from a French escape line stroll among unsuspecting German soldiers on leave in Paris in spring 1943. A Pathé News cameraman who belonged to the same line captured the scene on film.

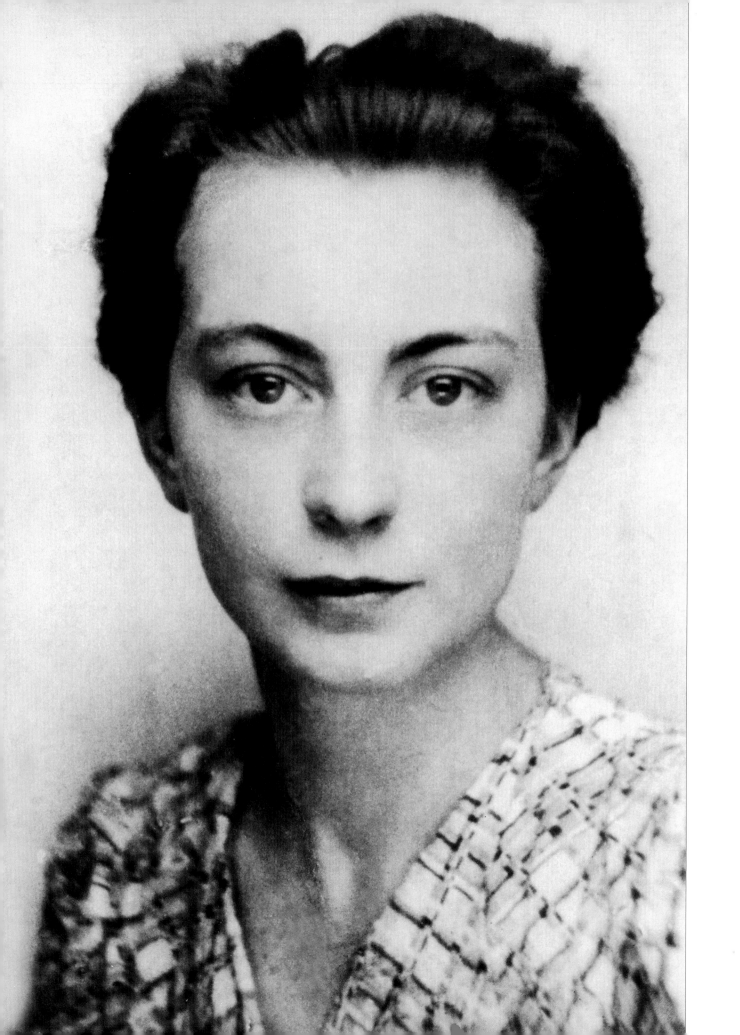

feeding, and equipping the line's passengers when they reached the frontier area. Like Dédée, she enlisted the help of family members. Her husband worked for the Germans as an interpreter and obtained official stamps and blank documents that were used to manufacture false papers for the passengers, in case they were stopped and interrogated en route. Her son served as a courier for the line, and her daughter conducted fugitives arriving at the local train station to safe houses. Tante Go seemed to know every smuggler in the area. Some dealt with German officers and provided her with incriminating information about them that she could use against them if they threatened her. Others agreed to guide the fugitives over the mountains to Spain.

The leading guide was a big, hard-drinking Basque named Florentino Goicoechea, who spoke neither French nor English but possessed an encyclopedic knowledge of the terrain. If a passenger was too weak to ford a rushing river, Florentino could carry the man across on his shoulders. And almost every time he led escapees along the steep, twisting pathways through the Pyrenees to the town of San Sebastián on the other side, Dédée went with him.

A young RAF pilot named John Hoskins, who rode the Comet Line across the border with some other downed airmen in 1942, later described what it was like. "We crossed the frontier between two blockhouses and could hear the Spanish frontier guards having a party," Hoskins recalled. "Florentino kept going at a murderous pace and we began to fall further and further behind. In the end, Dédée and Florentino were carrying all our packs. She was very annoyed that we simply could not keep up; she was only a slip of a girl, but she had enormous strength and courage. Finally, when we could go no further, she told us to hide in a ditch at the side of the road while she and Florentino went on into San Sebastián to get transport. We were so tired we were happy to agree and the three of us jumped into the ditch and fell asleep. We were later awakened by the sound of car doors slamming—Dédée had come back by taxi to pick us up!"

One night, as she and Florentino were crossing back hurriedly into France after being spotted by guards, Dédée fell and cut her legs so badly that she later required treatment. "You need some rest, young lady," a doctor told her in Paris. "You need a holiday in the mountains."

Dédée had no time for a holiday, but she returned to the mountains repeatedly, bringing with her Allied airmen downed in the Netherlands and Luxembourg as well as Belgium. By late 1942 she had made 16 round trips across the Pyrenees and had led more than a hundred Allied airmen to freedom. The British continued to provide her with assistance and advice, urging her to be wary of German agents who might attempt to infiltrate the line by pretending to be fugitives. But no escape line could defend

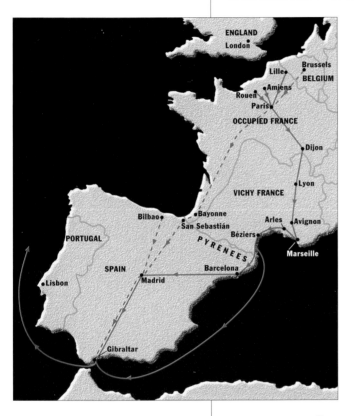

Two of the main escape networks, the O'Leary Line (solid lines) and Comet Line (dashed lines), led airmen and other fugitives out of several occupied territories to Vichy France in the south and then to freedom, either through neutral Spain, or directly, by boat.

❮ Andrée de Jongh

To change her appearance for clandestine work, 24-year-old Comet Line chief Andrée de Jongh dyed her blond hair black, as seen in the 1941 portrait at left. De Jongh escorted 118 fugitives into Spain before her arrest in early 1943, then survived two and a half years in prisons and concentration camps.

FINDING A WAY HOME

Specializing in assistance to both prisoners of war and downed airmen, Britain's MI-9 service was a pipsqueak of an agency next to the vast resources of MI-6 and MI-5, traditional spy services that could trace their bureaucratic ancestry to the early 1700s. While MI-6 controlled hundreds of agents overseas, MI-9 could spare only a handful. But what the feisty young upstart lacked in men and money, it made up in ingenuity and verve.

Headed by Major Norman R. Crockatt, an army officer who had been a prisoner during World War I, MI-9 helped create and support escape lines, including the famous O'Leary Line in France, to smuggle fugitives out of occupied countries. But its assignment didn't stop there. MI-9 also interviewed escapees to get new ideas; helped

the United States create a similar division, MIS-X; and trained British servicemen how to escape—or better yet, evade capture. And, like the larger spy services, it created ingenious devices, several of which are shown here.

Because of its focus on escape and evasion, MI-9's gadget shop had a knack for concealment and deception. Among other products, MI-9 developed uniform tunics that could be quickly converted into civilian jackets, radios made to look as if prisoners had assembled them by scrounging local components, and playing cards that split in half to reveal map sections. Other devices, like the radio below, were simply made tiny enough to be easily hidden.

The essential item for someone caught behind enemy lines was a compass, and for this purpose MI-9 turned to

Above, a German security officer poses in a secret tunnel discovered at a prisoner-of-war camp. Such photographs were used to train camp guards in how to prevent escapes.

HIDDEN RADIO
This compact radio receiver was made by MI-9 using American miniature components. Fitted into a cigarette tin, it included a pop-up wire antenna and attached headphone.

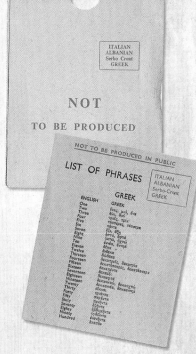

POCKET PHRASE BOOK
Issued by the American MIS-X service, this compact English-to-Greek translation booklet offers phrases that might be especially useful for a fugitive.

SILK MAP KIT
Issued to airmen on missions over enemy territory, kits like this one included detailed but easily concealed silk maps as well as a miniature compass and a hacksaw blade.

BUTTON COMPASS
This button from a Royal Engineers uniform conceals a miniature compass. The screw-on device on the back of the button was threaded in reverse to avoid its detection in a search.

ESCAPE KIT
Full of useful items that ranged from stimulant drugs and waterproof matches to chocolate, this MI-9 escape kit came packed in a plastic case that converts into a canteen when emptied.

the Blunt Brothers, a venerable London firm of instrument makers. Rising to the challenge, Blunt created an array of compasses, including some made in the form of collar studs, others embedded in combs, and still others built into the backs of buttons. MI-9's energetic gadget masters also eventually saw to it that all razor blades sold in British military canteens were magnetized so that they would function as crude compasses when suspended from a string.

Providing escape supplies for aircrew and others leaving on active operations was just a matter of issuing the gear, but getting equipment into enemy prisoner-of-war camps was more daunting. To solve the problem, both MI-9 and MIS-X created dummy prisoner-relief associations. On the surface, these organizations simply provided games, food, and other comforts. In reality, however, a carton of chess sets might hide a miniature radio receiver, while a shipment of books could conceal hacksaw blades and files. Combined with the prisoners' own desire to escape, such help was a powerful force. By the end of World War II, more than 35,000 Allied soldiers, sailors, and airmen had escaped from captivity, many of them as a result of either training or equipment provided by the escape agencies.

against the sort of disaster that befell Dédée's organization that autumn.

On November 19, 1942, two English-speaking strangers presented themselves at a Comet Line safe house in Brussels, claiming to be American airmen serving in the RAF. They wore khaki shirts rather than RAF blue, and one of them asked if he could use the "cabinet"—an odd way for an American to refer to the bathroom. When asked to write down their names and other information, they complied slowly and with some difficulty, explaining nervously afterward that they needed some fresh air and would return in an hour. Their hosts were by this time deeply suspicious—Allied servicemen on the run did not go strolling around Brussels for their health. But the damage had been done. Simply by welcoming the two men as prospective passengers, the occupants of the house had confirmed the suspicions of the Gestapo. Within hours they were under arrest.

Using torture to pry disclosures from those arrested, the Gestapo nabbed nearly a hundred members of the organization in Brussels alone. And the damage did not end there, for some knew the identities of other workers down the line. Dédée herself was caught in January 1943, just before she set off on yet another crossing to Spain, with three RAF airmen. Evidently, a Spanish farm hand whom she had once employed as a guide gave the Gestapo her name in return for money. At first, Dédée insisted to her interrogators that she was simply a guide, ignorant of the organization as a whole. But the Gestapo knew who she was and began asking questions about her father, who was still at large and whom they believed to be the leader of the Comet Line. At that, Dédée admitted her role as ringleader.

The Gestapo had the chief in their hands, but they refused to believe that a young woman could be the driving force behind a major escape line. Ultimately she was sent to the Ravensbrück concentration camp in Germany. She survived the war, largely because her captors persisted in their notion that she was simply her father's assistant. Frédéric de Jongh was betrayed and executed in 1944. Yet the Comet Line struggled on. The crafty Tante Go, overlooked by the Gestapo, remained active until 1944, when she escaped to Britain. The Basque guide Florentino continued to lead small parties through the mountains for as long as there was a need. Over the course of the war, perhaps a thousand airmen and other fugitives found their way to freedom on the indomitable Comet Line.

THE CAT'S MANY LIVES

Not all who worked secretly against the Germans in occupied Europe had Dédée's courage and conviction. Another woman active in the resistance responded far differently when her principles were put to the test. Her name was Mathilde Carré, but fellow resistance workers knew her as la Chatte ("the Cat"), for her feline habit of perching in an armchair and nervously clawing at the fabric with her long nails. Unfortunately for those who depended on her, she also possessed a catlike ability to shift loyalty and jump from one lap to another. The consequences in her case were far reaching, for she played a key role in an intelligence network that fed reports from French informants to the British.

Resistance Hero

For many, a Frenchman named Jean Moulin *(above)* represents the flame of the resistance at its brightest. As the personal representative of exiled general Charles de Gaulle, Moulin had the difficult task of pulling together France's diverse and fractious resistance groups, which ranged from Communist to conservative in sympathies and were often run by strong-willed, independent leaders. To do so, he traveled regularly and at great risk through occupied France.

The chances Moulin took in this vital work caught up with him in Lyon in June 1943, when the notorious Gestapo chief Klaus Barbie arrested Moulin and others at a secret meeting of resistance leaders. Although his captors tried hard to extract Moulin's invaluable knowledge of the French resistance, he remained silent under brutal torture and died in German custody. Ashes thought to be his remains now rest in the Panthéon in Paris.

Carré was in her early 30s when her country fell to Germany. Green eyed and vivacious, she was very much at loose ends. She had lived for a while in Algeria with her husband, who ran a school there, but the marriage had failed, as had her efforts to find fulfillment in wartime by working as a nurse. She craved adventure.

It was soon forthcoming. In October 1940, she encountered a dark, attractive Pole named Roman Garby-Czerniawski in a café in the southern French city of Toulouse. A former officer in the Polish Air Force, he had escaped to France after German forces overran Poland and now sought to create a spy network that would aid the British. His French was poor and his knowledge of the country limited, however, and he needed an assistant. Carré seemed to fill the bill. She impressed him as a "spitfire," ready to commit herself totally to his cause. "It's dangerous," he told her. "If you fail, you pay with your life for it or worse still, by prison, torture, God only knows what."

"Don't worry," she replied, as he later recalled. "I am ready for all sacrifices. Perhaps I will become a second Joan of Arc."

They went to work immediately, traveling to Paris to set up their spy headquarters. "I did not know what I was doing but I had complete faith in him," she said afterward, adding that life with him "had wings." Many assumed that the two were lovers, but both later denied it. Garby-Czerniawski, who took the code name Armand, certainly charmed the Cat—and many others who came in contact with him. He was a natural leader with great organizational talents. Soon, more than a hundred men and women had joined his network, dubbed Interallié (Inter-Allied). The number of informants and couriers would eventually grow to twice that number, with the members divided into cells covering much of France.

Interallié's harvest of intelligence was prodigious. Farmers reported on the movements of German troop trains and truck convoys. Dockworkers kept track of ship arrivals and departures. Observers at various points located and described German camps, airfields, and coastal defenses. They identified French factories that manufactured war matériel and pinpointed Gestapo headquarters. In the early days, the intelligence haul was microfilmed and hand-carried by a chain of couriers from Paris to Marseille and on to London. Later, radios made the flow instantaneous. The information was invaluable to the British, greatly increasing the efficiency of their bombing.

The Cat loved the work, and she was good at it—energetic, resourceful, and daring. She served as a courier and sometimes collected intelligence herself, visiting the port of Brest on one occasion to assess the damage done by RAF bombers. Once Interallié began communicating with London by radio, she spent much of her time encoding and transmitting messages, which placed her at the very heart of the operation.

The Germans knew that an espionage outfit in France was providing the British with reports that enabled them to conduct bombing raids of uncanny effectiveness. This was a matter of military intelligence, and the Abwehr took charge of the case, applying much the same techniques used to uncover the Soviet-linked agents of the Red Orchestra *(pages 44-71)*. Soon vans equipped with radio direction finders were prowling Paris in search of

Roman Garby-Czerniawski   Hugo Bleicher   Pierre de Vomécourt

the transmitters that linked Armand's group to London. In November 1941, however, before technicians pinpointed the locations, an informer betrayed one of Armand's top men. Facing torture, that leader directed authorities to other prominent members of the network—among them, Armand and the Cat, who were arrested separately.

Mathilde Carré found herself in the hands of an exceptionally shrewd spy catcher, Sergeant Hugo Bleicher of the Abwehr. First he consigned her to a cold, damp prison cell, where she spent a miserable night. Then he had her brought to the luxury hotel that served as the Abwehr's Paris headquarters, where he had a quiet chat with her over coffee and freshly baked rolls. "Madame Carré," he informed her according to her own account, "we have decided that you are far too intelligent and interesting to remain in prison."

The Abwehr had seized all the documents it needed to clinch the case in arresting Armand, he added, but he had only code names and a few real names of others in the organization and needed someone to identify them by sight. "You and I will work together and if you play no tricks,

Mathilde Carré

Mathilde Carré, code-named la Chatte, poses near a river in southern France in 1940, the year she began to work for Roman Garby-Czerniawski (top, left) as he built a Paris-based resistance network. When the Abwehr penetrated the network a year later, Carré betrayed her comrades to Abwehr sergeant Hugo Bleicher (center). Pierre de Vomécourt (right), an agent for the British Special Operations Executive (SOE), turned her again to the Allied side.

you can be assured that you will be at liberty this evening," he told his prisoner. "If you double cross me you will be shot immediately without trial."

She did as asked. At meetings with several unsuspecting confederates that day, she played her part, greeting them as though nothing was wrong, leading them on until they incriminated themselves, and then standing by as Bleicher arrested them. All were whisked off to prison before they could warn others that the Cat had changed sides.

She and Bleicher became lovers that night. "It was a purely animal cowardice," she later wrote, "the reaction of a body which had survived its first night in prison, had suffered cold, felt the icy breath of death and suddenly found warmth once more in a pair of arms—even if they were the arms of the enemy."

If she saw Bleicher as the enemy, however, she hardly acted that way. She soon told him everything she knew about Interallié and betrayed more of her compatriots. The Abwehr was now in possession of Interallié's five radio transmitters. Carré knew the codes and obligingly transmitted deceptive messages to London scripted by the Abwehr and signed, "La Chatte."

In late 1941 a new victim stumbled into Bleicher's web in the person of a French-born SOE agent named Pierre de Vomécourt. He was attempting to organize a resistance network in France but lacked a radio transmitter to coordinate his activities with London. A lawyer friend suggested that he seek help from Mathilde Carré, and he met with her at a café on the Champs Elysees. Sitting nearby was Sergeant Bleicher, sipping an apéritif and no doubt savoring the prospect of opening a new line to London.

De Vomécourt gratefully accepted Carré's offer to get his messages through to the SOE; this gave her the opportunity to continue sending German-scripted, misleading messages under his name as well. Carré did not fool him for long, however. Once, as a test, he asked her to obtain false identity papers, and she promptly supplied him with documents that were all too perfect, bearing authentic German stamps. When he accused her of working with the enemy, she promptly confessed. Claiming she had taken the Germans' side only under duress, however, she eagerly volunteered to reverse loyalties once again. De Vomécourt reluctantly accepted.

Soon after tearfully spilling her story to the SOE agent, Carré went to Bleicher, who still believed she was working just for him, and suggested that she accompany de Vomécourt on a covert trip he was planning to Britain for high-level consultations. The payoff for the Abwehr, she said, would be a glimpse of the innermost workings of the SOE. Convinced that his hold on her was unbreakable, Bleicher agreed to this plan. In February 1942, as German border forces carefully looked the other way, she and de Vomécourt were picked up at night by boat on the coast of Brittany and spirited to London, where she gladly told British intelligence everything she knew.

The Cat fully expected to be embraced by the British as that rarest of articles in the intelligence trade—a triple agent. In reality, however, agents like the Cat who had obviously gone over to the enemy and sold out their confederates were hard to trust and were seldom welcomed back into the fold. When the British had finished debriefing the Cat, they threw her in prison and kept her locked up for the rest of the war. Afterward, she was returned to France and tried for treason. She received a death sentence, but it was commuted to life imprisonment and she ended up serving only nine years, regaining her freedom as a mood of national forgiveness took hold. A devout Catholic by then, she retired to the French countryside and wrote a confessional about her wartime adventures, entitled *I Was the Cat.*

Her fate contrasted to that of her former partner Armand, the founder of Interallié. In October 1942 he appeared out of the blue in England, informing authorities there that he had escaped from his German captors in France. Under questioning, however, he admitted that the Germans had freed him only after he agreed to spy for them in England. He assured his interrogators that he never meant to honor that deal and was eager to deceive the Germans. In this case, MI-5 and the Double Cross Committee concluded that Armand could be trusted up to a point and decided to enroll him provisionally as a double agent under the code name of Brutus— a fitting name for a man who needed watching.

As the tangled story of la Chatte suggests, resistance leaders, and those who organized efforts in their behalf, had to contend with the fact that there were figures in their midst who were prepared to betray their superiors for any number of motives, including fear, greed, envy, and sheer spite. In 1943 one such traitor may have revealed the whereabouts of Jean Moulin, the most dedicated and respected of all French resistance leaders, leading to his capture by notorious Gestapo officer Klaus Barbie *(sidebar, page 139)*. Even the SOE found it hard to detect those agents within its ranks who had switched to the other side—or had fallen unwillingly under German control. Operating in a murk of uncertainty, agents found that every venture across the lines was a journey through a minefield, laden with explosive consequences.

CALLING NORTH POLE

Just how disastrous those consequences could be was illustrated when the SOE unknowingly matched wits with a highly experienced Abwehr officer: Major Hermann Giskes, commander of military counterintelligence in the Netherlands. His long-running scheme of radio deception, known to the Germans as Nordpol, or North Pole, was a great coup for the Abwehr—and among the most devastating setbacks for the SOE in the entire course of the war.

The stage for Operation North Pole was set in the Dutch capital of The Hague on March 6, 1942, when Giskes, acting on information supplied by radio-detection-finding squads, apprehended an SOE agent named Hubert Lauwers, along with his radio and three coded messages that he was about to transmit to headquarters in Britain. Lauwers was one of many Dutch volun-

Hermann Giskes

Transferred unwillingly from Paris to the Netherlands in late 1941, Abwehr major Hermann Giskes made the most of his assignment by devising the long-running North Pole ruse against the British SOE and Dutch resistance.

"With a little luck there exists a definite possibility that we can continue deceiving the enemy Secret Services in London."

—Hermann Giskes, 1942

Hubert Lauwers

Lieutenant Hubert Lauwers, a young Dutch recruit to the SOE, had been working with the Dutch resistance for four months when the Germans arrested him in March 1942. He then became the first unwilling pawn in Giskes's radio deception against the British.

teers recruited by the SOE from among those who had fled their country after the German occupation in 1940 or who were living abroad at the time. His instructions from London were to communicate by radio every other Friday at 6:30 in the evening, and Giskes had timed the raid to catch Lauwers in the act.

Giskes personally conducted the interrogation, hoping to turn Lauwers. "As a soldier," he told the agent, "I have the greatest respect for your courage and devotion to duty, but I must say nonetheless that the kind of job which you have been given by London is not very respectable." That job, he knew, involved organizing underground forces for a campaign of sabotage against the German occupiers. That campaign was just taking shape, and Giskes made it clear that the Germans would do everything in their power to prevent the British from furthering it by infiltrating supplies and additional SOE agents. "Any Army of Occupation, irrespective of its nationality, will crush such attempts by means of the shooting of hostages and the terrorizing of the population," he insisted, painting an ugly picture of what could lie ahead for Lauwers's native land. He gave Lauwers a choice: send scripted messages to London or face torture by the Gestapo.

Lauwers agreed to send the messages—but only because he was sure the SOE would realize something was amiss. He had been trained to include in his radio transmissions a so-called security check by inserting a deliberate mistake at regular intervals to show that he was not under duress and being "played back" to London by the Germans. Unfortunately, the coded messages captured during the raid contained his security check, and the agent had no doubt that the alert Giskes would be aware of it. By chance, however, the deliberate error he had inserted in two of those messages happened to occur within the word *stop,* used frequently as telegraphic punctuation. Lauwers told his captors that his security check was to misspell *stop* once in every message—and explained the absence of the error in the third message as an oversight he would have corrected, given the chance.

Giskes accepted this explanation, and Lauwers was confident that SOE headquarters in London would notice that he had switched from his assigned security check to a different pattern of errors. But the SOE missed his warning. Those who decoded such messages in London paid scant attention to security checks, having learned from experience that agents often forgot them or failed to use them properly.

As a result of this breakdown in security, SOE officers in London not only accepted as genuine the messages scripted by Giskes but also continued to send reports to Lauwers exposing their plans for this burgeoning movement of Dutch freedom fighters. Soon Lauwers received a message that an SOE agent would be parachuted in to organize sabotage. In the early morning hours of March 28, the agent dropped straight into enemy hands. Eight more agents were introduced over the next several months. All were met when they landed, not by the Abwehr or Gestapo but by Dutch collaborators posing as resistance workers. Thinking they were among friends, the agents divulged much useful information. Only then did the Germans swoop in and hustle them off to prison. London, meanwhile, was informed by radio that the agents had arrived safely and were now hard at work.

As Giskes learned the codes and transmission schedules assigned to the agents he captured, he established new radio links with London, making it seem as if the Dutch resistance was thriving. Maintaining that illusion was not easy. On one occasion, after London dispatched orders for Dutch saboteurs to attack a radar station, Giskes staged an abortive assault on the installation by men masquerading as resistance fighters. He then sent word to London that the saboteurs had done their best but come up short. He went even further to show the SOE that its agents were busy in Rotterdam by blowing up a barge there filled with scrap metal—a small price to pay to keep London from growing suspicious. When the SOE ordered an agent to come back to London to report on progress in the Netherlands, Giskes had one of his radio operators request information about an escape line—and used the reply to penetrate the line and arrest many of its members. London was then told that the agent in question had been killed in a traffic accident before he could return.

Like the British officers in charge of Double Cross who lived in constant fear that a German agent might slip through the net and expose their operation, Giskes knew how fragile his scheme was. A report from some independent source on the ground might well reveal as mere fantasy the Dutch resistance networks his false messages had described. "One single control group, dropped blind and unknown to us in Holland," he wrote later, "could have punctured in an instant the whole gigantic bubble of Operation Nordpol. This unpleasant possibility was always before our eyes during the long months of the play-back, and it kept us from getting too sure of ourselves."

In fact, at least one SOE code specialist, Leo Marks, had suspected almost from the beginning that something was rotten in the Netherlands. In a 1998 memoir, Marks detailed how he first became suspicious, not simply because of the missing security checks, but for a variety of other reasons. For example, SOE agents in other operations invariably sent in numerous unreadable messages—indecipherables, as they were known—that were coded incorrectly under the haste and stress of working in the field. Messages from the Dutch group, by contrast, were meticulously coded.

Fortunately for the Germans, however, Marks was never able to convince the heads of the Dutch section that the Netherlands operation had fallen under German control. Such a scenario stood in total contrast to the regular, eagerly believed reports of a growing resistance movement. It seemed so implausible—and, Marks noted, would have put the relatively new agency in such a bad light—that decision makers held out again and again for absolute proof of his suspicions. In the fog of war, of course, such complete certainty is rare indeed.

What seemed to Marks like the clincher came in February 1944 with the return to London of two Dutch SOE agents, Pieter Dourlein and Johan

In a forest clearing in the Netherlands, German security police accompanied by a Dutch collaborator in a dark coat load a trailer with weapons originally intended for the resistance. Convinced by false radio messages that an underground movement was flourishing in the Netherlands, the SOE made some 200 supply flights there but ended up arming the Nazis.

Ubbink. According to their report, upon his arrival in the Netherlands each man had been captured as part of a continuing German operation. Putting their SOE training to use, the two eventually managed to break out of their Dutch prison by squeezing through the bars of their cells, then lowering themselves from the window of a lavatory to the ground below with a rope Dourlein had fashioned from bedding. After scrambling painfully over a barbed-wire barrier, they made their way in the night to a nearby town, where they threw themselves on the mercy of the local priest. He in turn put them in touch with a former police inspector, who had quit his job rather than cooperate with the Nazis and had joined the Dutch resistance.

With the help of resistance workers, the fugitives reached safety in Spain by year's end. But their troubles were not over. Once back in London, they were grilled by intelligence officers, who had received a warning in a radio message scripted by Giskes that the two agents were in fact turncoats working for the Gestapo. After the interrogation, they were transferred to Brixton Prison, Dourlein recalled, "and put in cells alongside common criminals."

Despite the rough treatment accorded Dourlein and Ubbink, however, many at the SOE had by this time grown suspicious of the Dutch operation, as Marks had been all along. Even though SOE staff still could not agree on how extensive the problem was or who was to blame, contacts with the "Dutch resistance" were now handled more cautiously. Even before the escaped agents' return, Giskes had noticed that the radio messages from the SOE had grown "dull and colorless" and concluded that the British spymasters he had deceived for so long were growing wary. His greatest hope had been to learn from Operation North Pole when and where the Allied invasion forces would come ashore. That was one secret he never penetrated, and he had no hope of doing so now, when his foes were on their guard.

Finally, on April Fools' Day, 1944, he brought the game to an end, broadcasting a taunting message on all 10 radio transmitters under his control. No one who read the message could have any doubt that it came from

From the files of British intelligence, the aerial photograph above clearly shows the former priests' seminary at Haaren, the Netherlands, that was converted into a prison for the dozens of SOE agents caught in Operation North Pole. Despite reports that agents were held there, the SOE remained unconvinced that anything was wrong in the Netherlands.

Johan Bernard Ubbink

Pieter Dourlein

"Is this what I risked my life for, time and time again? Is this why I escaped from Haaren prison? Is this why I trekked across four countries hounded by the enemy?"

—Pieter Dourlein, on disbelief of his story

the Germans: "We understand that you have been endeavoring for some time to do business in Holland without our assistance. We regret this the more since we have acted for so long as your sole representatives in this country, to our mutual satisfaction. Nevertheless we can assure you that, should you be thinking of paying us a visit on the Continent on any extensive scale, we shall give your emissaries the same attention as we have hitherto, and a similarly warm welcome. Hoping to see you."

The British were in no mood to laugh at Giskes's joke. In attempting to fuel a nonexistent campaign of sabotage, the SOE had unwittingly supplied the Germans with more than 15,000 kilograms of explosives, 8,000 small arms, half-a-million rounds of ammunition, 75 radio transmitters, and much else besides. And then there was the appalling human cost. Fifty-two SOE agents had been captured; in 1944 nearly all were executed, on orders from Berlin. Nor were they the only victims. Hundreds of Dutch civilians had been arrested on the basis of information obtained through Operation North Pole.

So devastating were the results that some suspected treachery within the SOE—suspicions that lingered long after the war. But Dourlein, who was eventually exonerated and honored for his SOE service, concluded that the main causes of the disaster were "inefficiency, complacency, and negligence." A combination of wishful thinking and bureaucratic struggles within and around the SOE had simply overpowered its perception of the truth. Furthermore, Dourlein understood that campaigns of resistance, whether initiated within the occupied countries or planned abroad, were inherently risky because they relied on amateurs whose bravery and dedication could not always compensate for their lack of expertise. "Operation North Pole," he concluded, "was the victory of the professional Germans—who laid their plans long before the war, knew exactly what they were going to do and trained their people thoroughly—over the amateurs on our side, the majority of whom set to work full of enthusiasm but with little or no training, so that they had to learn by experience. This costs lives."

Despite the enormous risks, however, men and women in the occupied countries continued to actively resist their temporary conquerors. Operating escape lines, collecting intelligence, and performing other secret services for the Allied cause throughout the war, they played a courageous part in undermining Hitler's Fortress Europe and helped bring the walls down.

THE GADGET SHOPS

Stanley Lovell

Above, OSS research chief Stanley Lovell displays a specialized grenade and silenced pistol.

Charles Fraser-Smith

Charles Fraser-Smith, who devised gear for MI-6 and SOE agents, operated under cover of the British Ministry of Supply.

Christopher Clayton Hutton

Christopher Clayton Hutton headed a unit that made devices for MI-9, the British escape specialists.

From compact radios to silenced weapons, the equipment issued to Allied spies and saboteurs included a wide variety of specialized gear, some of it shown here and on the pages that follow. Creating such items was the task of secret "gadget shops," which produced items ranging from the grimly practical, such as suicide pills and explosives, to the near whimsical; included in the latter category was a never-realized scheme by American gadget-master Stanley Lovell to use migratory bats to transport incendiary materials into the flammable eaves of Japanese dwellings.

Lovell *(above, left)* headed the research and development branch of America's Office of Strategic Services. His British counterpart, former schoolmaster Charles Fraser-Smith *(above, center),* oversaw the purchase and creation of special tools for the MI-6 intelligence service and the sabotage experts of the Special Operations Executive. Fraser-Smith also worked closely with equipment experts in other British agencies, including Christopher Clayton Hutton *(above, right)* of the MI-9 escape and evasion service.

Fraser-Smith's operation ultimately employed hundreds of small machine shops, factories, and craftsmen. None left a clearer signature than a shop in the London suburb of Welwyn Garden City, which proudly gave the prefix *Wel* to its many creations, including the Welrod pistol *(page 151)* and the foldable Welbike motorcycle *(pages 158-159).*

SILENCED SUBMACHINE GUN
A modification of the standard 9-mm British Sten gun, the SOE's Mark II model—also used by commandos—fired only single shots when the silencer (far left) was attached.

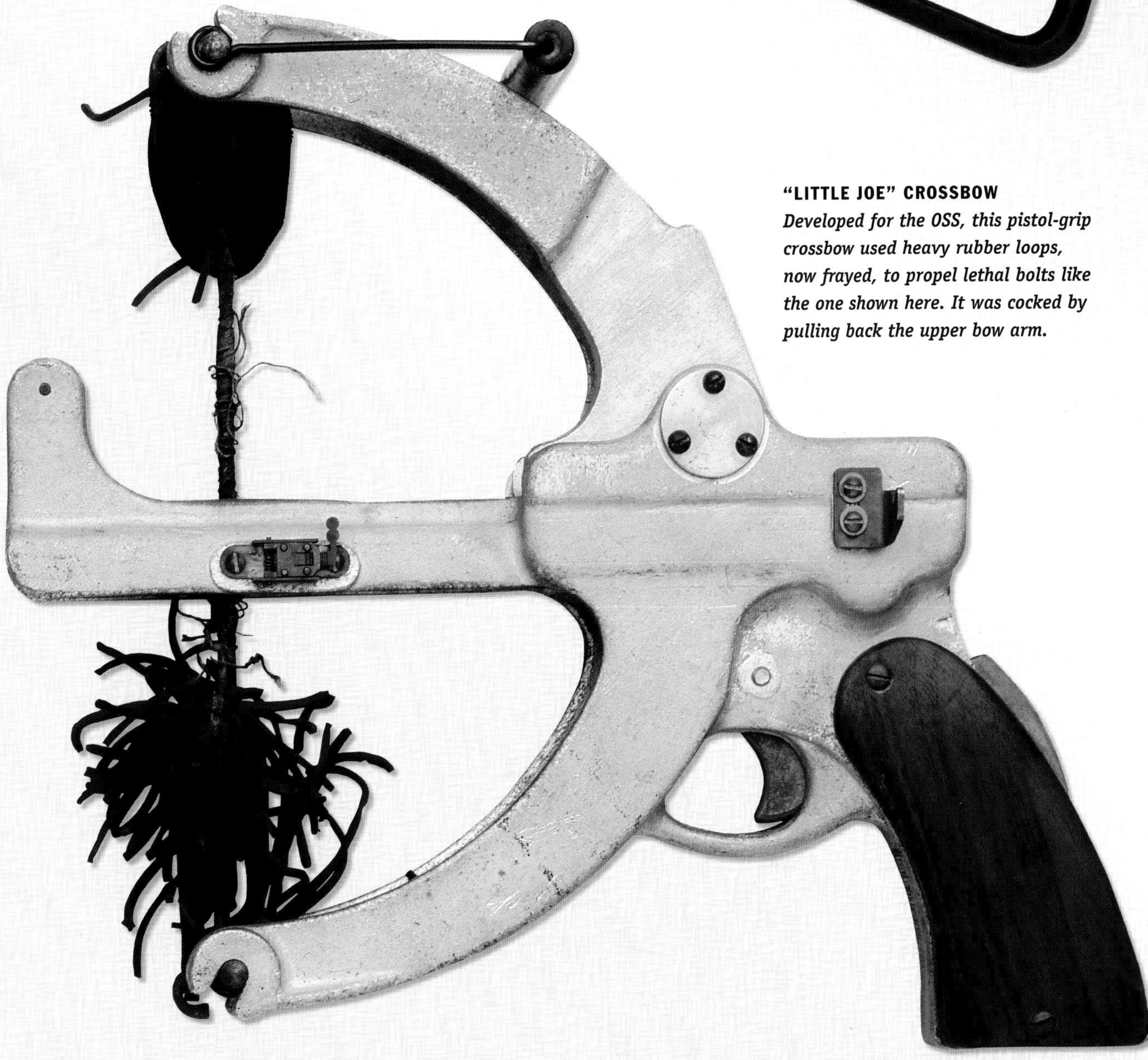

"LITTLE JOE" CROSSBOW
Developed for the OSS, this pistol-grip crossbow used heavy rubber loops, now frayed, to propel lethal bolts like the one shown here. It was cocked by pulling back the upper bow arm.

WILLIAM TELL CROSSBOW
Above, an OSS officer tries out a
"William Tell" crossbow at a test range.
Highly accurate, the aluminum crossbow could be
hand-cranked to 300 pounds of pull, and it released
its bolts (below) at 180 feet a second. Although the
OSS hoped the silent, flashless device would be an
effective weapon, it was never used in combat.

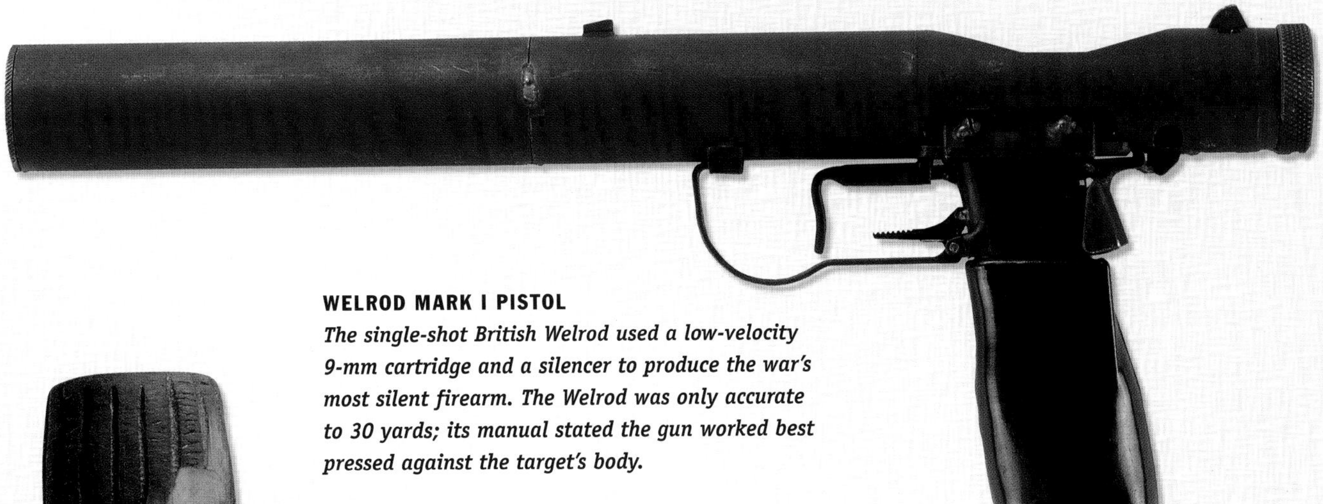

WELROD MARK I PISTOL

The single-shot British Welrod used a low-velocity 9-mm cartridge and a silencer to produce the war's most silent firearm. The Welrod was only accurate to 30 yards; its manual stated the gun worked best pressed against the target's body.

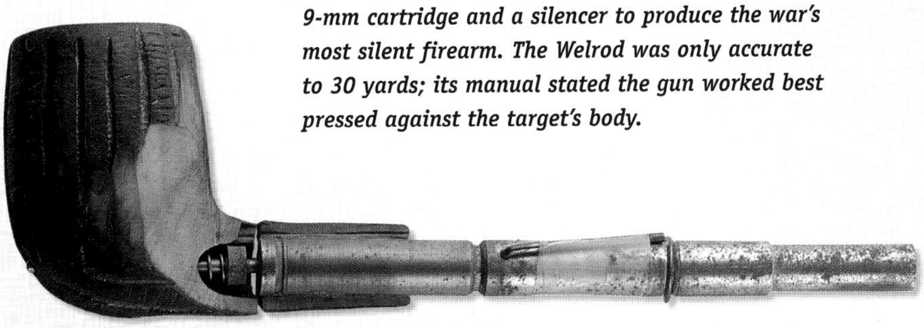

PIPE PISTOL

One of the many weapons disguised as everyday objects, this SOE pipe pistol was fired by holding the barrel and twisting the pipe bowl.

SHOOTING TO KILL

Although SOE and OSS agents openly confronted the enemy only rarely, situations could arise that called for direct action. Sabotage teams and operations groups sometimes needed silent weapons to eliminate enemy sentries from afar, and any agent might find it necessary to eliminate a dangerous informer or collaborator. In response, both the British and American gadget shops produced quiet shooting weapons that ranged from silenced guns to a variety of crossbows, although the latter did not prove popular in the field. American technicians also contrived arrowlike bolts that could be fired from the army's standard .45-caliber pistol. For assassination or personal defense, ingenious engineers from both nations disguised miniature firearms as everyday objects, from the pipe shown here to fountain pens or even cigarettes.

Equally effective in slashing or stabbing, this smaller, more concealable version of the Fairbairn-Sykes fighting knife (below) came with a leather arm scabbard. At left, two Free French commandos demonstrate how one could be used to dispose of an enemy sentry.

WEAPONS FOR CLOSE COMBAT

Because hand-to-hand combat was always a possibility in the secret war, the gadget shops issued a large variety of effective, easily concealed knives and other hand weapons. Although this gear ranged from odd inventions like the Peskit combination weapon to tiny, highly concealable lapel knives and push daggers, the most popular by far was the Fairbairn-Sykes knife. Two British officers, Captains W. E. Fairbairn and E. A. Sykes, had originally devised this two-edged weapon for the Shanghai police; in 1940, they came up with a smaller version for covert use. During the war more than 250,000 Fairbairn-Sykes knives were crafted by the Wilkinson Sword Company. The knife was so well received by commando, SOE, and OSS officers that Wilkinson's bladesmiths worked after-hours to fulfill orders for custom variations.

A KNIFE IN A LAPEL
Intended as a weapon of last resort, lapel knives could be sewn into a jacket lapel—or a pocket, like the one at right—to avoid detection. The SOE knife above, with its inlaid blade, was formally presented to the leader of a French resistance unit.

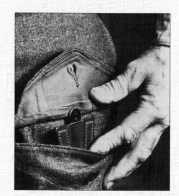

A TRIPLE-THREAT COMBINATION

Named for its inventor, John Peskit, the SOE's Peskit close-combat weapon was intended to provide a versatile weapon for hand-to-hand fighting. The Peskit included a retractable stiletto blade—shown extended here—and wire garrote; a steel ball at the end of the handle enabled it to be used as a club as well.

PUSH DAGGER

Based on World War I trench knives, the spike-bladed push dagger below easily penetrated thick clothing when thrust in with a straight arm punch. Used by both the SOE and OSS, push daggers could be readily concealed, as shown in the wartime photograph of a dagger wrist sheath (bottom).

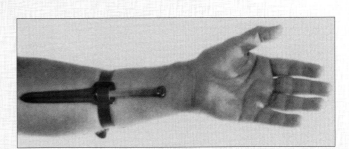

SABOTAGE TOOLS

Even before the war, military planners knew that sabotage devices would be key to clandestine resistance, and the first shots had not yet been exchanged when Section D of the British foreign office was asked to begin dreaming up as many as possible. The Section D shop, later part of SOE, spent the war producing items ranging from improved time fuses to devices disguised as coal or mule dung. Across the sea, the OSS gadget shops devised its own ingenious but deadly gadgets. Among the SOE and OSS sabotage gear airdropped to resistance forces were tire-slashing blades, percussion grenades, and numerous incendiary devices, including the versatile fuses shown below.

To create a firebomb, a Dutch resistance fighter (right) decants flammable material into empty cans of VIM cleaning powder.

GAMMON GRENADE
The grenade at left—named a gammon, the British word for ham, for its shape—had a cloth skirt that could be filled with plastic explosives.

BEANO GRENADE
Devised by the OSS for sabotage rather than combat, the baseball-sized "Beano" grenade above, right, contained a detonator that armed itself in flight and exploded on impact.

TIME-DELAY PENCIL FUSES
Time-delay fuses like those at left were built from brass tubes. Each contained a firing pin, a percussion cap, and a copper tube containing a glass vial filled with acid. Crushing the glass released the acid, which ate through a wire connected to the pin, allowing it to strike the cap; the strength of the acid controlled how long this delay lasted.

COAL-BOMB DISGUISE KIT

Because coal supplies vary in color and appearance, OSS gadget-developers found that shaping a bomb like a lump of coal (lower right) was only the first step. To make the bomb match the local fuel, a specialized paint kit (above), complete with several crafting tools, was provided to saboteurs. If all went well, the bomb exploded when shoveled into the firebox of a ship or locomotive.

CONCEALABLE TIRE RIPPER

The SOE tire ripper above, shown here with a sheath, fitted around a finger and could be concealed in the palm of the hand. Its razor-sharp, hooked blade allowed a saboteur to quickly slash open the rubber tires of an enemy vehicle.

RADIOS AND
SPECIAL GEAR

Among the nonlethal devices entrusted to agents, perhaps the most important were radios, which lay at the heart of the secret war. Agents needed easily concealed radios to transmit reports to their controllers, and resistance groups required long-range communication with headquarters. Among the classics produced by Britain's SOE shops were the SCR 1 "Biscuit Tin" radio below and the Mark II suitcase set at right. In the war's later years, miniature components developed in America allowed both SOE and OSS shops to produce even lighter, more powerful sets. Other devices the gadget shops created ran the gamut from tiny cameras to special-purpose escape tools. All devices meant for agents, even large items like the motorcycle on pages 158-159, had to be designed for easy transport as well as rugged wear.

At left, a British-trained Norwegian resistance fighter transmits a message on his Mark II suitcase radio in 1943 during a secret mission to sabotage a heavy-water plant in Vermork, Norway.

BISCUIT-TIN RECEIVER
The SOE receiver, power pack, and battery shown below were made to be concealed in biscuit tins like the one at right, which were then stripped of their English labels for use in occupied Europe. Nearly 5,000 such receivers were issued to the French resistance.

TYPE B.

BATTERY
HT./LT. 90V

Type No. F.K.M.

TLEY & PALMERS

FOR BISCUITS

BY APPOINTMENT
BISCUIT MANUFACTURERS
TO H.M.KING GEORGE VI

EADING & LONDON
ENGLAND

REACTION

TUNING

SENSITIVITY   AE TRIMMER

SUITCASE RADIO

Powered by a six-volt car battery, the British Mark II radio could transmit coded messages over a distance of 500 miles. Introduced in 1942, the 32-pound "B-2" type shown here came packed in an 18-inch-wide European-style civilian suitcase.

MATCHBOX CAMERA

The 16-mm miniature camera at left was produced for the OSS by Kodak and could be fitted into either Swedish or Japanese matchboxes for concealment. The shutter speed of the wide-angle lens, located just behind the opening at the front of the box, could be adjusted to allow for photographs or for document copying.

A KNIFE FOR ESCAPEES

The escape knife at left, a folding tool kit originally intended for downed airmen and escaping prisoners of war, was also issued to SOE personnel and intelligence agents. The handy device contained a knife, a wire cutter, a screwdriver, a small pry bar, and three hacksaw blades.

THE PORTABLE WELBIKE

A 70-pound collapsible motorcycle, the SOE Welbike at right could be folded, as shown in the upper photograph at far right, to fit the standard Allied parachute supply canister. Tested rather precariously in the wartime photograph at far right by SOE director major general Sir Colin Gubbins, the Welbike was meant to allow an agent to depart quickly from a dangerous drop zone. Powered by a small two-cycle engine, the motorcycle had a top speed of 30 miles an hour and a range, when fully fueled, of 90 miles.

C5152223

VICTORY THROUGH DECEPTION

n the morning of April 30, 1943, a fisherman noticed something strange bobbing in the Atlantic off Huelva, a port on the southwest coast of Spain. He hailed a nearby motorboat, which retrieved the object. It turned out to be a human body, in a state of decomposition. The corpse was wearing the battle dress of a British Royal Marine, a trench coat, and a life jacket. A locked briefcase was chained to the belt of the coat.

Spanish military authorities in Huelva took charge of the body, which was identified, based on the credentials in a tunic pocket, as that of 36-year-old William Martin, who held the acting rank of major. A doctor at the local mortuary concluded that Martin had entered the sea while still alive, perhaps as a result of a plane crash, and had died of drowning five to eight days before he washed ashore.

The authorities then turned the body over to the local British vice-consul, and Major Martin was buried without delay in the Cemetery of Solitude just outside Huelva. A funeral detail from the Spanish navy provided him with full military honors. A simple white marble tombstone engraved with his name and those of his parents, John and Antonia Martin of Cardiff, Wales, marked the grave, which was adorned with a wreath sent by his family and by his fiancée, Pam.

There was just one hitch to the orderly proceeding: Spanish officials had retained Martin's briefcase. The British naval attaché in Madrid promptly requested its return, having been informed by his superiors in London that it held papers of the utmost importance. But it was not until May 13—two weeks after the recovery of the body—that the Spanish complied with his request. Moreover, despite assurances that no one had tampered with the sealed envelopes inside the briefcase, scrutiny of the documents back in London proved otherwise. The creases in the letters did not match the original folds.

Those letters spelled out Allied plans for future operations in the Mediterranean. They would naturally be of great interest to the Germans, and Spain, although nominally neutral, leaned toward the

British soldiers easily hoist aloft an inflatable rubber Sherman tank, designed to resemble the real thing when spotted from above by German pilots. Such decoys were deployed along England's southeast coast in early 1944 to support the war's greatest deception campaign, aimed at misleading German commanders as to where the main Allied force would land on D-Day.

Axis. The British could only assume that the letters had been opened and photographed before being resealed, and that German officials were now fully informed of the contents.

Prime Minister Winston Churchill had approved the mission that entrusted those sensitive documents to Major Martin, and officials concluded that he should be informed at once in Washington, where he was conferring with other Allied leaders. Far from being alarmed by news that the letters had been intercepted, however, Churchill was delighted. For the documents were part of an ingenious British hoax called Operation Mincemeat, designed to feed false information to the Germans. The message that reached Churchill in Washington left no doubt in his mind that the enemy had taken the bait: "Mincemeat Swallowed Whole."

MAKING MINCEMEAT

Clever as it was, Operation Mincemeat was far from unique, for deception operations of one kind or another were a key part of the hidden history of the war. All required careful planning and more than a little daring. A hoax that went awry could alert the enemy to the very plans the scheme was meant to conceal. In the case of Mincemeat, intelligence officers hoped to divert attention from the upcoming invasion of Sicily by convincing the Germans that the Allies had other targets in mind.

That was a tall task. By the spring of 1943, vast quantities of men and matériel were assembling in North Africa across from Sicily. The buildup was sure to be spotted by the Germans. Furthermore, seizing Sicily was an obvious priority for the Allies, who wanted to eliminate air bases there that menaced Allied convoys and use the island as a steppingstone to the Italian mainland. As Churchill remarked of the invasion target, "Everyone but a bloody fool would *know* that it's Sicily." Hitler was no fool, but the fact that his forces were overextended and susceptible to attack at many points left him skeptical of the threat to Sicily and fearful that the real danger lay elsewhere.

The purpose of Operation Mincemeat was to play on those fears and keep Hitler and his aides guessing about Allied intentions until it was too late for them to concentrate their forces and repulse the looming threat to Sicily. Such trickery helped ease the way for the invasion forces and served as a model for an even greater deception to come—the vast D-Day smoke screen that kept the Germans from anticipating the Allied landing at Normandy and from responding effectively once troops came ashore there.

Mincemeat was part of a larger intelligence campaign code-named Barclay, masterminded by an outfit known as the London Controlling Section (LCS), which coordinated deception efforts. The game plan for Barclay was to keep German forces dispersed across the Mediterranean by presenting Hitler and his aides with many possible targets to worry about besides Sicily. Knowing that Hitler considered the Balkan Peninsula especially vulnerable to attack, Allied planners portrayed Greece as the primary objective. At the same time, they hinted at secondary assaults on the island of Sardinia and other points in the western Mediterranean to help explain the Allied

Ewen Montagu

Lieutenant Commander Ewen Montagu of naval intelligence was awarded the Military Order of the British Empire for planning Operation Mincemeat, the scheme enlisting a dead man to impersonate a deceased British courier.

"In life he had done little for his country; but in death he did more than most could achieve by a lifetime of service."

—Ewen Montagu, on Glyndwr Michael

buildup there. To inflate the apparent threat to targets other than Sicily, they staged misleading amphibious training exercises, generated bogus radio traffic from nonexistent units, and planted phony stories with double agents.

Operation Mincemeat was designed to reinforce this program of deception by offering the Germans written proof that any move toward Sicily would merely be a diversion. Orchestrating Mincemeat were Lieutenant Commander Ewen Montagu, a 41-year-old barrister serving with naval intelligence in London, and a colleague of his from the Royal Air Force, Flight Lieutenant Charles Cholmondeley. They gave a new twist to an old trick—planting misleading documents on a body and leaving it to be discovered by the enemy. Since most couriers carrying urgent papers overseas now traveled by plane, they had to arrange for a corpse to seemingly fall from the sky into enemy hands. One possibility was to parachute a body bearing false documents into enemy territory, but they opted for a subtler approach, one that called for the corpse of a staff officer to be discovered floating off the coast of Spain in a manner that suggested his plane had crashed at sea.

After receiving provisional approval for the plan, Montagu set out to find a suitable cadaver to play the part of the victim. He needed someone who looked the right age to fit the profile of an up-and-coming staff officer—roughly in his mid-30s—and who had died of a cause not obviously inconsistent with drowning, shock, or exposure, any of which might explain the death of a man wearing a life jacket whose plane had gone down at sea.

During his search, Montagu conferred with an old friend from his barrister days, Sir Bernard Spilsbury, Britain's foremost forensic pathologist. Sir Bernard was as closemouthed as "an oyster," Montagu wrote after the war, "absolutely secure from temptation to gossip." They met over a glass of sherry at the doctor's London club. Sir Bernard assured Montagu that it would require a great deal of skill to detect that a corpse plucked from the sea had been dead before entering the water. Such a conclusion, he said, would require "a pathologist of my experience—and there aren't any in Spain."

With the help of a London coroner, Montagu found a recently deceased man at a local mortuary who seemed to fit the bill. Montagu later claimed in his postwar account of Operation Mincemeat, entitled *The Man Who Never Was*, that the corpse chosen to play the part of Major Martin had succumbed to pneumonia and had fluid in the lungs, which would be conveniently mistaken for seawater by an inexpert pathologist. In reality, that story was itself a hoax, intended to disguise the man's identity out of consideration for his next of kin. Not until 1995 did documents released by the British government reveal that the dead man was a 34-year-old drifter from South Wales named Glyndwr Michael, who had committed suicide by swallowing rat poison—a cause unlikely to show up in a routine postmortem.

While the body lay in cold storage until needed, Montagu began fleshing out the character of the imaginary Major Martin. He placed Martin on the staff of the British Chief of Combined Operations as a landing-craft expert. Martin would be journeying to North Africa in that capacity—with the added assignment of carrying sensitive letters to top British commanders in the Mediterranean—when his plane went down off the coast of Spain. Supplying an identity card to match this story proved unexpectedly challenging: Montagu lacked a convincing photograph for Martin until he accidentally spotted someone at a meeting who, as he put it, "might have been the twin brother of the corpse." Having secured the photograph, Montagu then carried the phony identity card around for some time, occasionally rubbing it against his trousers to make it look well used.

Other items that would be found on the body suggested that Major Martin had had his share of human failings. He had carelessly let his pass to his London headquarters expire, for example, and he carried a letter from the manager of his bank notifying him that he was overdrawn. Martin's future plans were suggested by such items as letters from his fiancée, Pam, a fetching picture of Pam in a bathing suit, and a gruff letter from his father warning against hasty wartime weddings.

Although those effects established Martin's personality, it was the two official letters Martin carried in his briefcase that were crucial to the deception. One from General Sir Archibald Nye, vice chief of the Imperial General Staff, was addressed to his old friend General Sir Harold Alexander, commander of British forces in northwest Africa. Nye himself wrote this letter under guidance from Montagu, and it offered Alexander the informal sort of briefing that one "old boy" might expect from another.

Nye indicated that the Allies were preparing for two offensives—one aimed at Greece and the other at a target closer to Sicily. He did not specify that target, but the second letter carried by Major Martin *(page 169)* offered a broad hint. This document was written by Montagu but signed by Vice Admiral Lord Louis Mountbatten, and it purported to be a letter of introduction for Martin to the commander of the Mediterranean fleet. The message explained that Martin was carrying a very "hot" letter and asked that he be posted back to London "as soon as the assault is over." Mountbatten added that perhaps Martin "might bring some sardines with him," since those delicacies were being rationed back in England.

Montagu was confident that the enemy would interpret this last comment as a thinly veiled reference to Sardinia. "That sort of joke would appeal to the Germans," he wrote, "who would be able to see the point and understand the reference." Taken together, the Nye and Mountbatten letters were intended to confirm other signals sent to the Germans that Allied forces seemingly destined for Sicily would instead land on nearby Sardinia not long after the invasion of Greece began.

Montagu's superiors worried that the Germans would see through the Mincemeat scheme and take it as confirmation of the impending attack on Sicily. The chiefs of staff ultimately insisted that the plan go all the way to Churchill for approval. "*He* had no qualms," Montagu observed of the prime minister. "It was the kind of thing he enjoyed."

Having crafted the letters, Montagu made certain that they were not lost at sea or overlooked by Spanish authorities by placing them in a briefcase and chaining it to Martin's person. A briefcase containing only two thin letters might seem suspicious, so Montagu filled the space with proofs of a new edition of a manual on British commando operations.

"In wartime, truth is so precious that she should always be attended by a bodyguard of lies."

—Winston Churchill

The final step in the preparations was the most unpleasant. Montagu and his RAF associate, Charles Cholmondeley, went to the mortuary to dress Major Martin for action. The corpse had been lying there frozen for over two months. "By this time Major Martin had become a completely living person for us," Montagu wrote, and it was a shock to see him "lying stiff and cold." His feet were so rigid that they had to be thawed with an electric heater to get the boots on.

For the trip to Spain, Montagu and Cholmondeley packed the body in dry ice inside a heavy steel canister labeled "optical instruments," which was then bolted shut and loaded aboard a van on the evening of April 17, 1943. Climbing into the cab, the two officers—accompanied by a racecar driver named Jock Horsfall, who shared time behind the wheel—headed north toward Scotland and a rendezvous with the British submarine *Seraph*. It was a long trip, most of it made at night with headlights blacked out. At one point, instead of following the road around a traffic circle, they blindly drove straight across it. No harm was done, however, and they arrived next morning at the Holy Loch submarine base, where the mysterious canister was taken aboard the *Seraph*. The crew was told that the sub was deploying a secret weather-reporting buoy.

Shortly after 4 a.m. on April 30, the *Seraph* surfaced in the Atlantic a little more than a mile off Huelva—a destination chosen because a German agent with good contacts among the local Spanish authorities was known to operate in the area. The sub's commander, Lieutenant N. L. A. Jewell, had his four officers haul the canister topsides. Only then did he let them in on the secret.

Quickly adapting to their roles in this unconventional burial at sea, the men unbolted the canister cover, removed Martin, and fitted him with a life jacket, which they then inflated. The dry ice in the canister had retarded the process of decomposition during the two weeks the corpse was in transit, and its condition was consistent with that of a body that had been drifting at sea for several days. While Jewell intoned what he could remember from the Anglican burial service, his assistants cast Major Martin adrift.

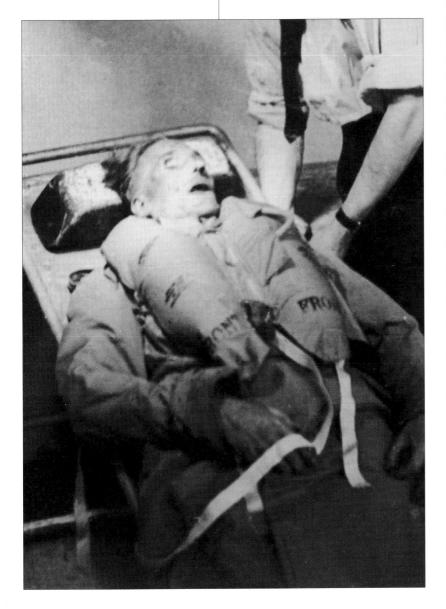

The corpse of 34-year-old Glyndwr Michael—a civilian who committed suicide in January 1943 and was later chosen by Montagu to represent a fictitious courier called Major William Martin—was fitted with a life jacket to make it look as if Martin died at sea as a result of a plane crash.

CREATING MAJOR MARTIN

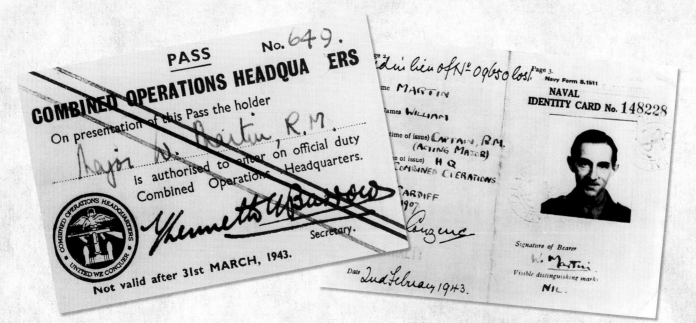

PASS   No. 649.

COMBINED OPERATIONS HEADQUA ERS

On presentation of this Pass the holder

Major W. Martin, R.M.

is authorised to enter on official duty
Combined Operations Headquarters.

Kenneth Stafford

Secretary.

Not valid after 31st MARCH, 1943.

Page 2.
ndu lieu of No 09650 lost.

me MARTIN

James WILLIAM

ime of issue) CAPTAIN, R.M.
(ACTING MAJOR)

e of issue) H Q
COMBINED OPERATIONS

CARDIFF
1907

Couzens

Date 2nd February 1943.

Page 3.
Navy Form S.1511

NAVAL
IDENTITY CARD No. 148228

Signature of Bearer

W. Martin

Visible distinguishing marks

NIL.

Headquarters pass

Naval ID card

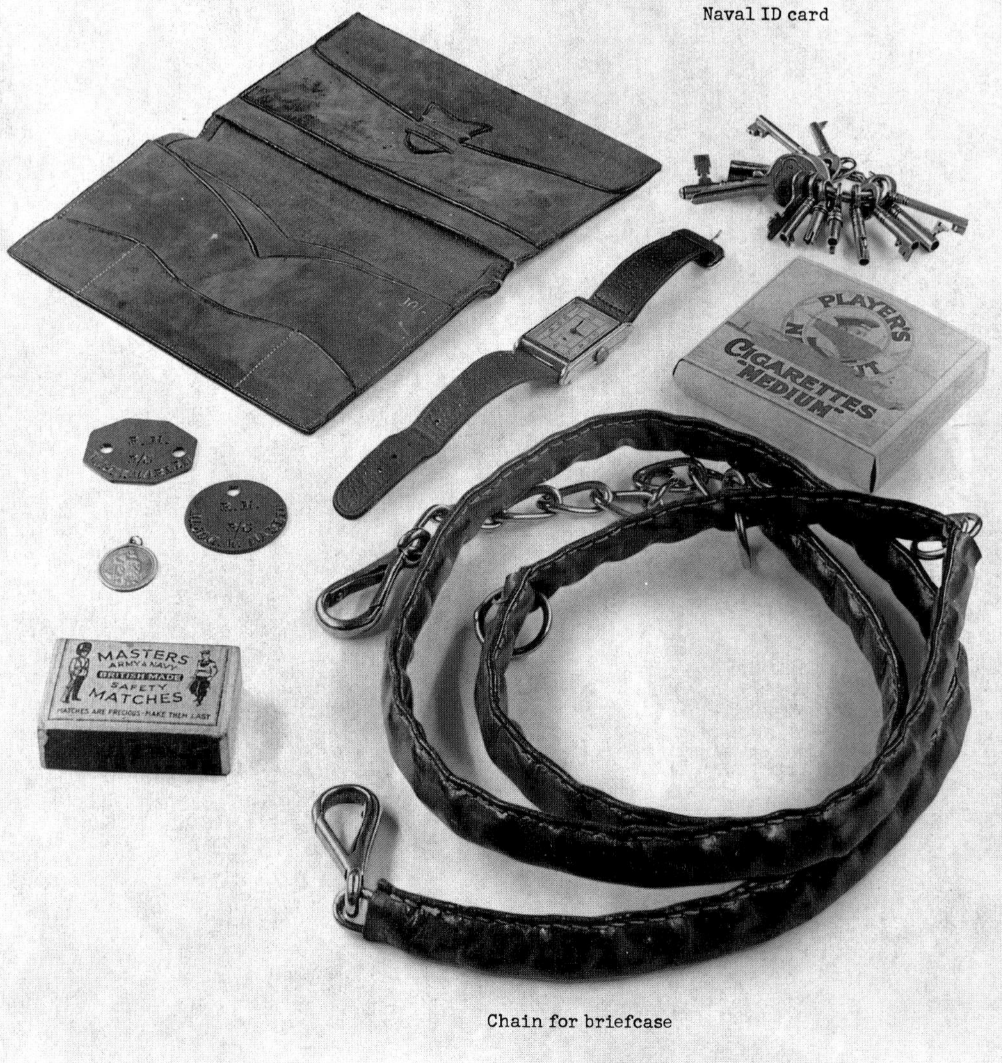

The planners of Mincemeat made Major Martin seem real by equipping him with the items shown here, including a pass to his London headquarters, which he had failed to renew amid the distractions of his coming trip and recent engagement (opposite). Spanish officials who retrieved the body found a wallet, keys, cigarettes, matches, watch, ID tags, and a Saint Christopher medal on his person—and the crucial confidential papers in a briefcase secured to him by a chain.

PLAYER'S
CIGARETTES
MEDIUM

MASTERS
ARMY & NAVY
BRITISH MADE
SAFETY
MATCHES
MATCHES ARE PRECIOUS · MAKE THEM LAST

Chain for briefcase

TELEPHONE Nº MAYFAIR 6261 (2 LINES)
TELEGRAMS EUCLASE WESDO LONDON.

113 New Bond Street

London. W. 1. 19ᵗʰ April 1943.

Major W. Martin, R.M.,
Naval + Military Club,
94, Piccadilly - W.1.

To S. J.

Sons of E. (Phillips

Silvers...

Jewels, Antique D...

15ᵗʰ April. 1943.   Single diamond ring
shoulders plat... (pre...

Engraving "P. L. from...

Bill for engagement ring

Fiancée, Pam

Letter from fiancée

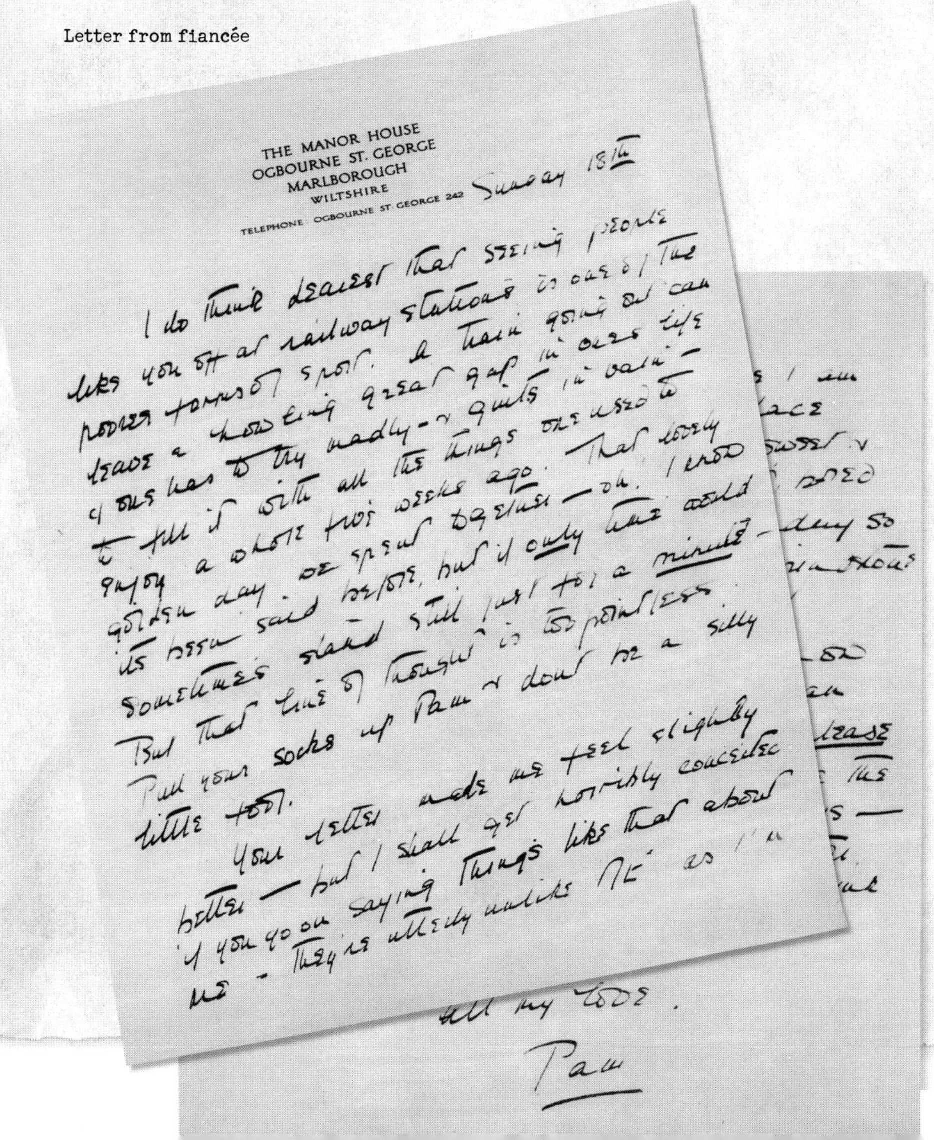

THE MANOR HOUSE
OGBOURNE ST. GEORGE
MARLBOROUGH
WILTSHIRE
TELEPHONE OGBOURNE ST. GEORGE 242   Sunday 18ᵗʰ

I do think dearest that seeing people
off at railway stations is one of the
poorer forms of sport. A train going out can
leave a howling great gap in ones life
& one has to try madly — & quite in vain —
to fill it with all the things one used to
enjoy a whole two weeks ago. That lovely
golden day we spent together — oh! I know
its been said before, but if only time could
sometimes stand still just for a minute — But
that line of thought is too pointless
Pull your socks up Pam & don't be a silly
little fool.

Your letter made me feel slightly
better — but I shall get horribly conceited
if you go on saying things like that about
me — They're utterly unlike ME as I...

all my love .

Pam

Prince of Wales Theatre
SECOND HOUSE
THURSDAY
April 2...
CIRCLE
C 10   10/6
NO TAX
TO BE RETAINED

Prince...
SECO...
TH...
A...
CIRCLE
C 1   10/6
NO TAX
TO BE RETAINED

Theater ticket stubs

Among the mementos in Martin's wallet were a photograph of his imaginary fiancée, Pam—actually a picture of a War Office employee—and an artful letter composed in her name by another young woman, in which Pam recalls a "lovely golden day we spent together." Completing the illusion were a bill for the engagement ring Martin bought Pam and ticket stubs for a London show the happy couple supposedly attended before he left on his ill-fated flight.

167

Just as predicted by a navy expert, the prevailing wind and tide pushed him swiftly toward shore—and into history.

As the drama unfolded, the German agents and their obliging Spanish contacts played their roles precisely as Montagu had hoped. German operatives telegraphed summaries of the letters to Berlin and forwarded photographic copies. Within two weeks, the information had passed from intelligence officers of the Abwehr up through the high command and reached Hitler himself. "The genuineness of the captured documents is above suspicion," said a report prepared for Admiral Karl Dönitz, commander in chief of the German navy.

The letters had the desired effect on Hitler, who refused to commit additional troops to the defense of Sicily and southern Italy. Instead, he ordered reinforcements to Sardinia and greatly bolstered the defenses of Greece, building up shore batteries and minefields along the coast, dispatching torpedo boats there from Sicily, and transferring the First Panzer Division from France to Greece. In late July, two weeks after the Allies invaded Sicily against little opposition, Hitler remained so concerned about an attack on Greece that he sent his most esteemed commander, Field Marshal Erwin Rommel, to deal with that perceived threat, which never materialized.

"The operation succeeded beyond our wildest dreams," Churchill's chief of staff, General Lord Hastings Lionel Ismay, wrote of Mincemeat after the war. "To have spread-eagled the German defensive effort right across Europe," he added, "was a remarkable achievement." In the end, few men unfit for service made a stranger or more significant contribution to the war effort than the late Glyndwr Michael, who lay forgotten in Huelva's Cemetery of Solitude under the tombstone of the man who never was.

END GAME EUROPE

The Allies' success in cloaking the invasion of Sicily offered a preview of the monumental deception campaign that was already taking shape in London as plans coalesced for a huge amphibious landing on the coast of France in 1944. Allied commanders chose Normandy as the landing site because it was less heavily defended than the region around Calais. To be sure, the Pas de Calais—known to the English as the Strait of Dover—offered the Allies both the shortest Channel crossing and the most direct route to the German industrial heartland. But as Ultra intercepts confirmed, Hitler considered the region around Calais the most likely landing site and had made it the

At top, Ewen Montagu (left) and driver Jock Horsfall stand by the van they used to transport a steel canister (above) holding the body of "Major Martin," preserved in dry ice, from a London morgue to a submarine base in Scotland.

Montagu drafted the misleading note at right, signed by Lord Louis Mountbatten, which told the Admiral of the Fleet that Major Martin was carrying a "hot" letter; the "VCIGS" referred to is the vice chief of the Imperial General Staff. A sly mention of sardines subtly supports other planted evidence in the briefcase that Sardinia might be the target for future Allied attacks.

Telephone :
WHitehall 9777

In reply, quote : R.1924/43

COMBINED OPERATIONS HEADQUARTERS,

1A, RICHMOND TERRACE,

WHITEHALL, S.W.1.

21st April,
1943.

Dear Admiral of the Fleet,

I promised V.C.I.G.S. that Major Martin would arrange with you for the onward transmission of a letter he has with him for General Alexander. It is very urgent and very "hot" and as there are some remarks in it that could not be seen by others in the War Office, it could not go by signal. I feel sure that you will see that it goes on safely and without delay.

I think you will find Martin the man you want. He is quiet and shy at first, but he really knows his stuff. He was more accurate than some of us about the probable run of events at Dieppe and he has been well in on the experiments with the latest barges and equipment which took place up in Scotland.

Let me have him back, please, as soon as the assault is over. He might bring some sardines with him - they are "on points" here!

Yours sincerely

Louis Mountbatten

Admiral of the Fleet Sir A.B. Cunningham, G.C.B.,D.S.O.,
Commander in Chief Mediterranean,
Allied Force H.Q.,
Algiers.

strongest point in his so-called Atlantic Wall, studded with fortifications of steel and concrete. Allied intelligence chiefs would use all the assets at their disposal—including the expert double agents controlled by MI-5 and the Double Cross Committee—to keep Hitler's best forces concentrated around Calais while the invasion of Normandy unfolded.

No double agent involved in this deception campaign ran greater risks than the one code-named Tricycle, whose real name was Dusko Popov. Since returning in 1942 from his unsuccessful mission to the United States, where he had clashed with FBI director J. Edgar Hoover, the cunning Yugoslav had endeared himself to his German overseers and was now considered one of their best agents in Britain. In February 1944, as troops and supplies gathered in England for the invasion of Normandy, he made a daring run to Lisbon to see his Abwehr controller, who went by the name of von Karsthoff. Popov brought with him intelligence seemingly of the utmost significance, consisting of the order of battle—or roster of units—for the entire First U.S. Army Group, or FUSAG. According to Popov, FUSAG was a formidable force, and it was assembling just across the Channel from Calais, suggesting that the Allies would cross in strength there, just as Hitler expected.

Much to Popov's surprise, von Karsthoff dismissed his report as "warmed-over gossip." For a moment, Popov feared the new Allied deception regarding Calais might crash on takeoff and that his own life might be in jeopardy. But then, adopting his haughtiest manner, he insisted to von Karsthoff that the information be forwarded to Berlin. While his report made its way up the chain of command, Popov returned safely to England, where Ultra decrypts revealed that Hitler and his aides had accepted his story.

In fact, there was some substance to Popov's report on FUSAG. Eleven genuine divisions had been assigned to this so-called army group, but they were not preparing to cross the Strait of Dover. Nearly all of those units would eventually be sent to support the invasion of Normandy and would be replaced by make-believe divisions, simulated by phony radio traffic and other ruses. The purpose of this elaborate hoax was to sustain the fiction that Normandy was merely a diversion, to be followed by the main invasion at Calais, thus keeping German forces frozen in place there. If the enemy saw through this scheme, the results might be disastrous, but Allied intelligence officers were prepared to chance it. "We had spent the earlier days of the war perfecting our system, building it up," Popov wrote afterward. "Now we were wagering everything, going for broke."

Convincing the Germans that Allied invasion forces would make their big push across the Strait of Dover was the crux of the deception, but the campaign did not stop there. The largest web of lies ever fabricated to deceive an enemy in wartime was taking shape under the label of Operation Bodyguard, which owed its name to a remark made by Winston Churchill as he conferred with Soviet dictator Joseph Stalin. "In wartime," observed the British prime minister, "truth is so precious that she should always be attended by a bodyguard of lies."

Operation Bodyguard embraced numerous programs of deception, each with its own code name—a network of ruses that stretched from Scandinavia to southern France and eastward as far as Greece. Included were efforts to suggest that the Balkan Peninsula or the Mediterranean coast of France were under imminent threat of attack from Allied troops in North Africa, forcing the Germans to leave troops in place to defend both areas. But the main element of Bodyguard, known as Operation Fortitude, was aimed at confusing the Germans about precisely where and when the invasion forces gathering in Britain would strike. Fortitude South was the code name for the crucial effort to keep enemy forces concentrated around Calais in anticipation of an attack, whereas Fortitude North was aimed at preventing the Germans from ruling out the possibility of an invasion of Scandinavia and shifting troops stationed there to the coast of France.

Hitler considered a northern invasion a real possibility and had stationed 27 divisions in Norway, Denmark, and Finland. To keep them there, the Allies simulated plans to land a sizable force on the coast of Norway in May 1944 with the supposed objective of pinning down German forces in the north until after the invasion of France. Reports reached Germany early

The massive buildup of matériel in southern England in early 1944 at sites like the ordnance depot below signaled that the Allies would soon send a huge invasion force across the Channel. Yet much of this went undetected by the Germans, in part because of misleading reports from Double Cross agents indicating that troops massing in Britain might land anywhere from Norway to southern France.

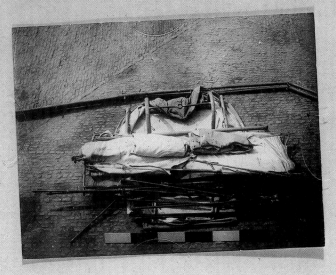

At left and below, shots from a wartime album illustrate several devices used to mislead reconnaissance flights that slipped through British air defenses. As shown here, the Allies devised a moving dummy tank by covering a Jeep with a metal framework and a realistic exterior (left). They also improved on flat dummy planes (lower right) by crafting three-dimensional models that cast more-convincing shadows and could better fool observers.

in the year that the British Fourth Army was organizing for that purpose near Edinburgh, Scotland. Said to number 350,000 troops, this purported army in fact consisted of just 334 men and 28 officers.

To project the image of a much larger force, deception planners filled local newspapers with reports of marriages and other social events involving Fourth Army troops. Dummy aircraft appeared at three airfields, along with phony fuel trucks. Real warships intended for the invasion of Normandy, but not needed for that purpose until later, anchored in the Firth of Forth, as if preparing for an attack on Norway. Commando raids of the sort that often preceded invasions struck military and industrial targets on the Norwegian coast. Sustaining the illusion of the Fourth Army was a barrage of radio traf-

THREE DIMENSIONAL SPITFIRE.
In this case built on old "Moth" undercarriage.

THREE DIMENSIONAL DUMMY

FLAT SPITFIRE

THREE DIMENSIONAL DUMMY BOSTON
SHOWING CONSTRUCTION

fic from what passed for its headquarters in the basement of Edinburgh Cas-tle, where operators sent messages to bogus units supposedly carrying out training exercises in skiing, rock climbing, and cold-weather operations. They knew the Germans were listening when a Luftwaffe fighter machine-gunned their headquarters, shaking up the occupants but injuring no one. It was the Fourth Army's first and only exposure to combat.

As summer approached and the invasion of Norway failed to material-ize, Fortitude North lost much of its credibility. Two make-believe divisions were transferred from Scotland to southeast England to bolster the notion that the big push across the Strait of Dover was imminent. This transfer was not convincingly simulated by British radio operators, who left the impres-sion that one of those divisions had completed a laborious move of 300 miles to its new base in a single day—an impossible feat. By then, however, For-titude North had achieved its objective by preventing any large-scale redeployment of German troops from Scandinavia to France.

Fortitude North was a modest deception compared with Fortitude South, which was designed not simply to lock German divisions in place across the Strait of Dover before the invasion of Normandy but to keep them around Calais for more than a month afterward, awaiting a follow-up attack by FUSAG that would never come. Although Allied planners made that threat seem more plausible by assigning to FUSAG 11 flesh-and-blood divi-sions—two with the First Canadian Army and nine with the Third U.S. Army—one unit after another would be sent to bolster the real invasion of Normandy, where their presence would surely be detected by the Germans. The scheme would collapse unless it appeared that fresh divisions were be-ing sent to England's southeast coast to replenish FUSAG.

As with Fortitude North and its phantom British army, local news-papers would convey the impression that the Dover area was swamped with Allied troops by featuring items such as notes from church vicars condemn-ing the moral collapse brought on by the presence of so many foreign sol-diers. Meanwhile, radio operators would transmit a steady stream of false signals from fictional divisions in the vicinity, following a script contained in a book eight inches thick that governed all such communications, beginning in the spring and continuing for several weeks after D-Day.

Visual deception played a vital role as well. Although the Allies now had control of the skies over Britain, German reconnaissance aircraft some-times got close enough to the coast to survey sites where an invasion might be in the offing. To guard against that possibility, dummy landing craft con-structed of plywood and papier-mâché at a motion-picture studio lined har-bors and estuaries along the southeast coast, with smoke pouring from their fake stacks. A phony oil storage dock and refinery took shape in the harbor at Dover. Farmers were astonished to see tanks in their pastures that deflat-ed when impaled by the horns of angry bulls. Tank and truck tracks led into the woods, suggesting that vehicles were hidden under the trees.

An eyewitness report from a top German officer also provided seeming confirmation of FUSAG's strength and readiness. General Hans Kramer, the last commander of the Afrika Korps, had been taken prisoner by the British

The impressive-looking warplanes pictured in this aerial view of a base in Scotland in 1943 were in fact dummies, meant to provide German observers with false evi-dence of preparations for an inva-sion of Norway. Such visual decep-tion, combined with contrived radio signals from a bogus army in Scotland and misinformation from double agents, helped keep German divisions from being shifted out of Norway to oppose the real threat to Hitler's forces in France.

in Tunisia. Now he was to be repatriated through the Swedish Red Cross because of failing health. On the way from a detention camp in Wales to the Swedish ship that would carry him home, Kramer was driven through southwestern England, where large numbers of troops were gathering across from Normandy for the real invasion. Kramer was told by his escorts that he was traveling through the southeastern part of the country, where FUSAG was assembling. He had no way of knowing the truth because all signposts and place names in England had been taken down in 1940 for the duration of the war to foil German invaders or saboteurs.

Before embarking for Germany, the clueless General Kramer stopped to dine with the man who was serving both as the real commander of the U.S. Third Army and as the purported chief of FUSAG, Lieutenant General George S. Patton. Although the celebrated Patton privately resented the FUSAG charade because it put him temporarily on the sidelines, the Germans assumed that he had won command of the crack invasion forces bound for Calais with his bravura performance in Sicily, where his armored units had distinguished themselves. His presence added credibility to the idea that the Allies were mustering their strength for a crossing at Dover.

Perhaps the strangest—and least effective—of all the hoaxes carried

Below, hard-fighting lieutenant general George S. Patton, known as Old Blood and Guts, inspects troops of his so-called First U.S. Army Group (FUSAG) in April 1944. Patton's commanding presence at FUSAG headquarters near the Strait of Dover was advertised to the Germans to make them believe he had plans to lead his forces across the strait to invade the Calais region.

Bernard Law Montgomery

M. E. Clifton James

Lieutenant M. E. Clifton James, an actor by trade, proved so adept at impersonating General Bernard Law Montgomery that the British sent the lowly army paymaster to Gibraltar and North Africa in May 1944 in the commander's uniform—including his trademark beret—to foster the illusion that Montgomery was planning an invasion of southern France. After the war, James appeared in pageants and a movie in a reprise of his role as Monty.

out to divert attention from the forthcoming landing at Normandy involved the assignment of a former actor, Lieutenant M. E. Clifton James of the Royal Army Pay Corps, to impersonate British general Bernard Law Montgomery, the hero of El Alamein. While the real Monty joined in the planning for Normandy, James was sent to Algiers in his stead in late May 1944 to make it appear that the Allies were planning something big in the Mediterranean, perhaps an invasion of southern France. The goal was to keep the Germans from redeploying forces from the Mediterranean coast to the threatened Atlantic Wall—and to make them think an Allied push across the English Channel was unlikely any time soon if a commander as important as Montgomery was off in Africa.

James bore a striking resemblance to Montgomery and quickly learned to imitate Monty's jaunty salute, his high-pitched voice, and his characteristic long stride with hands clasped behind his back. Even men who knew the field marshal well were nearly fooled. But unlike Monty, who abstained from tobacco and alcohol, James was reportedly fond of both. By one account, he smuggled a hip flask of gin aboard the plane for the flight to Algiers and barely sobered up in time for a conspicuous appearance at the Gibraltar airfield, which was known to be under surveillance by a German agent, watching through field glasses from just across the border in Spain.

As it turned out, James's performance made little impression on the Germans. No theatrics at this stage could disguise the fact that a major storm was brewing along the Atlantic Wall. The Germans knew as much from reports they were receiving from their trusted agents in Britain—spies who faithfully reported that an invasion of France was imminent while deceiving their German controllers about where the big blow would fall.

D-DAY FOR DOUBLE CROSS

By the spring of 1944, MI-5 and the Double Cross Committee were in an unrivaled position to feed false information to the enemy. They had perfected their system and felt reasonably confident that every spy reporting to Germany from England was under their complete control. Indeed, they had more double agents at their disposal than they knew what to do with and had the luxury of selecting the cream of the crop. To reduce the risk of foul-ups, only agents in high standing among the Germans figured in the D-Day deceptions. An agent whom the enemy viewed as untrustworthy "might wreck the whole enterprise," wrote John Masterman, chairman of the Double Cross Committee. "Even worse, his messages might be 'read in reverse' and the true target of attack be exposed instead of concealed by him."

One sign that an agent was esteemed in Berlin was the willingness of the Germans to supply him with a radio. Few female agents were entrusted with radios, however, and even those who were well regarded by their controllers usually had to resort to writing letters with invisible ink or sending coded telegrams. Such was the case with a beautiful young Argentinian, known to MI-5 by the code name Bronx, who pretended to spy for the Germans in Britain by getting close to men in high positions.

Bronx was instructed by her German spymaster to communicate any

intelligence she acquired on Allied invasion plans in the form of coded telegrams to the Bank of the Holy Ghost in Lisbon, where she had an account, requesting funds to pay for medical expenses. Her telegram on May 15, 1944, asking for £50 to cover her bill at the dentist, signaled that she had learned Allied forces would come ashore at Bordeaux in southwestern France within the month. In a letter that followed, penned in secret ink, she reported hearing this news from a drunken American officer in a London nightclub. Although the Germans fully expected the main Allied invasion to come at Calais, they could not rule out the possibility of other landings, and Bronx's report was evidently taken seriously enough to keep the 11th Panzer Division pinned down near Bordeaux for weeks to come.

Another female Double Cross agent, code-named Treasure, claimed to have access to such vital intelligence on FUSAG that the Abwehr did decide to equip her with a radio. Treasure's real name was Lily Sergueiew. A young Frenchwoman of Russian origin, she had reached England in late 1943 after persuading her Abwehr controller, with whom she was intimate, that she could be trusted to operate on enemy ground. She now reported to the Ger-

At low tide, German field marshal Erwin Rommel leads an inspection of barriers designed to snag Allied landing craft along the Atlantic Wall, where he took charge of troops in late 1943. Rommel had orders to repulse an invasion anywhere along the coast within "a matter of hours or, at the most, days," but Hitler complicated that task by bolstering defenses around Calais, while leaving other areas like Normandy vulnerable.

"If the enemy succeeds in breaching our defenses along a wide front, consequences of staggering proportions will follow."

—Adolf Hitler

mans that she was having an affair with an American staff officer attached to FUSAG—and arranged a trip to Lisbon to collect a radio from her controller for relaying the precious secrets she extracted from her source.

During this trip, Treasure became distressed when the British quarantined her pet dog in Gibraltar, where it later died. She already had a reputation for being "exceptionally temperamental and troublesome," according to Masterman. Perhaps her erratic behavior arose from her fear that she was dying of leukemia. In any event, the loss of her pet so angered her that, upon returning to England, she planned to alert the Abwehr that she was under British control. Before taking the plunge, however, she had a change of heart and confessed to her British handler. In response, MI-5 dispensed with her services and assigned someone else to imitate her signature as a radio operator and send false reports to the Germans on her hard-won equipment.

This was not the only close call for MI-5. Tricycle, a key player in the effort to conceal Allied intentions, came perilously close to being exposed as a double agent shortly before D-Day. Popov himself was not to blame. Despite his free-wheeling manner, he was a careful agent who did all he could to avert suspicion. Many of his reports were made by radio from the safety of England, and he and his MI-5 handlers were ever so subtle. "Never did we say anything directly about the Pas de Calais," Popov wrote later. Instead, the idea was to give out "indications" and fragmentary clues that the Germans would then put together themselves, leading them to conclude the target site was Calais. These false leads, as in previous Double Cross deceptions, were carefully interspersed with actual facts of little real strategic value. Because they could verify the truthful items, the Germans were more inclined to believe the remaining false ones.

In addition to his broadcasts, however, Popov continued to make regular runs to Portugal and Spain to confer with his German controller, and those visits were fraught with peril. The dashing Popov had "the steel within," a British colleague observed, "the ruthlessness and the cold-blooded courage that enabled him to go back to the German secret service headquarters in Lisbon and Madrid time and again. It was like putting his head into the lion's mouth." He was accustomed to mixing business with pleasure during these forays, but even his love affairs carried risks. On one Lisbon visit, he went to bed with a young woman he described as "a statuesque, dark-blond Belgian girl," who searched his apartment when she thought he was asleep. He concluded that she was an enemy agent sent to check up on him.

In April 1944 Popov unexpectedly had to deal with Nazi spymasters who were new to him. By this point in the war, the Abwehr was being absorbed into the SD, the security service of Heinrich Himmler's SS. Popov's Abwehr controller, von Karsthoff, had been replaced in Lisbon by two surly SD men, who struck Popov as "a couple of faithful party hacks." They gave Popov a grilling that lasted for most of the night, he recalled, but in the end they accepted as genuine his report on the FUSAG invasion force. "You Nazi supermen," Popov thought triumphantly afterward, "I've done you in."

But Popov was not out of danger. One spy in Lisbon knew full well that he was working for the British, and if that man spilled his story the results

could be disastrous. His name was Johann Jebsen, and he and Popov had been friends since their student days in Jebsen's native Germany before the war. Later, Jebsen had recruited Popov for the Abwehr. Jebsen eventually recognized that Popov's true loyalties lay with the Allies, and Popov in turn came to suspect that Jebsen despised his Nazi overlords and was prepared to offer his services to London. By 1944 Jebsen had crossed that line and enlisted with the British as a double agent under the code name Artist.

Jebsen offered the British valuable information, but he also presented them with a terrible dilemma. To prove his loyalty, he was willing to name Abwehr agents in England—including the Spaniard Juan Pujol, or Garbo, whose contribution to the deception campaign surpassed even Popov's. Jebsen did not know that Garbo was in fact working for the British. But he did know that Popov was a double agent, which made it dangerous for Jebsen to remain in Lisbon, where the Germans might come to suspect him and pry the truth from him. One option was to offer Jebsen sanctuary in Britain, but then the Germans would assume that he had betrayed both Pujol and Popov and the Double Cross Committee would have to drop the two top performers in its deception scheme.

To resolve the dilemma, the committee considered having Artist assassinated. That option was rejected, however, not because it was deemed improper—thousands of lives would be at risk if the enemy saw through the deception—but because it would spark a German investigation that might bring to light Jebsen's illicit contacts with the British and cast suspicion on Popov. Reluctantly, the committee simply left Jebsen in place.

Not long after Popov completed his perilous run to Lisbon and returned to London, the worst fears of the Double Cross Committee seemed to be realized. On April 28 Jebsen was summoned to the German embassy in Lisbon on the pretext of being awarded a medal for his services to the Reich. Once inside the building, he was interrogated, beaten, drugged, and bundled unconscious into the trunk of a limousine with diplomatic plates before being spirited away to Berlin. News of his arrest reached London via Ultra decrypts of German radio traffic and created an atmosphere of almost unbearable tension at MI-5. Would Jebsen tell all he knew, betraying Popov and revealing the FUSAG threat as a hoax? If so, the Germans might well conclude that Normandy was indeed the target.

As it turned out, Jebsen had been arrested on suspicion of involvement in currency swindles. His captors may never have questioned him about Popov or MI-5. If they did, Jebsen evidently revealed nothing of significance before he was shot to death in late 1944 as he allegedly tried to escape from the Oranienburg concentration camp near Berlin.

Jebsen's arrest, however, meant retirement for Popov. With Artist behind bars and subject to torture, Tricycle's secret was no longer safe. He shut

At left, members of the British Royal Engineers struggle ashore at Normandy on D-Day, June 6, 1944. Double Cross agents helped shield the vulnerable invasion forces from a potentially devastating counterattack by portraying the landing as a diversionary action.

down his transmitter on May 19, explaining to the Germans by letter that he thought himself under suspicion by the British.

Some of the slack left by Popov's retirement was taken up by the double agent Brutus, the former Polish officer and French resistance leader Roman Garby-Czerniawski, known in the resistance as Armand. Garby-Czerniawski had persuaded German authorities to let him "escape" from a French prison by agreeing to spy for them in Britain and had then become a Double Cross agent. Despite MI-5's initial suspicions, he proved his loyalty to the Allies by contributing to the Fortitude North deception. And so, after Popov stepped down, Brutus informed Berlin by radio that he had been appointed to General Patton's headquarters as liaison between the exiled Polish high command and FUSAG. This allowed him to pick up where Popov left off, keeping the Germans abreast of the latest developments as Patton's force supposedly prepared to smash through the Atlantic Wall at Calais.

GARBO TAKES THE PRIZE

Of all the Double Cross agents, none did more to conceal Allied intentions before, during, and after the Normandy landing than Juan Pujol—Garbo—who now ranked as MI-5's greatest asset. His value to the British was directly proportionate to his standing among the Germans, who trusted him implicitly and considered him their best agent in Britain. Garbo's German controller in Madrid regarded him as a quarrelsome genius to be humored at all costs and always gave him what he asked for, whether it was more money to satisfy a greedy subagent or the latest in German ciphers to render his radio transmissions more secure.

By the spring of 1944, he was claiming in his carefully falsified reports, coauthored with his MI-5 handler Tommy Harris, that he had 14 subagents scattered about Britain. All 14, of course, were wholly imaginary. One fictitious operative was a British sailor with Communist leanings based in Scotland, who had supposedly been deceived by Pujol into thinking that he was supplying information to a Soviet espionage network. Another was a fiery Welsh nationalist and Fascist who belonged to a shadowy organization called the Aryan World Order and was said to have lured several of its members into Pujol's web. Among the loose-tongued sources exploited by other subagents was a fictional American army sergeant whose father was a senior officer on Eisenhower's staff.

Garbo's agents purportedly sent him messages in invisible ink. He then relayed their reports on the most powerful radio operated by any of the double agents—a set provided by the British, who wanted to be sure his signals were received loud and clear. In the first five months of 1944, he transmitted no fewer than 500 messages to Madrid from atop the London headquarters of MI-5. Like other Double Cross agents' broadcasts, they were free of any obvious bias. They simply laid out the raw intelligence Garbo had collected—including stories from various subagents that were sometimes inconsistent, as might be expected—and let the Germans draw their own conclusions. Only careful analysis of the reports would reveal that the evidence in them weighed slightly in favor of Calais as the main landing area.

Fighting with Dummies

Early on June 6, 1944, the Nazi press agency Transocean broke the news of the D-Day invasion by reporting landings by enemy paratroopers north of the Seine. Those landings had occurred in the dark, obscuring the fact that the supposed fighting men were lifeless dummies like the one at right, deployed by Britain's Special Air Service (SAS) to divert German attention from operations elsewhere by real paratroopers and by invasion forces coming ashore at the beaches.

Well before dawn, the SAS dropped 500 of the dummies—only three feet tall but large enough to look convincing in the dark at a distance—at four sites. Some of them came down north of the Seine and others near the American zone of operations in Normandy. The dummies were rigged to explode on landing with a bright flash and a noise resembling gunfire.

At each site, a few real SAS men landed to enhance the effect by playing recordings of battle sounds or setting off explosives. In Normandy, this small investment in deception paid big dividends, keeping an entire German regiment of 1,750 men busy until late morning searching for phantom paratroopers, which prevented them from reaching nearby Omaha Beach in time to repulse the oncoming Americans.

Ultra intercepts made clear that the deceptions broadcast by Garbo and other double agents were paying off. German intelligence greatly overestimated the number of Allied divisions in Britain, making the idea of more than one invasion seem plausible. The Germans were not blind to the possibility of an impending assault on Normandy, and some of the beaches there were strongly defended. But overall, Normandy remained far more vulnerable to attack than the area around Calais, where Hitler had kept his strongest forces in place to repulse the imagined threat from FUSAG.

The D-Day landing in Normandy on the morning of June 6, 1944, was no diversion. The Allies had assembled the mightiest invasion armada in history—5,000 vessels of every type, carrying more than 150,000 assault troops and 20,000 vehicles. Far from the embattled Normandy beaches, meanwhile, nearly one million German troops were deployed at various points around Europe awaiting invasions that never came. The enemy, as American general Omar Bradley wrote later, was "paralyzed into indecision."

For Garbo, D-Day marked the beginning of the most crucial phase of his operation, aimed at maintaining the apparent threat to Calais even as the Allies tried to break out of their Normandy beachheads and reclaim France. To preserve the Germans' trust in Garbo for that ultimate deception, the Double Cross Committee—with Eisenhower's express approval—authorized Pujol to transmit a warning of the Normandy invasion at 3 a.m. on June 6, a few hours before landing craft disgorged the first wave of assault troops. This notice would come too late to allow the Germans to reinforce the targeted beaches but would help avert suspicions that Garbo had deliberately downplayed the threat to Normandy.

As it turned out, Garbo was unable to reach Madrid on the radio until past dawn on D-Day because those manning the listening post had gone to bed at midnight, disregarding Garbo's earlier recommendation that they stand a 24-hour watch. The failure permitted Garbo to deliver one of his patented scoldings to Madrid. "This makes me question your seriousness and your sense of responsibility," he signaled. His German controller was suitably apologetic, and Garbo's stock in Berlin remained high.

Meanwhile, Brutus had signaled the Germans on June 6 that FUSAG had no involvement in the Normandy landing. "Received this morning news of the beginning of the invasion," he radioed in his guise as a Polish liaison at Patton's headquarters. "Extremely surprised because our FUSAG remains unmoved." He concluded that FUSAG was being held in readiness for "an independent action."

This helped set the stage for Garbo's greatest performance. On June 8, he pretended to assemble in London all his available agents. Out of their conference grew his longest radio message ever—one in which he departed from form and offered his opinions. "It is perfectly clear that the present attack is a large-scale operation but diversionary in character," he stated. The purpose was "to draw the maximum of our reserves," he added, "so as to be able to strike a blow somewhere else with ensured success." FUSAG remained in southeast England, Garbo concluded, ready when ordered to cross the Pas de Calais and deliver the knockout blow. This report was well received, and Hitler refrained from sending divisions in the Calais area to meet the threat in Normandy.

Garbo kept up the Calais charade for seven more weeks, during which time Patton and his Third U.S. Army were sent to reinforce the Allies in Normandy. Garbo reported that a new commander had been named to replace Patton as chief of FUSAG and that the army group was being replenished with incoming divisions—some of them from the fictional Fourth British Army in Scotland. Finally, in August, Garbo announced the cancellation of the planned assault by FUSAG. The German general staff remained convinced that Normandy had indeed been a diversion that by luck grew into something bigger, precluding the need for a landing at Calais.

Far from blaming Garbo for faulty intelligence, his handlers sent him a reward of $3,000. A short time later, as Allied forces swept across France, Garbo received one of Germany's highest military awards. "With great happiness and satisfaction," reported his controller, "I am able to advise you today that the Führer has conceded the Iron Cross to you for your extraordinary merits." Since this decoration was intended for "first-line combatants," Pujol was enrolled honorarily in a Spanish division fighting with German forces on the Russian front.

Before Germany went down to defeat in 1945, Pujol won a prize that meant much more to him—the honor of becoming a Member of the British Empire. The award was kept secret, and he gladly remained an obscure figure after the war, moving to Venezuela and living quietly there with his wife and children under an assumed name for fear that someone on the losing side might learn of his treachery and seek retribution. "I wanted to be forgotten, to pass unnoticed and to be untraceable," Pujol explained later.

Not until 1984, when he was past 70 and felt sure that all who wished him ill had either "died or disappeared," did he emerge from the shadows, after being located by a journalist, to take credit for his contribution to the Allied victory. During ceremonies marking the 40th anniversary of D-Day, the duke of Edinburgh thanked him personally at Buckingham Palace. And on June 6, 40 years to the day after the troops came ashore, he joined in observances of the landing on the Normandy beaches. Looking back, he took pride in the fact that his deceptions had furthered a cause he regarded as just and had saved Allied lives. "Many, many more would have perished," he reflected, "had our plan failed and the Germans counterattacked in force."

Shielded by barrage balloons against low-flying enemy aircraft, Allied ships disgorge reinforcements onto Omaha Beach after D-Day. Double Cross agent Garbo helped convince the Germans that the invasion— the largest amphibious assault in history—was a trap, meant to lure German forces away from Calais, where the real action would occur.

ACKNOWLEDGMENTS & PICTURE CREDITS

ACKNOWLEDGMENTS

The editors wish to thank the following for their assistance in the preparation of this volume:

Carl Boyd, Old Dominion University, Norfolk, Va.; Jeff Cutting, Australian War Memorial, Canberra, Australia; Cyndy Gilley, Do You Graphics, Woodbine, Md.; Laura Given, Henninger Media Services, Arlington, Va.; Regina Griebel, Berlin; Toni Heily, CIA Exhibit Center, Washington, D.C.; Heidrun Klein, Bildarchiv Preussischer Kulturbesitz, Berlin; Prudence Lawday, Bibliothek für Zeitgeschichte, Stuttgart; Dean Love, Bethesda, Md.; Marti Mercer, National Security Agency, Fort Meade, Md.; Helga Müller-Steinhäuser, Bildarchiv J. K. Piekalkiewicz, Rösrath-Hoffnungsthal; Art Ronnie, Altadena, Calif.; Christopher Staerck, London; John Taylor, National Archives at College Park, Md.; Johannes Tuchel, Gedenkstätte Deutscher Widerstand, Berlin; Thorsten Zarwel, Bundesarchiv, Berlin.

PICTURE CREDITS

The sources for the illustrations in this book appear below. Credits from left to right are separated by semicolons, from top to bottom by dashes.

COVER: Bildarchiv J. K. Piekalkiewicz, Rösrath-Hoffnungsthal. **3:** Bildarchiv J. K. Piekalkiewicz, Rösrath-Hoffnungsthal. **6-8:** CORBIS/Bettmann. **9:** National Archives, Neg. No. RG 373. **10:** Bildarchiv Preussischer Kulturbesitz, Berlin. **11:** Süddeutscher Verlag, Bilderdienst, Munich—Murry Sill/Silver Image, courtesy H. Keith Melton, TheSpyMuseum.com (2). **12:** From *At Dawn We Slept, The Untold Story of Pearl Harbor*, by Gordon W. Prange, McGraw-Hill Book Co., New York, 1981, courtesy Donald M. Goldstein; National Archives, Neg. No. 80-G-413507. **14:** Bildarchiv J. K. Piekalkiewicz, Rösrath-Hoffnungsthal. **16:** AP/Wide World Photos—Bildarchiv J. K. Piekalkiewicz, Rösrath-Hoffnungsthal; Murry Sill/Silver Image, courtesy H. Keith Melton, TheSpyMuseum.com. **18:** From *Spy/CounterSpy*, by Dusko Popov, Grosset & Dunlap, New York, 1974 (2). **19:** Courtesy of the publisher, Yale University Press. **20, 21:** Public Record Office, Kew, Surrey, England—Octopus Publishing Group, London. **22:** Bildarchiv J. K. Piekalkiewicz, Rösrath-Hoffnungsthal. **23-26:** Imperial War Museum, London. **27:** Maurey Garber. **28:** From *Spy/CounterSpy*, by Dusko Popov, Grosset & Dunlap Publishers, New York, 1974, adapted by John Drummond, © Time-Life Inc.; courtesy H. Keith Melton, TheSpyMuseum.com—Murry Sill/Silver Image, courtesy H. Keith Melton, TheSpyMuseum.com. **29:** AP/Wide World Photos. **31:** © 1999 Owen/Black Star. **32:** From *Operation Garbo*, by Juan Pujol and

Nigel West, Weidenfeld and Nicolson, London, 1985—Public Record Office, Kew, Surrey, England. **34:** National Archives, courtesy Kevin Mahoney. **35:** AP/Wide World Photos—Robin Reid/courtesy H. Keith Melton, TheSpyMuseum.com. **36, 37:** National Archives, Neg. No. 226-FPL-T-117; National Archives, courtesy Kevin Mahoney, Neg. No. 226-FPL-P-20. **38, 39:** National Archives, courtesy Kevin Mahoney (2); from *OSS*, by R. Harris Smith, University of California Press, Los Angeles, 1972 (2)—courtesy Time Inc. Picture Collection. **40, 41:** National Archives, courtesy Kevin Mahoney. **42, 43:** Brooke Dolan, U.S.A.; Allan Squires, U.S.S.C., both images from *OSS*, by R. Harris Smith, University of California Press, Los Angeles, 1972. **44:** Private collection. **46, 47:** Nederlands Instituut voor Oorlogsdocumentatie. **48:** Bayerische Staatsbibliothek München. **49:** TRH Pictures, London. **50, 51:** Süddeutscher Verlag, Bilderdienst, Munich—Bildarchiv Preussischer Kulturbesitz, Berlin (2). **52-54:** Bildarchiv J. K. Piekalkiewicz, Rösrath-Hoffnungsthal. **55:** Bildarchiv Preussischer Kulturbesitz, Berlin—Bildarchiv J. K. Piekalkiewicz, Rösrath-Hoffnungsthal—Bildarchiv Preussischer Kulturbesitz, Berlin (2). **56:** Bildarchiv J. K. Piekalkiewicz, Rösrath-Hoffnungsthal. **57:** Süddeutscher Verlag, Bilderdienst, Munich—Murry Sill/Silver Image, courtesy H. Keith Melton, TheSpyMuseum.com. **59:** Johannes Haas-Heye—Gedenkstätte Deutscher Widerstand, Berlin (2). **60, 61:** Bundesarchiv, Berlin. **62:** From *The Red Orchestra*, by Gilles Perrault, Simon & Schuster, New York, 1967. **63:** Bildarchiv J. K. Piekalkiewicz, Rösrath-Hoffnungsthal. **64:** Courtesy John Eppler—from *The Cat and the Mice*, by Leonard Mosley, Harper & Brothers, New York, 1958. **65:** Dar Al-Hilal; George Rodger/Magnum Photos. **66:** Prof. Günter A. Peis, Innsbruck, Austria. **67:** AP/Wide World Photos. **68:** FBI, courtesy Art Ronnie. **69:** CORBIS/Bettmann. **70:** National Archives, Neg. No. 65-HM-20A. **71:** National Archives, Neg. No. 065-HM-68. **72, 73:** Ullstein Bilderdienst, Berlin. **74:** Ullstein Bilderdienst, Berlin; Bundesarchiv, Koblenz, photo 146/99/3/1A—Bildarchiv Preussischer Kulturbesitz, Berlin; Imperial War Museum, London; Ullstein Bilderdienst, Berlin. **75:** Ullstein Bilderdienst, Berlin—Süddeutscher Verlag, Bilderdienst, Munich; Bildarchiv Preussischer Kulturbesitz, Berlin; Ullstein Bilderdienst, Berlin. **76, 77:** AKG, Berlin (2); Ullstein Bilderdienst, Berlin—Keystone Pressedienst, Hamburg; AKG, Berlin; Süddeutscher Verlag, Bilderdienst, Munich (2); Keystone Pressedienst, Hamburg; Süddeutscher Verlag, Bilderdienst, Munich. **78:** Bundesarchiv, Koblenz, photo 146/72/109/18a—Süddeutscher Verlag, Bilderdienst, Munich;

Bildarchiv Preussischer Kulturbesitz, Berlin (2). **79:** Ullstein Bilderdienst, Berlin. **80:** National Archives, Neg. No. 242-JRB-12-75. **82:** National Cryptologic Museum/National Security Agency (NSA), Fort Meade, Md. **83:** National Archives, Neg. No. SRDJ-013011. **84:** Sally Wilson, Tarrant Monkton, Dorset, England—© Express Newspapers, London. **87:** From *Enigma*, by Wladyslav Kozaczuk, University Publications of America, Bethesda, Md., 1984—Bundesarchiv, Berlin. **88:** Larry Sherer, courtesy NSA, Fort Meade, Md. **89:** Art by Linda Richards, based on artwork by William J. Hennessy, Jr., © Time Life Inc., 1991.—Larry Sherer, courtesy NSA, Fort Meade, Md. **90:** From *Enigma*, by Wladyslav Kozaczuk, University Publications of America, Bethesda, Md., 1984. **92:** Art by Linda Richards, based on diagram from *The Enigma War*, by Jozef Garlinski, Charles Scribner's Sons, New York, 1972. **93:** From *Seizing the Enigma*, by David Kahn, Houghton Mifflin, Boston, 1991—courtesy Margaret and Robin Denniston, Oxford, England. **94:** From *Alan Turing: The Enigma*, by Andrew Hodges, Simon & Schuster, New York, 1983; from *Seizing the Enigma*, by David Kahn, Houghton Mifflin, Boston, 1991. **95:** Bildarchiv J. K. Piekalkiewicz, Rösrath-Hoffnungsthal—courtesy Barbara Eachus. **97:** Public Record Office, Kew, Surrey, England. **98, 99:** Aerofilms Limited, Borehamwood, Hertfordshire, England; Bletchley Park Trust/Science and Society Picture Library, London (3). **100:** © Hulton Getty/Liaison Agency. **102, 103:** Imperial War Museum, London. **104:** The Friedman Collection, George C. Marshall Research Foundation—NSA, Fort Meade, Md. **106:** U.S. Navy, Neg. No. W-PH-67-13982. **107:** From *Double Edged Secrets*, by W. J. Holmes, Naval Institute Press, 1979, courtesy Mrs. Janet Rochefort Elderding. **109:** National Archives, Neg. No. 80-GO-414422. **111-123:** Background book, photo by Robin Reid. **111:** Bildarchiv J. K. Piekalkiewicz, Rösrath-Hoffnungsthal. **112:** Bildarchiv J. K. Piekalkiewicz, Rösrath-Hoffnungsthal—Ullstein Bilderdienst, Berlin. **113:** AKG, Berlin—Murry Sill/Silver Image, courtesy H. Keith Melton, TheSpyMuseum.com. **114:** Bildarchiv J. K. Piekalkiewicz, Rösrath-Hoffnungsthal—Archives Drago Arsenijevic. **115:** Rivett Collection, from *Cast No Shadow*, by Mary S. Lovell, Pantheon Books, New York, 1992; Library of Congress, Neg. No. LCUSZ62-101779. **116:** CORBIS/Bettmann (2); from *Cast No Shadow*, by Mary S. Lovell, Pantheon Books, New York, 1992 (2). **117:** *France Soir* (DR)—CORBIS/Bettmann. **118:** Australian War Memorial, Neg. No. 306807—Royal Australian Navy/copied by Henry Groskinsky. **119:** Australian War Memorial, Neg. No. 306817—map by John Drummond, Time Life Inc.;

from *Lonely Vigil, Coastmasters of the Solomons*, by Walter Lord, Viking Press, New York, 1977. **120:** From *I Was Cicero*, by Elyesa Bazna, Harper & Row, New York, 1962—Hart Preston/LIFE Magazine © Time Inc. **121:** Roger-Viollet, Paris—Bill van Calsem/courtesy H. Keith Melton, TheSpy-Museum.com. **122:** Roger-Viollet, Paris (2)—CORBIS/Bettmann. **123:** Thomas Veres/courtesy USHMM Photo Archives—Lena Kurtz Deutsch/courtesy USHMM Photo Archives; Thomas Veres, New York. **124:** Roger-Viollet, Paris. **127:** © Stephen Howarth, Shelton, Nottinghamshire, England—map by John Drummond, Time Life Inc. **128, 129:** Keystone, Paris. **130, 131:** Courtesy Secrétariat d'Etat à la Défense Chargé des Anciens Combattants D.M.I.H.—Erich Lessing/Magnum Photos. **132:** Vincent Brome, London. **133:** Courtesy Secrétariat d'Etat à la Défense Chargé des Anciens Combattants D.M.I.H. **134:** Courtesy Librairie Académique Perrin, Paris. **135:** Map by John Drummond, Time-Life Inc. **136, 137:** Imperial War Museum, London; Murry Sill/Silver Image, courtesy H. Keith Melton, TheSpyMuseum.com. **139:** Keystone Pressedienst, Hamburg. **140:** Bildarchiv J. K. Piekalkiewicz, Rösrath-Hoffnungsthal; from *Colonel Henri's Story,* by Hugo Bleicher, William Kimber, London, 1954; reproduced with thanks to Duncan

Stuart, CMG, SOE Adviser, Foreign and Commonwealth Office, London—Archives Tallandier, Paris. **142:** Bildarchiv J. K. Piekalkiewicz, Rösrath-Hoffnungsthal. **143:** Reproduced with thanks to Duncan Stuart, CMG, SOE Adviser, Foreign and Commonwealth Office, London. **144, 145:** Nederlands Instituut voor Oorlogsdocumentatie. **146:** Public Record Office, Kew, Surrey, England. **147:** Reproduced with thanks to Duncan Stuart, CMG, SOE Adviser, Foreign and Commonwealth Office, London; Public Record Office, Kew, Surrey, England. **148, 149:** Courtesy of the Trustees of the Imperial War Museum/© Dorling Kindersley Ltd., London—courtesy H. Keith Melton, TheSpyMuseum.com (3)—Fil Hunter, courtesy Joseph F. Canole. **150, 151:** Courtesy H. Keith Melton, TheSpy-Museum.com; Robin Reid/courtesy CIA Exhibit Center—Robin Reid/courtesy H. Keith Melton, TheSpyMuseum.com—Dorling Kindersley Ltd., London/RAF Museum, Hendon. **152, 153:** Robin Reid/courtesy H. Keith Melton, TheSpyMuseum. com—Imperial War Museum, London; Murry Sill/Silver Image, courtesy H. Keith Melton, TheSpyMuseum.com—Robin Reid/courtesy H. Keith Melton, TheSpyMuseum. com (2)—courtesy H. Keith Melton, TheSpyMuseum. com **154, 155:** Cas Oorthuys/The Nederlands Photo Archives—Murry

Sill/Silver Image, courtesy H. Keith Melton, TheSpyMuseum. com. **156:** Courtesy H. Keith Melton, The SpyMuseum.com—Murry Sill/Silver Image, courtesy H. Keith Melton, TheSpy Museum.com. **157:** Murry Sill/Silver Image, courtesy H. Keith Melton, TheSpy Museum.com—Robin Reid/courtesy H. Keith Melton, TheSpy-Museum.com. **158, 159:** Murry Sill/Silver Image, courtesy H. Keith Melton, TheSpy-Museum.com; Robin Reid/courtesy H. Keith Melton, TheSpyMuseum.com (2)—Lady Gubbins, Middleton Stoney, Oxfordshire, England. **160:** Courtesy of Dunlop. **162:** From *The Man Who Never Was,* by Ewen Montagu, Evans Brothers Ltd., London, 1953. **165:** Public Record Office, Kew, Surrey, England. **166, 167:** Public Record Office, Kew, Surrey, England. **168, 169:** From *MI5, British Security Service Operations 1909-1945*, by Nigel West, Stein and Day, New York, 1981—Public Record Office, Kew, Surrey, England (2). **171:** U.S. Army. **172-175:** Public Record Office, Kew, Surrey, England. **176:** TRH Pictures, London. **177:** CORBIS/Bettmann—Bildarchiv J. K. Piekalkiewicz, Rösrath-Hoffnungsthal. **78, 179:** S.I.R.P.A./E.C.P.A., France. **180:** Imperial War Museum, London. **183:** Murry Sill/Silver Image, courtesy H. Keith Melton, TheSpyMuseum.com. **184, 185:** U.S. Coast Guard, Neg. No. 2517.

BIBLIOGRAPHY

BOOKS

Accoce, Pierre, and Pierre Quet. *A Man Called Lucy.* Trans. by A. M. Sheridan Smith. New York: Coward-McCann, 1966.

Andrew, Christopher. *Her Majesty's Secret Service.* New York: Viking, 1986.

Andrew, Christopher, and David Dilks (eds.). *The Missing Dimension.* Chicago: Univ. of Illinois Press, 1984.

Baker, Jean-Claude, and Chris Chase. *Josephine.* New York: Random House, 1993.

Baker, Josephine, and Jo Bouillon. *Josephine.* Trans. by Mariana Fitzpatrick. New York: Harper & Row, 1977.

Bazna, Elyesa. *I Was Cicero.* Trans. by Eric Mosbacher. New York: Harper & Row, 1962.

Bennett, Ralph. *Ultra in the West.* New York: Charles Scribner's Sons, 1979.

Best, S. Payne. *The Venlo Incident.* New York: Hutchinson, 1950.

Boyd, Carl:
American Command of the Seas. Newport News, Va.: The Mariners' Museum, 1995.
Hitler's Japanese Confidant. Lawrence: Univ. Press of Kansas, 1993.

Breuer, William. *Hitler's Undercover War.* New York: St. Martin's Press, 1989.

Brome, Vincent. *The Way Back.* New York: W. W. Norton, 1958.

Brown, Anthony Cave. *"C."* New York: MacMillan, 1987.

Calvocoressi, Peter. *Top Secret Ultra.* New York: Pantheon Books, 1980.

Carré, Mathilde-Lily. *I Was "the Cat."* London: Souvenir Press, 1959.

The Center of the Web (The Third Reich series). Alexandria, Va.: Time-Life Books, 1990.

Conquest, Robert. *The Great Terror.* New York: Oxford Univ. Press, 1990.

Cruickshank, Charles. *Deception in World War II.* New York: Oxford Univ. Press, 1979.

Darling, Donald. *Secret Sunday.* London: William Kimber, 1975.

Deacon, Richard:
A History of the British Secret Service. London: Frederick Muller, 1969.
A History of the Russian Secret Service. New York: Taplinger, 1972.
Kempei Tai. New York: Beaufort Books, 1983.

Dourlein, Pieter. *Inside North Pole.* London: William Kimber, 1953.

Drea, Edward J. *MacArthur's Ultra Codebreaking and the War against Japan, 1942-1945.* Lawrence: Univ. Press of Kansas, 1992.

Ehrlich, Blake. *Resistance: France.* New York: New American Library, 1966.

Farago, Ladislas. *The Game of the Foxes.* New York: David McKay, 1971.

Foot, M. R. D.:
Resistance. London: Eyre Methuen, 1976.
Six Faces of Courage. London: Magnum, 1980.

SOE in France. Frederick, Md.: Univ. Publications of America, 1984.

Foot, M. R. D., and J. M. Langley. *MI9: Escape and Evasion, 1939-1945.* Boston: Little, Brown, 1980.

Garby-Czerniawski, Roman. *The Big Network.* London: George Ronald, 1961.

Garlinski, Józef. *The Enigma War.* New York: Charles Scribner's Sons, 1977.

Gisevius, Hans Bernd. *To the Bitter End.* Boston: Houghton Mifflin, 1947.

Giskes, H. J. *London Calling North Pole.* New York: British Book Centre, 1953.

Haswell, Jock. *The Intelligence and Deception of the D-Day Landings.* London: B. T. Batsford, 1979.

Hinsley, F. H., and Alan Stripp. *Codebreakers.* Oxford: Oxford Univ. Press, 1993.

Hinsley, F. H., and C. A. G. Simkins. *British Intelligence in the Second World War* (Vol. 4). London: Her Majesty's Stationery Office, 1990.

Hodges, Andrew. *Alan Turing.* New York: Simon and Schuster, 1983.

Hoffmann, Peter. *German Resistance to Hitler.* Cambridge: Harvard Univ. Press, 1988.

Holmes, W. J. *Double-Edged Secrets.* Annapolis: Naval Institute Press, 1979.

Howard, Michael:
British Intelligence in the Second World War (Vol. 5). New York: Cambridge Univ.

Press, 1990.

Strategic Deception in the Second World War. London: Pimlico, 1992.

Howarth, David:

Pursued by a Bear. London: Collins, 1986.

The Shetland Bus. London: Thomas Nelson, 1952.

Jeffreys-Jones, Rhodri. *American Espionage.* New York: Macmillan, 1977.

Kahn, David:

Hitler's Spies. New York: Macmillan, 1978.

Seizing the Enigma. Boston: Houghton Mifflin, 1991.

Kesaris, Paul L. (ed.). *Classified Studies in Twentieth-Century Diplomatic and Military History.* Washington, D.C.: Univ. Publications of America, 1979.

Kozaczuk, Wladyslaw. *Enigma.* Edited and translated by Christopher Kasparek. Washington, D.C.: Univ. Publications of America, 1984.

Ladd, James D., Keith Melton, and Peter Mason. *Clandestine Warfare.* New York: Blandford Press, 1988.

Laffin, John. *Special and Secret.* Sydney: Time-Life Books (Australia), 1990.

Langley, J. M. *Fight Another Day.* London: Collins, 1974.

Lee, Bruce. *Marching Orders.* New York: Crown, 1995.

Leverkuehn, Paul. *German Military Intelligence.* New York: Frederick A. Praeger, 1954.

Lewin, Ronald:

The American Magic. New York: Farrar Straus Giroux, 1982.

Ultra Goes to War. New York: McGraw-Hill, 1978.

Lovell, Mary S. *Cast No Shadow.* New York: Pantheon Books, 1992.

McKee, Alexander. *El Alamein.* London: Souvenir Press, 1991.

Manvell, Roger, and Heinrich Fraenkel. *The Men Who Tried to Kill Hitler.* New York: Coward-McCann, 1964.

Marks, Leo. *Between Silk and Cyanide.* New York: Free Press, 1998.

Masterman, J. C. *The Double-Cross System in the War of 1939 to 1945.* New Haven: Yale Univ. Press, 1972.

Melton, H. Keith.

OSS Special Weapons and Equipment. New York: Sterling, 1991.

The Ultimate Spy Book. London: Dorling Kindersley, 1996.

Michel, Henri. *The Shadow War.* New York: Harper & Row, 1972.

Montagu, Ewen:

Beyond Top Secret Ultra. New York: Coward, McCann & Geoghegan, 1978.

The Man Who Never Was. New York: J. B. Lippincott, 1954.

Neave, Airey:

Little Cyclone. London: Hodder and Stoughton, 1954.

Saturday at M.I.9. London: Hodder and Stoughton, 1969.

The Overseas Targets War Report of the OSS (Vol. 2). New York: Walker, 1976.

Paine, Lauran. *Mathilde Carré.* London: Robert Hale, 1976.

Parrish, Thomas. *The Ultra Americans.* Briarcliff Manor, N.Y.: Stein and Day, 1986.

Peden, Murray. *A Thousand Shall Fall.* Stittsville, Ontario: Canada's Wings, 1979.

Peis, Günter. *The Mirror of Deception.* London: Weidenfeld and Nicolson, 1977.

Perrault, Gilles. *The Red Orchestra.* New York: Simon and Schuster, 1969.

Piekalkiewicz, Januz. *Secret Agents, Spies and Saboteurs.* New York: William Morrow, 1973.

Polmar, Norman, and Thomas B. Allen. *Spy Book.* New York: Random House, 1998.

Popov, Dusko. *Spy/Counterspy.* New York: Grosset & Dunlap, 1974.

Pujol, Juan, with Nigel West. *Operation Garbo.* New York: Random House, 1985.

Rachlis, Eugene. *They Came to Kill.* New York: Random House, 1961.

Radó, Sándor. *Codename Dora.* London: Abelard, 1977.

Read, Anthony, and David Fisher. *Operation Lucy.* New York: Coward, McCann & Geoghegan, 1981.

Ronnie, Art. *Counterfeit Hero.* Annapolis: Naval Institute Press, 1995.

Rosenfeld, Harvey. *Raoul Wallenberg.* New York: Holmes & Meier, 1995.

Rossiter, Margaret L. *Women in the Resistance.* New York: Praeger, 1986.

Rout, Leslie B., and John F. Bratzel. *The Shadow War.* Frederick, Md.: Univ. Publications of America, 1986.

Russell, Francis, and the Editors of Time-Life Books. *The Secret War* (The World War II series). Alexandria, Va.: Time-Life Books, 1981.

Sergueiev, Lily. *Secret Service Rendered.* London: William Kimber, 1968.

Seth, Ronald. *The Undaunted.* New York: Philosophical Library, 1950.

The Shadow War (The Third Reich series). Alexandria, Va.: Time-Life Books, 1991.

Smith, Bradley F.:

The Shadow Warriors. New York: Basic Books, 1983.

The Ultra-Magic Deals. Novato, Calif.: Presidio Press, 1993.

Smith, R. Harris. *OSS.* Berkeley: Univ. of California Press, 1972.

Spector, Ronald H. (ed.). *Listening to the Enemy.* Wilmington, Del.: Scholarly Resources, 1988.

The SS (The Third Reich series). Alexandria, Va.: Time-Life Books, 1988.

Stripp, Alan. *Codebreaker in the Far East.* Totowa, N.J.: Frank Cass, 1989.

Sullivan, George. *In the Line of Fire.* New York: Scholastic, 1996.

Tarrant, V. E. *The Red Orchestra.* New York: John Wiley & Sons, 1996.

Trepper, Leopold. *The Great Game.* New York: McGraw-Hill, 1977.

Van Der Rhoer, Edward. *Deadly Magic.* New York: Charles Scribner's Sons, 1978.

Vomécourt, Philippe de. *An Army of Amateurs.* Garden City, N.Y.: Doubleday, 1961.

West, Nigel:

MI5: British Security Service Operations. New York: Stein and Day, 1982.

MI6: British Secret Intelligence Service Operations. New York: Random House, 1983.

Whymant, Robert. *Stalin's Spy.* New York: St. Martin's Press, 1996.

Winterbotham, F. W. *The Nazi Connection.* New York: Harper & Row, 1978.

Winton, John. *Ultra in the Pacific.* Annapolis: Naval Institute Press, 1993.

PERIODICALS

Fenyvesi, Charles, and Victoria Pope. "The Angel Was a Spy." *U.S. News & World Report,* May 13, 1996.

Filby, P. William. "Bletchley Park and Berkeley Street." *Intelligence and National Security,* Apr. 1988, Vol. 3, no. 2.

Goren, Dina. "Communication Intelligence and the Freedom of the Press." *Journal of Contemporary History,* Oct. 1981, Vol. 16, no. 4.

Lashmar, Paul, and Chris Staerck. "Spy Fiasco Cost Britain 50 Agents." *The Independent* (London), Sept. 21, 1998.

Masterman, John. "The XX Papers." *Yale Alumni Magazine,* Feb. 1972.

Morgan, Roger. "The Second World War's Best Kept Secret Revealed." *After the Battle,* 1996, no. 94.

Prior, Leon O. "Nazi Invasion of Florida!" *The Florida Historical Quarterly,* Vol. 49, Oct. 1970, no. 2.

Swanberg, W. A. "The Spies Who Came in from the Sea." *American Heritage,* Apr. 1970, Vol. 21, no. 3.

Tolstoy, Ilia. "Across Tibet from India to China." *National Geographic,* Aug. 1946.

Trefousse, Hans L. "Failure of German Intelligence in the United States." *The Mississippi Valley Historical Review,* June 1955, Vol. 42, no. 1.

Yoshikawa, Takeo. "Top Secret Assignment." *United States Naval Institute Proceedings,* Dec. 1960, Vol. 82, no. 12.

OTHER SOURCES

Fenton, Ben. "Stalin's Fifth Man from Cambridge Spy Ring Dies." www.telegraph.co.uk, Oct. 9, 1995.

Grigg, John. "A Soviet Spy Makes His Excuses." www.telegraph.co.uk, Oct. 11, 1997.

"Report of Team George." OSS London, 1944, and DSC citation for Paul Cyr. NARA, RG 226.

"Report of Team James." OSS London, 1944. NARA, RG 226.

Smith, Michael:

"Enigma of KGB's Third Man at Bletchley Park." www.telegraph.co.uk, June 26, 1997.

"Fifth Man Cairncross Gave Stalin the Atom Bomb." www.telegraph.co.uk, Jan. 12, 1998.

"Graham Greene Backed Second Spy for Soviets." www.telegraph.co.uk, June 21, 1999.

TIME LIFE Time-Life Books is a
division of Time Life Inc.

TIME LIFE INC.
PRESIDENT and CEO: Jim Nelson

TIME-LIFE BOOKS
PUBLISHER/MANAGING EDITOR: Neil Kagan
SENIOR VICE PRESIDENT, MARKETING:
Joseph A. Kuna
VICE PRESIDENT, NEW PRODUCT
DEVELOPMENT: Amy Golden

SECRETS OF THE CENTURY
World War II: War in the Shadows

Editor: Esther Ferington
Design Directors: Tina Taylor (principal), Cynthia
Richardson

Deputy Editor: Harris J. Andrews III
Text Editor: Stephen Hyslop
Assistant Art Director: Janet Dell Russell Johnson
Associate Editor/Research and Writing:
Nancy C. Blodgett
Senior Copyeditor: Mary Beth Oelkers-Keegan
Picture Associate: Amanda Stowe
Editorial Assistant: Patricia D. Whiteford
Photo Coordinator: David M. Cheatham

Special Contributors: Charlotte Anker, Ronald H.
Bailey, George Constable, James M. Lynch,
Susan Perry, Ellen Phillips (text); Charlotte
Fullerton, Kevin Mahoney, Rosanne Scott
(research/writing); Arlene Borden, Christine
Hauser, Maggie J. Sliker, Terrell Smith, Robert
H. Wooldridge Jr. (research); Janet Cave, Lee
Hassig (editing); Christopher Register (design);
John Drummond (art); Norma Shaw (over-
read); Indexing Partners (index)

Correspondents: Maria Vincenza Aloisi (Paris),
Christine Hinze (London), Christina Lieberman
(New York); valuable assistance also provided
by Elizabeth Kraemer-Singh, Angelika Lemmer
(Bonn)

Separations by the Time-Life Imaging
Department

NEW PRODUCT DEVELOPMENT: Director,
Paula York-Soderland; Project Manager, Karen
Ingebretsen; Director of Marketing, Mary Ann
Donaghy; Marketing Manager, Paul Fontaine;
Associate Marketing Manager, Erin Gaskins

MARKETING: Director, Peter Tardif; Marketing
Manager, Nancy Gallo; Associate Marketing
Manager, Terri Miller

Executive Vice President, Operations: Ralph Cuomo
Senior Vice President and CFO: Claudia Goldberg
Senior Vice President, Law & Business Affairs:
Randolph H. Elkins
Vice President, Financial Planning & Analysis:
Christopher Hearing
Vice President, Book Production: Patricia Pascale
Vice President, Imaging: Marjann Caldwell
Director, Publishing Technology: Betsi McGrath
Director, Editorial Administration: Barbara Levitt
Director, Photography and Research:
John Conrad Weiser
Director, Quality Assurance: James King
Manager, Technical Services: Anne Topp
Senior Production Manager: Ken Sabol
Manager, Copyedit/Page Makeup: Debby Tait
Production Manager: Virginia Reardon
Chief Librarian: Louise D. Forstall

ISBN 0-7835-1950-8

10 9 8 7 6 5 4 3 2 1

OTHER PUBLICATIONS

COOKING
Weight Watchers® Smart Choice Recipe Collection
Great Taste~Low Fat
Williams-Sonoma Kitchen Library

DO IT YOURSELF
Custom Woodworking
Golf Digest Total Golf
How to Fix It
The Time-Life Complete Gardener
Home Repair and Improvement
The Art of Woodworking

HISTORY
Our American Century
World War II
What Life Was Like
The American Story
Voices of the Civil War
The American Indians
Lost Civilizations
Mysteries of the Unknown
Time Frame
The Civil War
Cultural Atlas

TIME-LIFE KIDS
Student Library
Library of First Questions and Answers
A Child's First Library of Learning
I Love Math
Nature Company Discoveries
Understanding Science & Nature

SCIENCE/NATURE
Voyage Through the Universe

For information on and a full description of
any of the Time-Life Books series listed above,
please call 1-800-621-7026 or write:
Reader Information
Time-Life Customer Service
P.O. Box C-32068
Richmond, Virginia 23261-2068